# Contents

Preface     1

Abbreviations     11

The Infancy Prologue: Roots and
Shadows Cast Before (1:1–2:23)     13

Book One: Proclaiming the Kingdom (3:1–7:28)     33

Book Two: Mission in Galilee (8:1–11:1)     107

Book Three: The Gathering Storm (11:2–13:53)     135

Book Four: Preparing for the
Passion and the Church (13:54–18:35)     164

Book Five: Collision Course
and the Final Times (19:1–25:46)     209

The Climax: Jesus' Passion
and Resurrection (26:1–28:20)     285

# Preface

It had been fourteen years since I had set foot in the library of the divinity school at St. Louis University, where I had once taught in the Scripture department. Then it had been crammed into the basement of the general library. Now I found myself like a crew member of the space ship Enterprise punching buttons to a maze of elevators and sliding doors until I finally found myself in the new library standing before the interminable shelves of the New Testament section, ready to plunge into my sabbatical and write my commentary on Matthew. During those intervening fourteen years I had been a seminary rector, teaching Scripture in Toronto, then serving on the Provincial Administration of the Marianists, and the last six years as director of novices in Nepal, in sight of Mount Everest. Still in the throes of re-entry to the developed world, I stood before the Matthew section and, overwhelmed at the number of commentaries before me, asked myself why I ever dreamed of writing another commentary on Matthew.

As I paged through one commentary after another, my courage and conviction gradually returned. For one thing, I realized once again how each new commentator brings new insights, correctives, challenges and enrichments to previous views. But I also realized the freshness of each approach emerged not merely out of new discoveries in research but also—particularly in the more popular commentaries—from the writer's own experience of life. And there I knew I had some modest claim to uniqueness.

I had just returned from six years living in Nepal and India, sinking roots in a culture vastly alien to my native America. That experience, painful at times but immensely enriching, has convinced me how much my own biblical commentaries until now have been conditioned by the preoccupations of the developed western world and how enlightening, on the other

1

hand, are the insights available—imposed, I would rather say—by living in a culture much closer to biblical times than our own. Footwashing, arranged marriages, animal sacrifices, a festival duplicating in many details the Jewish Passover (even to blood on the doorposts), week-long weddings, the extended family, tribal traditions, widespread leprosy, smothering hospitality are just a few experiences that for me have thrown new light on numerous biblical passages. I have drawn on these experiences here, and that, along with challenges to our nominally Christian western culture, is a major claim to the uniqueness of this commentary, which otherwise reflects modern biblical scholarship with a view to its practical meaning for the Christian life.

Even had I not been blessed with the Asian third-world experience, I have long wanted to journey as a writing pilgrim through Matthew's gospel, because my fascination with it has grown over the years, many of which I have spent teaching the gospel to a wide variety of students. Their positive response to my presentation has been added encouragement to me to share it with a wider audience.

There are a number of introductory comments that appear to me essential if we are to read Matthew intelligently. For many Christians, the only exposure they have had to Matthew has been the selections used by the liturgy or the preacher. However valid and powerful the message of an individual passage may be, it is quite a different experience to read the gospel from beginning to end and to see each unit in the light of the whole. It is the difference between focusing on a detail of Michelangelo's general judgment fresco and viewing the majestic whole. When we take the wide-angle view of Matthew's gospel we find not only the work of a consummate artist but of a theologian and pastor as well. By his selection, editing, and arrangement of passages Matthew communicates a strong message to the church of his day and ours.

## From Jesus through Matthew to Us

Heidegger once said, "A man is who he is, and his history." We could say that a gospel is what it is *because* of its history.

Jesus died, we know, around the year 30 of our era. He wrote nothing, nor did he command any of his disciples to write. He preached and ministered to people, and told his disciples to do the same. As the communities of his disciples multiplied and grew in the ensuing years, two concerns emerged: on the one hand, a desire to recall and retain the events and the words of Jesus' life and, on the other, a concern to proclaim these events and words in a way that would be meaningful to new audiences with new problems often quite removed from the original context of the historical Jesus. The "gospel" in this oral period had its roots in Jesus but it was a living message. It lived in the hearts of those who proclaimed it and developed as it was shared with others.

Gradually, however, as the first generation of disciples thinned out through missionary expansion or death, a need was felt to capture the memories of Jesus in written form. At first this was done in fragmentary units, as they were remembered, the most important being the passion story, which has a remarkable common structure in all four of our evangelists. At the same time, Jesus' sayings were gathered, the most enduring collection being a document called "Q," from the German *Quelle*, meaning "source." It disappeared as a separate source when it was later ensured permanent existence by being incorporated into the gospels of Matthew and Luke. Now "Q" refers to those passages which are common to Matthew and Luke but are not found in Mark.

The first person to organize the traditions about Jesus into a continuous story was Mark. His was the first written "gospel." Mark's interest, however, was not that of an archivist. He was proclaiming the good news for a specific community, which most scholars say was the Christian community in Rome, and thus he shapes the tradition, even as he transmits it, in such a way as to tell the Christians of Rome, under persecution, what Jesus means for them *now*.

The same can be said for Matthew. Most scholars today hold that Matthew wrote his gospel after the fall of Jerusalem (70 A.D.), during the period when the only surviving Jewish party, the Pharisees, striving to re-organize the decimated and distraught nation, came into serious conflict with the Jewish

Christians over their claims about Jesus. Because of the split between church and synagogue, many Jewish Christians were experiencing alienation from their family members who had not become Christian. There are even echoes of persecution in Matthew's gospel. It was also a period in which the Jewish Christian community was incorporating more and more gentiles and experiencing the growing pains which such multi-cultural pressures were putting on the community. In addition, within Matthew's community there were two opposing groups, the laxists who, especially in view of the delay of Jesus' second coming, were throwing off the yoke of Jesus' high ethical demands; and the rigorists, whose impatience with the weak and straying members was also dividing the community. Finally, though the charism of prophecy continued to be exercised in Matthew's community, considerable harm was being done by false prophecy, leading community members away from the orthodox teaching of the original disciples of Jesus. I would wager no modern bishop had the tangle of problems that Matthew had!

There was, in Matthew's view, only one way to meet all these problems: Back to Jesus! His words, his example, his ministry, and especially his surrender to the Father's will in his passion, death and resurrection, contained the solution to every problem, pastoral and theological. The going back to Jesus, however, was a creative endeavor, for Matthew would organize and mold his reconstruction of the gospel according to the needs he perceived in his community, and this is where his inspired creativity appears.

Matthew had before him Mark, on the one hand, and Q, the sayings source. He uses nearly all of Mark, cleaning up Mark's style and shaping it to his theological concerns. That is why in this commentary we will be frequently comparing Matthew's text with Mark's; the differences will reveal much about Matthew's specific message. Since he shares the Q source with Luke, we will also be able, where relevant, to make similar comparisons. But in addition, Matthew had some sources of his own—for example, the infancy accounts—which scholars group under "M" for "Matthew's proper source." The genius of Matthew is his combination of these sources into a masterpiece, which makes one think of a mosaic in which each tiny stone has been carefully selected, honed and placed. If Matthew's gospel is divinely inspired, as the church of all ages has maintained, that inspiration touches not only the individual blocks but the work as a whole. The reader will be able to see the magnificent unity of the whole as the commentary unfolds.

An important conclusion follows: In the text of Matthew before us, there are three different levels of historical development: (1) The events and the words of the historical Jesus; (2) The reshaping of those events and words by the oral and early written tradition of the early church in the first decades after Jesus; (3) The final shape of the tradition under the pen of Matthew. The only level immediately available to us is the third. Recovering the first two levels is a difficult process and sometimes it is guesswork. Thus, while there is no serious reason to doubt Matthew's fidelity to the *meaning* of Jesus, we must remember that the Jesus we are seeing and hearing in this gospel, is *Matthew's* Jesus. But why should that surprise us? Those converted to Christianity by the preaching of the apostles were always hearing Jesus through the interpretation of Peter, or Paul, or John or James. The word of God that is "living and effective" (Heb 4:12) is not the word that sits on a library shelf. God's word lives in living people who share it with living people.

The difference, of course, is that we meet the Jesus of Matthew here not in a living voice but in a *text*. Even so, that text becomes living in the church that lives and preaches it and in the person who reads it with faith. So there is a fourth level of meaning in Matthew's gospel, and that is the here-and-now meaning for today's reader. In this commentary, I occasionally share what the text means to me personally, and what I believe it is saying to the modern church, in the hopes that this will facilitate the reader's own appropriation of the text for his life. For only when this fourth step is completed is it possible for the reader to say he has encountered the word of God, that is, Jesus, the revealer of the Father.

## *The Author*

It has been traditionally believed that the Matthew credited with authoring this gospel is the same as the apostle Matthew. There are serious problems with this view, however.

For one thing, if Matthew the apostle were the author, why would he not use his own memories of Jesus rather than depending almost totally upon Mark? Some of the non-Markan passages may indeed go back to Jesus' disciple Matthew, and that could account for the attribution of the gospel to the apostle. But that is far from certain. In any case, the church accepted and used this gospel as its favorite from an early hour (being more complete, it almost crowded out Mark), and it would have done so only because it was convinced of the genuineness of the gospel's apostolic tradition. For the question of Levi's name appearing in this gospel as Matthew, see our commentary on 9:9–13.

## Jesus' Teaching in Matthew

Matthew's gospel is so full of the teachings of Jesus that one might almost conclude that for Matthew Jesus is teacher before all else. That is not true, of course, for the word "teacher" or "rabbi" is used in the gospel only on the lips of those coolly or unfavorably disposed towards Jesus. Nevertheless, the teaching of Jesus predominates in the five great discourses into which Matthew gathers Jesus' sayings. Of these, the Sermon on the Mount gives the most extensive, lapidary teaching on the kinds of attitudes Jesus expects of his disciples. And in this commentary, within the Sermon on the Mount, I have given extensive space to the beatitudes and the Lord's prayer, both because I believe we touch there a major vein of Jesus' teaching and also because of their immediate relevance for the Christian of today.

## A Caution: The Struggle with the Pharisees

One of the elements which stands out more prominently in Matthew's gospel than in any other is the extremely unfavorable picture of the Pharisees and of the Jewish people as a whole. It is very important to understand this in the highly specialized context out of which this comes. The Pharisees traced their origin back to the *hasidim*, those Jews most faithful in time of persecution by the Greeks. They were basically a fervent lay movement that sought to make the written law a living thing, touching every element of human life. Thus, with the aid of their scribes, they evolved a comprehensive oral tradition in which every question of life in human society could be resolved by relating it somehow to the law. In this they differed from the Sadducees, who rejected the authority of this oral tradition and of the prophets as well, holding only to the authority of the first five books of the Bible, the Torah. The Sadducees were intimately associated with the temple priests, who, according to the gospels, were the ones who instigated the death of Jesus. But Jesus also collided with the Pharisees, at least with many of them, as all the gospels show. Amazingly, however, the early church counted among its members an important group of Pharisees (Acts 15:5) and of priests (Acts 6:7).

After the destruction of Jerusalem and the temple by the Romans in 70 A.D., the only Jewish party remaining was the Pharisees, who then took up the spiritual leadership of the people. Jewish Christians who in the early days had continued to frequent the temple and, we may presume, even the synagogue, were eventually excommunicated by the Jewish community. Obviously, that action could not have happened overnight. There was a progressive build-up of hostility until, by the time John's gospel was published, the break was complete. The picture we see in Matthew's gospel reflects the hostilities during the build-up period, probably shortly before the complete break, in the 80's according to most scholars today. The Pharisees were in an understandable struggle to gain spiritual control of the Jewish community and for their rabbis to be recognized as the unique teaching authority. The Jewish Christians saw this as a threat to the unique authority of Jesus and his authorized disciples; and the threat was no doubt mutually felt by the Pharisees. In this period, then, it was important for Matthew to buttress the unique authority of Jesus and his first disciples (and their successors) and to paint the Pharisees in the least favorable light. To do so, it was not necessary to create an anti-Pharisaic polemic out of thin air, for Jesus himself had often clashed with them. Thus Matthew built on the earlier tradition and reinforced it in various ways throughout his gospel, most strongly in chapter 23, the seven woes against the scribes and the Pharisees. Even there, though, Matthew is also using the woes to warn the members of his own community of false attitudes, to which today's Christians are no less vulnerable.

Though it was the priests rather than the Pharisees who were the primary instigators of the crucifixion of Jesus, since they were, with the elders and the scribes, the supreme authority, Matthew sees them, along with the crowd they control, as speaking for the people as a whole in their demand for the death of Jesus (27:25). Neither Paul (Rom 9–11) nor Matthew is thinking of individual Jews but only of the collectivity as such in its rejection of Jesus; for Matthew's community, like Paul's, contained many Jews.

This historical context hopefully will liberate us from blindly transferring to Jews today the polemics of the first century. The Second Vatican Council made this quite clear: "Even though the Jewish authorities and those who followed their lead pressed for the death of Christ (cf. John 19:6), neither all Jews indiscriminately at that time, nor Jews today, can be charged with the crimes committed during his passion." (*Declaration on Non-Christian Religions, #4*)

## Structure of the Gospel

Various alternatives of dividing the gospel have been proposed. One of the most ingenious is the symmetrical pattern, in which chapters or groups of chapters are balanced in a chiastic fashion (e.g. *a b c d c b a*) with the result that the keystone of the arch is the central chapter 13, the parables of the kingdom. Thus, Chapters 1–4 are *narrative* dealing with birth and beginnings; balancing the end chapters 26–28, also narrative, dealing with death and rebirth. Chapters 5–7 are *sermon* about blessings and entering the kingdom, balancing the sermon material in chapters 23–25 which are woes and the coming of the kingdom. And so forth.

Now there are obvious chiastic patterns within individual units of Matthew, and the commentary will illustrate that pattern in chapter 18. But as a theory for the structure of the entire gospel, the proposal falters for two reasons: (1) Often a very disproportionate amount of material must be gathered under one heading to achieve the symmetry; (2) While important, chapter thirteen cannot compare in content with the Sermon on the Mount, and moreover the symmetrical pattern overlooks the developing plot and the essential primacy of the passion-death-and-resurrection of Jesus, which is certainly the climax of Matthew's gospel.

Consequently, I prefer the more traditional division which sees the gospel arranged, after the infancy stories as a prologue, in five major books, each with a narrative and discourse, leading climactically to the passion-resurrection narrative and concluding with the final commissioning of the disciples. As follows:

### PLAN OF THE BOOK

THE INFANCY PROLOGUE: ROOTS AND SHADOWS
CAST BEFORE    1:1–2:23

BOOK ONE: PROCLAIMING THE KINGDOM    3:1–7:28
   *Story:* The New Creation    3:1–4:25
   *Discourse:* The New Law-Giver and the
     New Law    5:1–7:28

BOOK TWO: MISSION IN GALILEE    8:1–10:42
   *Story:* Jesus the Burden-Lifter    8:1–9:38
   *Discourse:* Mission    10:1–11:1

BOOK THREE: THE GATHERING STORM    11:2–13:53
   *Story:* Invitation and Response    11:2–12:50
   *Discourse:* The Switch to Parables    13:1–53

BOOK FOUR: PREPARING FOR THE PASSION AND
     THE CHURCH    13:54–18:35
   *Story:* Continuing his Ministry, Jesus
     Predicts his Passion    13:54–17:27
   *Discourse:* The Shepherding Community    18:1–35

BOOK FIVE: COLLISION COURSE AND THE FINAL
        TIMES                            19:1–25:46
   *Story:* Ministry in Judea and Jerusalem    19:1–22:45
   *Discourse:* Conflict with the Pharisees/
            The Final Times                23:1–25:46
   *The Future:* Known and Unknown        24:1–36
   *The Present:* Watch!                24:37–25:30

CLIMAX: JESUS' PASSION AND RESURRECTION    26:1–28:20

CONCLUSION: THE GREAT COMMISSION       28:16–20

# Abbreviations

| | |
|---|---|
| JB | The Jerusalem Bible |
| KJV | King James Version |
| NAB | New American Bible |
| NABR | New American Bible, Revised New Testament |
| NIV | New International Version |
| NT | New Testament |
| OT | Old Testament |
| RSV | Revised Standard Version |
| TEV | Today's English Version |

# Roots and Shadows Cast Before
## (1:1–2:23)

*Origin of the Infancy Gospel*

In the earliest stage of the gospel tradition, to which Mark is the closest, we find no interest in the details of Jesus' infancy. The gospel tradition, in fact, developed backwards. The apostles first preached the astounding fact of the resurrection of Jesus as a sign of the end-times and an urgent call to conversion.

But the man who was raised was not just a good and holy man. He had suffered the shameful death of a criminal, a role that many Jews found a stumbling block since that is not how the scribes and authorities read the "script" for the Messiah. Thus the second and immediately necessary step was to show that such a role was indeed in the "script" (see Luke's frequent statement, "it was necessary that the Christ should suffer") and that Jesus' resurrection was in fact God's reversal of the verdict of the Sanhedrin. "The stone which the builders rejected has become the cornerstone" (Mk 12:10). The passion story then was a necessary preface to the glory of Easter morning. In its turn, the passion story demanded an explanation of how a man "approved among you by signs and wonders" (Acts 2:22) should fall foul of the authorities. Thus the need for illustrations of Jesus' teaching and healing ministry on the one hand and the progressive hostility of the authorities on the other led to an outline of Jesus' public life and teaching, which eventually each evangelist would work up in his own unique gospel. It sufficed for this purpose to begin with the baptism of Jesus by John in the Jordan.

What then of Jesus' thirty years of obscurity in Nazareth? The memories of those years were meager, at least by the time Matthew and Luke came to compose their gospels for second generation Christians. Yet even these became the meditation of the Christian community as they began to see in them *fulfillment* and *forecast*. For Matthew and the tradition behind him, everything in the Old Testament was prophetic—history, law and prophets (Mt 11:13). That is, not only those statements that were in prophetic form but every law and every event recorded pointed to something greater to come. In this way Matthew in his first two chapters presents a summary of Old Testament history relived in the infancy of Jesus. We shall see this in detail momentarily. But there is a second purpose to the infancy stories: they are a preface and prelude to the gospel, shadows cast before. There is even a little passion story in the persecution by Herod, forecasting the rejection and suffering Jesus will experience in his public life. In the visit of the Magi the role of the gentiles is forecast. The infancy stories, then, were not just tacked on to Matthew's gospel to satisfy pious Christian curiosity. Nor are they strictly biographical accounts. They are a theological commentary on the whole economy of God, and a prelude to the great themes of the gospel. In this sense they function, in a narrative way, exactly as the prologue of John does in a brief, hymnic way. They insert the gospel into the great sweep of biblical history, and we, the readers, are given both subtle hints and explicit cues as to who this Jesus is that we shall soon see on the public stage.

## Son of David, Son of Abraham (1:1–17)

1 THE BOOK of the genealogy of Jesus Christ, the son of David, the son of Abraham.

2 Abraham was the father of Isaac, and Isaac the father of Jacob, and Jacob the father of Judah and his brothers, ³and Judah the father of Perez and Zerah by Tamar, and Perez the father of Hezron, and Hezron the father of Ram, ⁴and Ram the father of Amminadab, and Amminadab the father of Nahshon, and Nahshon the father of Salmon, ⁵and Salmon the father of Boaz by Rahab, and Boaz the father of Obed by Ruth, and Obed the father of Jesse, ⁶and Jesse the father of David the king.

And David was the father of Solomon by the wife of Uriah, ⁷and Solomon the father of Rehoboam, and Rehoboam the father of Abijah, and Abijah the father of Asa, [8]and Asa the father of Jehoshaphat, and Jehoshaphat the father of Joram, and Joram the father of Uzziah, [9]and Uzziah the father of Jotham, and Jotham the father of Ahaz, and Ahaz the father of Hezekiah, [10]and Hezekiah the father of Manasseh, and Manasseh the father of Amos, and Amos the father of Josiah, [11]and Josiah the father of Jechoniah and his brothers, at the time of the deportation to Babylon.

12 And after the deportation to Babylon: Jechoniah was the father of She-alti-el, and She-alti-el the father of Zerubbabel, [13]and Zerubbabel the father of Abiud, and Abiud the father of Eliakim, and Eliakim the father of Azor, [14]and Azor the father of Zadok, and Zadok the father of Achim, and Achim the father of Eliud, [15]and Eliud the father of Eleazar, and Eleazar the father of Matthan, and Matthan the father of Jacob, [16]and Jacob the father of Joseph the husband of Mary, of whom Jesus was born, who is called Christ.

17 So all the generations from Abraham to David were fourteen generations, and from David to the deportation to Babylon fourteen generations, and from the deportation to Babylon to the Christ fourteen generations.

A modern journalist would be appalled at the way Matthew begins his gospel. Where is the electrifying headline? Where the catchy opening paragraph? Instead we have a droning list of "begats" or "was the father of" (depending on your translation), which even devout Christians often find numbing to listen to.

There is good reason for this reaction. Western culture, particularly in North America, has come to idolize the self-made person, the immigrant of obscure origins who has made it to the top, who pulled himself up by his own bootstraps, who proved that all the vaunted heraldry and highborn nobility of the old world was no real title to greatness, who showed instead that one could even "come up from slavery" and claim dignity in society by one thing only: hard work and achievement. Tell me the story of a Horatio Alger or a Booker T. Washington, if you will. But a genealogy? No, thank you.

Achievement gives us our identity—and our heart attacks.

Matthew's beginning collides head on with this strategy of achievement, not because it has a prejudice for nobility or caste, but because for Matthew, as for the Bible in general, and indeed for most tribal cultures as well, identity is not a matter of achievement but of relationship. Our cook in Nepal was named *Maela* ("second-born"), and his brother who brought our morning supply of fresh milk was named *Kancha* ("younger brother"), and they both looked up to *Jheto*, their elder brother, the "first-born." Each had other names, of course, but rare was the person who remembered them, because the identity of each brother was conceived in terms of his place in the family order. Similarly, one of my novices, a Santhal tribal, was known at home as *Sanjela* because he was the "third born." When a tribal candidate would write us requesting admission to our community, the letter would often read like this: "You want to know about me. My father is fifty years old, a farmer, in good health. My mother is also living, housewife at home. My oldest brother is in the army. My next oldest brother works with my father at home. I have two younger sisters, one is going to school and the little one is at home. *Now that you know all about me*, please let me enter your community." A western candidate would tell us his age, his education, his work experience, his hobbies, his achievements, because that is what western culture has taught us to consider as giving us our identity. He would never think of introducing us to his family as an adequate response to our question, "Who are you?"

In the Bible, a man is always the son of his father. The recurrence of *ben-* or *bar-* (Isaiah ben Amoz or Simon bar Jonah) shows that in biblical culture one always belongs to someone, and this family identity is much stronger in ancient consciousness than it is in western, achievement-oriented culture. So that is the first challenge the genealogy puts to us: do we get our identity from what we *do*—or from our relationships? Is my importance something I have to prove or merit—or something I begin with because of the galaxy of relationships into which I am born? Each culture, of course, has its angels and its demons, and I am far from suggesting all the angels are on the one side and the demons on the other. But from the first line of Matthew's gospel we are confronted by a value system that challenges the very roots of much of "the developed world."

A second challenge resulting from this litany of names is a consoling one. The God of the Bible is a God of history and of historical persons. He is not a God revealed in myth but a God revealed in time and place and event. And while the biblical tradition has certainly often dramatized, enlarged and embellished events to exploit their religious significance, the tradition is anchored in history. The persons whose names appear here are neither gods nor heroes. Some of them belong in a rogues' gallery. The hero who writes straight with the crooked lines of their history is the Lord. He is the *Gibor*, the champion and the redeemer of Israel. He reveals himself in the mirror of the human experience of his people. He is the God of Abraham, of Isaac and of Jacob (Ex 3:6), the God of Jesus Christ, the God of Mary and Peter, the God of you and me. In their experience and ours we can find God.

Out of the litany of ancestors Matthew selects two and uses them as titles of Jesus. He is *Son of David*, that is, the Messiah-King descended from David and as such, the fulfillment of all the Jewish hopes. But he is also *Son of Abraham*. By reaching back to Abraham, Matthew prepares us to understand how the promised blessing of the gentiles will be fulfilled in a way beyond expectations, when the disciples are missioned to all the nations (28:19).

The number 14 is probably a memory technique for oral recitation. But scholars have also suggested other purposes. In Hebrew, the letters of the alphabet are also used as numbers. If such were the case in English, A would equal 1, B = 2, C = 3 and so on. If David's name were spelled DVD, D being equal to 4 and V to 6, the letters would add up to 14. The problem with this ingenious suggestion is that we are not sure of the exact Hebrew spelling of David's name in Jesus' day. It may have been DVYD. More plausible is the proposal that Matthew was working in apocalyptic categories like those of Dan 9:1–27, in which the week has a value for dividing human history. In this computation, a history that began with Abraham would count six weeks ($3 \times 14 = 6 \times 7$), and Jesus would open the seventh week, the perfect age of the Messiah. It is equally likely, though, that Matthew copied the genealogy of David straight from Ruth 4:18–22, where ten ancestors are given going back to Perez; Matthew then prefaced the names of the four patriarchs going back to Abraham. Once he had the number 14, he arranged the other series to match.

Biblical genealogies are often less interested in biological generation than in showing the transmission of the blessing from one person to a community of persons, a process that can involve immigration, marriage, adoption, covenant or conquest. This aspect will be important to Matthew in the surprises he underlines. The Lord's plan does not always follow human expectations. The firstborn is normally the heir, but such was not the case with Jacob nor with Jacob's son Judah who was the fourth son (Gen 49:3–8). But the major surprises concern the four women Matthew explicitly mentions: Tamar, Rahab, Ruth and Bathsheba (Uriah's wife). Why does Matthew name these four and pass over more prominent women like Sarah, Rebecca or Rachel? Is it because they were sinners, Matthew thus intending to show that Jesus came for sinners? This proposal should be discarded, since Ruth was certainly not a sinner, and the Rabbis venerated Tamar, though guilty of incest by modern standards, as a heroine determined to share the divine blessing which her husband refused her.

Is it because they were foreigners, a forecast of the call of the gentiles? Rahab was a Canaanite, and so probably was Tamar, Bathsheba was the wife of Uriah the Hittite, and Ruth was a Moabitess. Or was it that the unusual circumstances of their childbearing forecast and in a way legitimated the surprising way Jesus was conceived? Both these explanations would play well into Matthew's purpose, and there is no need to choose between them. Matthew thus would be telling his readers: Gentiles are in your future because they are in your past. And our history shows that, even in the biological transmission of the promise we can expect surprises.

And here is the ultimate surprise. At the end of the line, after all the male begetters, it is a woman who brings forth the Messiah. If transmission of the promise were a matter merely of biological generation, this would be God's supreme feminist joke. But far from being bypassed, Joseph benefits from this surprise too, for his fatherhood, no less real for being celibate, transmits the Davidic heritage to Jesus. To this event we now turn.

## A FAITHFUL GOD

If we look carefully at the structure of the narrative from this point to the end of chapter 2, we will notice five scenes, each with a citation from the Old Testament. It seems that Matthew has used stories handed down to him and added to each of them a "fulfillment citation." Luke's infancy gospel is equally concerned to show Scriptural fulfillment, but he uses the more subtle method of allusion. Matthew doesn't leave the fulfillment identification to chance, giving explicit citations as if to say *Nota Bene*. For Matthew the Jew, as for Paul the rabbi, Jesus is more than the burst of a supernova in human history. He is the fulfillment of promises made long ago. One must be a Jew, perhaps, to fully appreciate this, but even in our lives as we celebrate golden weddings and golden jubilees, we can appreciate the particular beauty of promises fulfilled.

## *The Role of Joseph (1:18-25)*

18 Now the birth of Jesus Christ took place in this way. When his mother Mary had been betrothed to Joseph, before they came together she was found to be with child of the Holy Spirit; [19]and her husband Joseph, being a just man and unwilling to put her to shame, resolved to divorce her quietly. [20]But as he considered this, behold, an angel of the Lord appeared to him in a dream, saying, "Joseph, son of David, do not fear to take Mary your wife, for that which is conceived in her is of the Holy Spirit; [21]she will bear a son, and you shall call his name Jesus, for he will save his people from their sins." [22]All this took place to fulfil what the Lord had spoken by the prophet:

[23]"Behold, a virgin shall conceive and bear a son,

and his name shall be called Emmanu-el"
(which means, God with us). ²⁴When Joseph woke from
sleep, he did as the angel of the Lord commanded him; he
took his wife, ²⁵but knew her not until she had borne a son;
and he called his name Jesus.

In Jewish society, betrothal or engagement was a serious,
public and legal matter. A fiancee unfaithful to her promised
union was guilty of adultery and was to be stoned to death (Lev
22:23). The groom already bore the name "husband" and the
only proper way to break the union was divorce, just as if they
had been married. There might be a lapse of time, however,
between the betrothal and their actually coming to live together, just as today in cultures where there are still arranged
marriages the agreement to marry may be settled long before
the couple come together. It was precisely in this situation that
Mary "was found to be with child by the Holy Spirit." Matthew's use of the passive "was found" and the immediate mention of the Holy Spirit indicate how concerned he is to protect
Mary before his Christian audience from any suspicion of mis-
conduct. He does not say by whom she was found, but this
information eventually gets to Joseph.

He is a just man. But what precisely is the challenge to
his justice here? To divorce her? Or to do it privately? Or both?
These questions depend on another: What was the purpose of
the angel's message? Was it to reveal to Joseph the *mystery*
of the virginal conception by the Holy Spirit? Or, does the angel's message presume Joseph knows the mystery and then go
on to reveal *Joseph's role* in it?

The traditional explanation is the former. Joseph did not
know of the virginal conception until the angel informed him
of it. But grammatically it is equally possible to translate the
message: "Do not fear to take Mary as your wife, for although
what is begotten in her is the work of the Holy Spirit, she will
bring forth a son and you will name him Jesus." This translation
presumes that Joseph knew of the mystery prior to the angelic
annunciation, presumably from Mary herself. If this is the case,
then Joseph's problem of conscience is not about a possible
adultery. It is rather religious fear: if the Lord has chosen

Mary to be mother of the Messiah and has bypassed human fathering in the conception of the child, then Joseph feels he must withdraw from this sacred economy. The angel's message is to assure him, on the contrary, that he has a key role.

Critics of this interpretation are quick to ask how Joseph's divorcing Mary, even privately in this case, could be an act of justice towards *her*. Would it not precisely expose her to reproach? But the same objection could be raised against the other alternative. Any kind of divorce, even private, would ultimately end in her pregnancy being revealed. So on this point we end up with obscurity in either case.

The importance of Mary's role is assumed, for it is the fulfillment of the prophecy of Isaiah 7:14. Originally addressed to King Ahaz when Jerusalem was threatened by the Syro-Ephraimite league, on Isaiah's lips it seems to have meant that the Lord would transfer the Davidic promises from faithless Ahaz to another Davidic king, presumably his son Hezekiah soon to be born of his young wife Abijah. At this original stage of the text, the Hebrew word *almah* means a young girl of marriageable age. When centuries later the Septuagint translators put the text into Greek, they translated it with a much more precise term *parthenos* meaning *virgin*. But even there, the text could mean nothing more than that the girl would be a virgin at the time of her marriage. When some critics claim that the origin of the virgin birth idea for Jesus derived from these texts rather than from a historical event, they have to deal with the serious objection that nowhere in Jewish or textual tradition was the text understood to mean a virginal conception. Thus, on purely critical grounds alone (to say nothing of a previous stance of faith or doctrine), it is just as likely that belief in Mary's virginal conception of Jesus came first, and this text was then seen to be fulfilled beyond expectations.

With Mary's role clearly in place, Matthew can proceed to focus on his primary objective, the role of Joseph. Accordingly, he departs from his usual procedure and inserts the Isaiah citation after the angel's message rather than at the end of the story, thus allowing the narrative to climax with Joseph's obedience to his vocation. If there had not been a virgin birth in the tradition known to Matthew, it would have been easier to establish Jesus' Davidic descent—through Joseph, naturally. But the virgin birth presents a problem, for it would seem to cancel the whole paternal lineage at the very last link. In fact, however, this only highlights the exceptional and unique vocation given to Joseph. *He* is Son of David (the only place in the NT where the title is used of anyone else but Jesus), and *he* will name the child.

The significance of the naming by Joseph should not be lost. Nowadays it is possible to establish descent by genetic tests. In Jewish tradition, since this was not possible, and other procedures were ambiguous, the law simply based paternity on the man's acknowledgement of the child as his. "If a man says, 'This is my son,' he is to be believed" (Mishna *Baba Bathra* 8:6). By naming Jesus, Joseph acknowledges him and thus becomes his legal father, handing on to Jesus the title *Son of David*.

When God stands some human procedure on its head, there must be something to be learned. There is no degradation of sexuality here, only a corrective. Sexuality as a gift of the divine was highly prized in all ancient cultures. Pantheons were filled with male deities and their consorts, some of them behaving quite "humanly" in their sexual relationships. In the Bible, the distinction of sexes is something found in creatures, not in the creator. Yet it enjoys God's blessing and the command to "increase and multiply." Human fertility, as well as fertility of land and livestock, was thus seen to be a mark of God's favor, and sterility a curse. In Israel, sexuality was understood to be the normal channel for the transmission of the promise made to Abraham and to the royal house of David. In this patriarchal culture it was the male progenitor who got the attention, and circumcision was the chief outward sign of this covenant promise.

Yet already in the OT there are occasions when the mother is mentioned along with the promised Messiah and the father is passed over in silence. In Micah 5:2 this is the case, but it is particularly striking in Isaiah 7:14, for there by omitting the father, Ahaz, in preference to the future queen mother, the oracle shows God's fidelity to his promise despite the failure of the male progenitor. The Lord may not have bypassed Ahaz's physical cooperation, but the king gets no consideration in the transmission of the promise. It is not physical generation that assures the promise, but faith. Thus while cherishing the gift of sexuality as bearer of the promise, Matthew uses the virginal conception by Mary and the celibate fatherhood of Joseph to humble the vaunted claims of sexuality and its patriarchal form in Israel as the transmitter of the promise.

There is good news here for those who through circumstance or choice do not have children of their own. God wants everyone to know that biological generation means nothing if parents and children do not know how to relate to one another. And God wants orphans, adopting parents and adopted children to know that it is love, not genetics, that is the real transmitter of life. Those in the ministry of education, nursing, counseling and the other helping professions need to know that they can truly parent others who are not physically their children. Religious who choose celibacy for the kingdom have no sterility to bewail, for they can transmit life to a multitude of children as part of the hundredfold Jesus promised (Mk 10:30) and as Paul himself experienced: "You are my children!" (Gal 4:19). The day I left south Asia one of my novices, who had lost his father during his novitiate year, burst into tears as we exchanged a parting hug and said, "You have been a real father to me." I could say the same about many others who have fathered me into life as Joseph did for Jesus.

## Adoration by the Gentiles (2:1–12)

2 NOW WHEN Jesus was born in Bethlehem of Judea in the days of Herod the king, behold, wise men from the East came to Jerusalem, saying, [2]"Where is he who has been born king of the Jews? For we have seen his star in the East, and have come to worship him." [3]When Herod the king heard this, he was troubled, and all Jerusalem with him; [4]and assembling all the chief priests and scribes of the people, he inquired of them where the Christ was to be born. [5]They told him, "In Bethlehem of Judea; for so it is written by the prophet:

[6]"And you, O Bethlehem, in the land of Judah,

are by no means least among the rulers of Judah;
for from you shall come a ruler
who will govern my people Israel.' "
7 Then Herod summoned the wise men secretly and
ascertained from them what time the star appeared; [8]and he
sent them to Bethlehem, saying, "Go and search diligently
for the child, and when you have found him bring me word,
that I too may come and worship him." [9]When they had
heard the king they went their way; and lo, the star which
they had seen in the East went before them, till it came to
rest over the place where the child was. [10]When they saw
the star, they rejoiced exceedingly with great joy; [11]and
going into the house they saw the child with Mary his mother, and they fell down and worshiped him. Then, opening
their treasures, they offered him gifts, gold and frankincense and myrrh. [12]And being warned in a dream not to
return to Herod, they departed to their own country by
another way.

This story is the centerpiece of Matthew's infancy narrative, and centerpieces for Matthew are important keys to the
meaning of the larger units of his work. We will briefly discuss
details of the passage, then reflect on its meaning.

Matthew's casual, subordinate way of introducing Bethlehem supposes that Jesus' birthplace was well known to his audience. So too the reference to Herod the Great, whose memory
was still fresh to second generation Palestinians, surrounded
as they were by structures or ruins of structures he built: the
vast temple of Jerusalem, the fortress Antonia, a theater and
amphitheater in Jerusalem, the crater-cupped fortress Hero-
dion, the refuge fortress at Masada, the Hellenistic cities of
Sebaste, Caesarea, Antipatris and Pharsaelis. From their parents and grandparents the Jewish readers of Matthew would
also have heard of Herod's paranoid brutality. Josephus describes the king's agonizing death with gruesome detail, telling
how he locked up the nobles of the land, giving orders that at
his death they should all be slain so that instead of general
rejoicing at the death of the tyrant "all Judea. . . will weep
over me whether they want to or not" (*Jewish Wars* I, 33).

Though we have no independent account of the event, the slaying of the innocents of Bethlehem is perfectly in keeping with Herod's capricious, barbarous character.

Who are these *magoi* from the East? In our Christmas songs and traditions they are called "wise men" or "kings" or "magi." Some recent translations, like the NAB, render the term less romantically and more accurately "astrologers," although in deference to Christian piety the NABR reverts to "Magi." Coming from the direction of Babylon, they would have been acquainted with Jewish messianic hopes, for there had been a Jewish community in Babylon since the time of the exile, now composed of descendants of those Jews who chose to settle there instead of returning to their homeland. They may also have been magicians of sorts, but if so they were not charlatans. They were seekers in faith.

They go to Jerusalem first rather than to Bethlehem. This can be understood at two levels. One, on the level of common sense: foreigners coming to worship a new-born king might indeed be suspect to the reigning king were not the new-born the incumbent king's son. Though these foreigners do not anticipate any trouble, they are keenly aware of the canons of eastern protocol. At a deeper level, however, they are led first to Jerusalem because the salvation of the gentiles "comes from the Jews" (John 4:22). That they come to Jerusalem and discover the Jewish scriptures first means that they enter into the salvation history of the chosen people. The infant king they will find is not only the fulfillment of their alien hopes but the culmination of a long history of a particular people. The earliest gentiles thus model the catechumenate of the later gentiles, who will be instructed in the Greek OT before they receive Christian baptism.

What is the star? Many have sought to identify a cosmic event, such as a supernova, or Halley's comet known to have appeared in 12–11 B.C. or the conjunction of Jupiter, Saturn and Mars in 7–6 B.C. Others consider the star simply to be a legendary element recalling the prophecy of Balaam in Num 24:17. Popular Jewish religion tried somehow to accommodate the stars to its beliefs, for excavated synagogues in Palestine and Rome have revealed signs of the zodiac. And Qumran's

Cave IV yielded fragments of an astrological treatise in Aramaic. Thus, whatever the origin of this story, that well-intentioned astrologers would have sought the meaning of an unusual constellation fits well the popular beliefs of the times.

The giving of gifts symbolic of their trade could mean the astrologers are leaving their old occupation behind in favor of their new found faith. If so, the gifts are seen as worthy manifestations of sincere seeking hearts. The Tropar of the Ukrainian liturgy of the Nativity expresses the transformation of the astrologers this way: "Your nativity, O Christ our God, has shed the light of understanding upon the world. Through it, those who had been star-worshippers learned through a star to worship you, the Sun of truth and to recognize in you the one who rises in the East and comes from on high."

The prostration of the astrologers is more than reverence for a king, though in royal eastern protocol the distinction between honor given to a king and divine worship was not at all clear, at least for non-Jews. But Matthew's audience, who believe in the divinity of Jesus, would understand their reverence to be worship in the strict sense, just as they would when Matthew uses it elsewhere of persons well-disposed towards Jesus (2:8, 11; 4:9, 10; 8:2; 9:18; 15:25, etc.).

That the visit of the astrologers should gain such notoriety that "all Jerusalem" is troubled and that Herod should summon "the chief priests and scribes *of the people*" may surprise us, until we realize that Matthew is forecasting the passion, in which official Jerusalem will ally with the imperial power against Jesus, in fulfillment of messianic Psalm 2:2, "The kings of the earth rise up and the leaders conspire together against the Lord and against his anointed."

The Scripture text concerning Bethlehem is a creative Matthaean fusion of Micah 5:1 and 2 Sam 5:2. The star, not visible to the eyes of unbelieving Jerusalem, is seen again by those seeking in sincere faith. "When they saw the star, they *rejoiced* with *exceedingly great joy*" (v. 10). Matthew's redundance here is intentional. The expression anticipates the "great joy" of the women on Easter morning (28:8).

They find the child "with Mary, his mother." Why the omission of Joseph? He is surely not dead, for he will re-appear in the next scene. No doubt Matthew here wishes to focus on the kingship of Jesus. In the Davidic messianic tradition the Queen Mother was intimately associated with the king. The "queen" in Judah was never the king's bride but his mother. Matthew himself had evoked this role for Mary in the Isaian prophecy in 1:23. In the Roman catacombs of Priscilla, the earliest painting of Mary (second century) is of this scene.

Gold, frankincense and myrrh were common stock of magicians, but Jewish tradition also saw them as gifts suitable for a king (Ps 45:8; 72:10, 11, 15; Is 60:6; Sg 3:6) and that is probably Matthew's understanding of them here. Because of this, later Christians, helped by reflection on Ps 72:10, assumed the astrologers themselves were kings. The church fathers saw the gold as symbol of royalty, the incense that of divinity, and the myrrh that of the coming passion of Jesus.

What does this story say to the church today, for whom the Jewish-Gentile tension is only of archival interest? I see the following applications:

1. For Matthew there was on the one hand the "established group" who were challenged out of their comfort by the new, foreign element. Today there are baptized Christians who form a church of sorts but one that has little interest in sharing the faith beyond its own comfortable confines. A church or a community that is not interested in evangelization is, in Matthew's view, no longer the church of Jesus Christ, as we shall see most dramatically in chapter 28.

2. In the interface with persons of other religions, we must respect the ways that they seek God, aware that the intensity of their longing for God may well shame our pusillanimity and smug self-contentedness. On the other hand, to assume the attitude that "everyone will be saved anyhow," that Christianity has no unique message, that there is no value in the disturbance (*mutual* disturbance!) which the interaction of religious faiths causes—is to reject the very e sence of *gospel*—which means good news to be shared.

3. Many Christians in the developed world or in Christian countries will have little opportunity to interact with those

of non-Christian origin. But a "gentile" can also be, in our daily experience, any person or group we have consciously or unconsciously written off. Luke's first adorers of the infant Savior are not astrologers from afar but poor, outcast shepherds from nearby. To be a Christian is to be called to make community with those who are not automatically attractive. It is a call to put love where there is none and in doing so to find it. Matthew will develop this program in detail in chapter 18.

4. Though this story is often used in support of mission to foreign countries, the scene here is not the sending scene of chapter 28. Rather it is the *coming* of the gentiles on their own—or at least not by human intermediaries—to Christ. The application should rather, therefore, be to the interface of the Christian community with those who knock on its doors. How much warmth of welcome do we give those seeking the Lord in our midst? Or, how well do we welcome newcomers to our church—or the lapsed who choose one day to "try it again"? The ministry of welcome and support to the catechumen and the seeker is a missionary ministry indeed.

5. Finally, the seeking attitude of these foreigners, who have so little external help to guide them and yet respond with wholehearted devotion and undertake a long, persevering journey to find the Lord-King, challenges all who are comfortably ensconced at some point of their own spiritual journey and have not moved for years, whether they be in or outside the Christian fold. Walter Buhlmann in *The Coming of the Third Church* relates how he was non-plussed when a Hindu lady in an Indian train leaned forward and asked him, "Can you tell me how to find God?" Finding God, even for Christians, is not a once-for-all event. It is a daily journey, where there are few resting places and no permanent dwellings.

## Refugee Family (2:13–18)

13 Now when they had departed, behold, an angel of the Lord appeared to Joseph in a dream and said, "Rise,

take the child and his mother, and flee to Egypt, and remain
there till I tell you; for Herod is about to search for the child,
to destroy him." ¹⁴And he rose and took the child and his
mother by night, and departed to Egypt, ¹⁵and remained
there until the death of Herod. This was to fulfil what the
Lord had spoken by the prophet, "Out of Egypt have I
called my son."

16 Then Herod, when he saw that he had been tricked
by the wise men, was in a furious rage, and he sent and
killed all the male children in Bethlehem and in all that
region who were two years old or under, according to the
time which he had ascertained from the wise men. ¹⁷Then
was fulfilled what was spoken by the prophet Jeremiah:
¹⁸"A voice was heard in Ramah,
  wailing and loud lamentation,
  Rachel weeping for her children;
  she refused to be consoled,
  because they were no more."

Having climaxed the identification of Jesus with David in
the coming of the astrologers to worship "the king of the Jews,"
Matthew now picks up the hostility of Herod implied in 2:12
and uses it to identify Jesus with Moses, who, though threatened in his childhood by a paranoid ruler, was God's chosen
lawgiver and savior. Beyond that identification, however, Jesus
relives in a brief interval of his childhood the centuries-span-
ning story of Israel's migration to Egypt and return. "Out of
Egypt I called my son" was originally the prophet Hosea's description of the exodus of the entire nation from Egypt (Hos
11:1), but now more fittingly fulfilled in the singular son, Jesus.

In saying that Herod will "search to destroy" the child,
Matthew evokes Pharaoh's searching to destroy Moses (Ex
2:15) and Solomon's attempt to kill Jeroboam (1 Kgs 11:40). It
is also a forecast of the plot of the priests and elders "to destroy
Jesus" (27:20).

If Matthew lacks Luke's details of poverty in the birthplace and the first visitors, he makes up for it by describing
the insecurity that faces Joseph, Mary and the child as they
set out for Egypt. Though there were certainly Jews living in

Egypt, a pious Israelite could hardly think of going there unless he had no choice, for Egypt represented the old life of
slavery and sin, the oppressor from whom the Lord delivered
his people to settle them in the promised land. So the family
becomes refugee, another way by which Jesus shares an experience so frequently repeated in our day. Anyone who has
been a refugee or worked with refugees knows the uncertainty,
the humiliation, the reduction to dependency, the alienation
from homeland, relatives and friends which exile brings. It is
a terrible fate for the parents who feel responsible for their
children's welfare yet often are at a loss to provide it. During
the civil war in Sri Lanka, I was involved in helping a refugee
family whose name—would you believe—was Joseph. The
father had been stationmaster in Jaffna. Their home was
bombed, the school the children attended was hit by mortar
fire, even the local hospital had been shelled. They were among
the fortunate ones to escape, but they had been tricked by an
"agent" who promised them paradise, taking their money but
not producing results. I will never forget the look in the father's eyes as I read his anxiety primarily for his children, their
safety, nurture and care. Joseph's and Mary's must have been
similar.

Jeremiah poetically described the exile of earlier Israelite
refugees to Babylon as Rachel, Jacob's wife, weeping over her
children. He places her at Ramah, six miles north of Jerusalem,
near her traditional burial site on the road the exiles took to
Babylon. But a very ancient scribal gloss on Gen 35:19 places
her tomb at "Ephrath, that is, Bethlehem." So for Matthew
Ramah is synonymous with Bethlehem. The sorrow of Rachel
at the disappearance of her children is repeated and intensified
in the slaughter of the innocents. Matthew cannot conceive of
this tragedy as directly willed and planned by God. Thus he
departs from his usual citation formula, "This took place to
fulfill what the Lord had spoken. . ." and says instead, "Then
was fulfilled what was spoken through the prophet Jeremiah."

## Homecoming (2:19–23)

19 But when Herod died, behold, an angel of the Lord
appeared in a dream to Joseph in Egypt, saying, ²⁰"Rise,

take the child and his mother, and go to the land of Israel,
for those who sought the child's life are dead." [21]And he rose
and took the child and his mother, and went to the land of
Israel. [22]But when he heard that Archelaus reigned over
Judea in place of his father Herod, he was afraid to go there,
and being warned in a dream he withdrew to the district of
Galilee. [23]And he went and dwelt in a city called Nazareth,
that what was spoken by the prophets might be fulfilled,
"He shall be called a Nazarene."

Again Joseph receives guidance in a dream. We would expect v. 20 to read: "for he who sought the child's life is dead."
Matthew uses the plural *those* intentionally to evoke the Lord's
command to Moses in Ex 4:19, "Go back to Egypt, for all those
who sought your life are dead." Archelaus was no improvement
over his father Herod. During his ten year reign he succeeded
in alienating his own people as well as the emperor Augustus,
who exiled him to Gaul. Galilee was in the hands of Herod
Antipas, and history agrees with Matthew that his rule there
was more peaceful. Joseph "withdrew"—a verb used consis-
tently by Matthew to indicate withdrawal from a faithless or
hostile environment. Galilee is important for Matthew because
it was a country mixed with gentiles, a good seed-ground for
the more inclusive kind of religious attitude for which Jesus
would be known and condemned.

"He shall be called a Nazorean" is not a quotation from
any specific OT text. Matthew hints that he knows this by at-
tributing it not to a single prophet but to "the prophets." This
legitimizes the opinion of scholars that Nazareth suggested to
Matthew the words *Neser*, the "branch" of the House of David
in Isaiah 11:1, and *Nazir* for "Nazirite," meaning "holy one of
God" (combining Is 4:3 with Judges 16:17).

Matthew's infancy gospel is a tapestry of OT motifs. There
are echoes of Moses' infancy as well as that of Samson the
Nazirite. Jesus relives the history of Israel in the brief span
of his early years. He is the Messiah, Son of David and King,
born of the virgin Mary in fulfillment of Isaiah's prophecy. But
he is also destined to bring salvation to the gentiles (foreign
women in the genealogy; the astrologers; the settling in Galilee

of the gentiles). There are also preludes to the major themes
of the gospel: Jesus will be teacher and lawgiver, rejected and
persecuted by the leaders of his people, yet welcomed by believing gentiles. In particular, elements of these first chapters
will be repeated in the concluding chapter 28. Jesus is God-
with-us (1:23; 28:20). The Jewish authorities are convened (2:4;
28:12), gentiles are welcomed or sought out (2:1–12; 28:19), Jesus is adored (2:11; 28:11,17), angels convey the divine message
(1:20; 28:5). We are already given a taste, then, of Matthew's
favorite devices: Old Testament fulfillment, foreshadowing and
symmetrical use of themes.  ■

# Book One:

---

# Proclaiming the Kingdom
# (3:1–7:28)

*Call to Repentance (3:1–6)*

3 IN THOSE days came John the Baptist, preaching in the wilderness of Judea, ²"Repent, for the kingdom of heaven is at hand." ³For this is he who was spoken of by the prophet Isaiah when he said,
"The voice of one crying in the wilderness:
Prepare the way of the Lord,
make his paths straight."
⁴Now John wore a garment of camel's hair, and a leather girdle around his waist; and his food was locusts and wild honey. ⁵Then went out to him Jerusalem and all Judea and all the region about the Jordan, ⁶and they were baptized by him in the river Jordan, confessing their sins.

"In those days" is chronologically vague, but Matthew uses the expression in its OT sense as a sign post for narrating sacred history. John is neither a guru nor a wisdom teacher. He is a prophet. Clothed like Elijah (2 Kgs 1:8), with whom Jesus will later identify him (11:13), he loves the desert as a place of encounter with the Lord (1 Kgs 19:1–18). But unlike Elijah he shuns the cities and preaches only in the desert.

Near the mouth of the Jordan on the northwest bank of the Dead Sea stood the monastery of Qumran, where a number of devout Jews lived in anticipation of the final cosmic battle of God against the forces of evil. John surely knew of the place, but whether he spent any time there or how he was related to the Essenes we do not know. He shared their love of the desert and their attitude towards the Pharisees and the Sadducees but

not their predestinarian doctrine nor their expectation that
only in the desert could salvation be found.

That he was in the desert does not mean he was out of
contact with people, for one of the great trade routes from the
East to Jerusalem crossed the Jordan just north of the Dead
Sea. It was the major "truck stop" of the region. But John's
choice of the desert is also symbolic. The Lord had spoken
through Hosea: "I will lead her into the desert and speak to
her heart" (Hos 2:16). For Amos (5:25) and Jeremiah (2:2–7)
the desert represented the time of Israel's honeymoon with the
Lord, the period of her pristine fidelity before she fell into the
corruption of the land. For Hosea it would be the place for
Israel's return to her covenant with the Lord. From there he
would lead her, renewed and purified, once again into the promised land (Hos 2:17–25). It was also the place for building a
highway on which the Lord would bring home the exiles from
Babylon (Is 40:3). All four gospels interpret that Isaian text to
be fulfilled in John's preaching, which prepares the way for
Jesus.

But John is more than a prophet, as Jesus will later say
(11:9). He is a herald, an announcer of an event, the inbreaking
of the kingdom. Unlike Mark and Luke, Matthew places on the
Baptist's lips the same words Jesus will use to begin his ministry: "Repent, for the kingdom of heaven is at hand" (4:17).
Thus the good news begins already with John the Baptist.

And that means it begins with repentance. There is no
experience of the kingdom without it. If for so many today the
"kingdom" seems an antiquated, foreign concept, is it perhaps
because today we hear so little about judgment, sin and repentance? We hear a lot about guilt as a crippling thing. Ther-
apists try to rid their clients of it—often by the pain-killer
method rather than the specific antidote. False guilt is one
thing, healthy guilt is another. And the way to get rid of
healthy guilt is not to excuse it or pretend it isn't there, or,
worse yet, to revise the law of God. The way to freedom, joy
and new life is to repent and receive the forgiveness of God.

For Matthew this forgiveness comes with Jesus. Mark and
Luke say that John preached a "baptism of repentance for the
forgiveness of sins" (Mk 1:4; Lk 3:3). Matthew, wanting to

make it clear that only the sacrifice of Jesus makes possible the total and universal forgiveness of sins, reserves this expression for Jesus' words over the cup of his blood at the Last Supper: "This is my blood of the covenant, which is poured out for many for the *forgiveness of sins*" (26:28).

For the first time in Matthew we encounter the expression *kingdom of heaven*, the evangelist's typically Jewish way of avoiding direct mention of God. Matthew does not mean the kingdom *in* heaven but the kingdom *from* heaven, God's rule which is established on earth. God rules over the whole universe, of course, but the kingdom of humankind is in revolt against God's rule, and the Lord-King is coming to set everything right. Jesus builds his preaching on this current concept but modifies it dramatically, as we shall see.

### Repentance Must Be Sincere (3:7–10)

7 But when he saw many of the Pharisees and Sadducees coming for baptism, he said to them, "You brood of vipers! Who warned you to flee from the wrath to come? ⁸Bear fruit that befits repentance, ⁹and do not presume to say to yourselves, 'We have Abraham as our father'; for I tell you, God is able from these stones to raise up children to Abraham. ¹⁰Even now the axe is laid to the root of the trees; every tree therefore that does not bear good fruit is cut down and thrown into the fire.

Among those who come for John's baptism are two groups whose sincerity he doubts. The Sadducees, found mainly in and around Jerusalem, accepted only the written law. The Pharisees, in addition, accepted the later oral tradition which sought to apply the law to the many details of daily life. John attacks their religious complacency. "Brood of vipers" is language Jesus will later use (12:34; 23:33). Relying on their descent from Abraham, the stone from which they were quarried (Is 51:1–2), they lack the good works which would make them acceptable to God and immune to the coming judgment. John plays on the words *banim*, meaning "children" and *abanim* meaning "stones." The real children of the kingdom will be the ones God

makes, not those who expect their own religiosity to be rewarded.

The greatest obstacle to genuine repentance is found in
those who somewhere got just enough religion to be inoculated
against its further demands. There is such a thing as "plateau
religion"—when a person reaches an "arrangement" with the
disturbing questions of life and defends his or her immobility
with an arsenal of rote answers and rituals. That person has
channeled the river of life into a moat. Such was the attitude
John attacked then. Such is the attitude Matthew warns us
against as we enter his gospel.

## The Messiah-Judge (3:11-12)

11 "I baptize you with water for repentance, but he
who is coming after me is mightier than I, whose sandals I
am not worthy to carry; he will baptize you with the Holy
Spirit and with fire. [12]His winnowing fork is in his hand, and
he will clear his threshing floor and gather his wheat into
the granary, but the chaff he will burn with unquenchable
fire."

John's ministry prepares not only for the inbreaking of
God's rule but also for the "mightier one" to come. The term
is a frequent one in the Greek OT for the divinity itself. In the
non-canonical Psalms of Solomon it is applied to the awaited
Messiah. In comparison with him, John has the role of the slave
who, after untying the thongs of his master's sandals (as in Mk
and Lk), carries them after him into the house. Not only is the
coming one of greater authority, but his baptism will be different. It will be a baptism of judgment. The image of fire and
the winnowing fan both make this clear. And, surely at the
level of John's preaching, even the mention of the Holy Spirit
suggests judgment. In Isaiah 4:4 the expression "spirit of fire,
spirit of burning" (translated appropriately by the NAB as
"blast of his searing judgment") depicts God's spirit or breath
or wind as a fire of judgment or cleansing. The monastery at
Qumran also referred to the purification of humankind "of all
impurity by the holy spirit" (*Community Rule* 4:20–21).

It appears then that in John's preaching the Holy Spirit was not meant to evoke grace but judgment, John's baptism by water being the last chance to avoid being burned with the chaff. Later when John sends his disciples to Jesus to ask him whether indeed he is "the one who was to come," Jesus will emphasize his compassion and mercy as a revision of John's portrait. For the moment, however, it will not be amiss to understand the text as a call to the reader today to prepare for purification. If "our God is a consuming fire" (Heb 12:29), if "fire goes before him and consumes his foes" (Ps 97:3), if "the day of his coming . . . is like the refiner's fire" (Mal 3:3), then to meet God is to be burned free of all that does not befit his holiness. The hardened sinner might hear this as bad news, but since this fire is nothing else than God's love, it will, like the fire that burns the forest, merely clear the way for new life.

## Jesus the Penitent (3:13–17)

13 Then Jesus came from Galilee to the Jordan to John, to be baptized by him. [14]John would have prevented him, saying, "I need to be baptized by you, and do you come to me?" [15]But Jesus answered him, "Let it be so now; for thus it is fitting for us to fulfil all righteousness." Then he consented. [16]And when Jesus was baptized, he went up immediately from the water, and behold, the heavens were opened and he saw the Spirit of God descending like a dove, and alighting on him; [17]and lo, a voice from heaven, saying, "This is my beloved Son, with whom I am well pleased."

If the Messiah John predicted was to come with the fire of God's judgment, there could be no more surprising scene than the one that now follows. Jesus queues up with the penitents approaching John to confess their sins and be baptized. Matthew more than the other evangelists stresses the shock of John, reflecting also perhaps a scruple of the later Christian community, that the Christ should so confound the expectations of even the most saintly of the Jewish people. The Messiah does not come in a fiery chariot, not even in a royal one. He, the baptizer with the Holy Spirit, comes barefoot and lost in the crowd, one penitent among many.

When John seeks to prevent this reversal of roles, Jesus explains, "Let it be so for now; for in this way it is fitting for us to fulfill all justice." What is the meaning of this mysterious phrase, "to fulfill all justice"? The Greek word *dikaiosune* is sometimes translated "righteousness" (KJV, RSV, NABR) or "all that God requires" (Phillips) or "all God's demands" (NAB). It is a favorite word on the lips of Jesus in Matthew. Those who hunger and thirst for it and those who are persecuted for it are blest (5:6,10). The "righteousness" of Jesus' disciples must surpass that of the scribes and Pharisees (5:20). In 6:1 it is equivalent to "religious acts." In 21:32 it is the way of life preached by John the Baptist. Thus some translations render it simply "holiness," as in the NAB version of 6:33: "Seek first [the Father's] kingship over you, his way of *holiness* . . ."

But here at the Baptism scene, the word means a specific plan or call of God which Jesus is to fulfill. In the OT and in Paul the "justice of God" often means his plan of salvation for his people. That would suit the context very well here, as Jesus has come to fulfill that plan in a way different from what John has expected. Jesus does not come from outside human experience but from within. Though not a sinner, his love for sinners leads him to take on their sinful state, to enter into their repentance and make it his own, to be "God with us" in that area of life we would judge farthest from God, sin. Repentance at least would seem to be something the sinful human heart brings to God; instead it is something God himself is a part of, something Jesus himself experiences and leads in—or, more exactly, brings up the rear in! If the penitent despairs of finding in his own heart repentance appropriate to his sin, he may look to Jesus to find his sin already repented for and take that repentance as completing the inadequacies of his own. "For our sake he made him to be sin who knew no sin, so that in him we might become the righteousness (*dikaiosune*) of God" (2 Cor 5:21).

There is a distant anticipation of the passover mystery here. As Jesus fulfills the justice of God by descending into the water, the Father fulfills his justice by a theophany, not only illustrating Jesus' teaching that "he who humbles himself will be exalted," but anticipating the Father's response to Jesus' submission in his passion and death by the glory of the resurrection.

Here the theophany involves the Spirit and the voice. The Spirit with which Jesus will baptize appears above the Penitent, reassuring John that baptizing Jesus was what God wanted. In Hosea 7:11; 11:11 and the Song of Solomon, the dove is a symbol of Israel or the beloved. If that is the symbolism being evoked, the dove is a symbol of Jesus. But since the dove is explicitly identified as "the Spirit of God," it is more likely that we are being invited to remember the spirit of God that hovered over the primeval waters at the first creation. Ben Zoma, a younger contemporary of the apostles, in reflecting on Genesis 1:2, said, "The Spirit of God was brooding on the face of the waters like a dove which broods over her young but does not touch them" (*B.Hag.* 15a). The dove then signals that the world is being created anew in the baptism of Jesus, a meaning which Paul and later Christian liturgy will richly exploit.

The Father's voice is addressed not to Jesus (as in Mark and Luke) but to the world. Whether there was an audience to hear the voice at the actual baptism of Jesus is irrelevant to Matthew. What is important is that we, the readers, hear it. The words are a combination of several OT texts. Isaiah 42:1 is the most obvious: "*This is my* servant whom I uphold, my chosen one *with whom I am pleased,* upon whom I have put my spirit; he shall bring forth justice to the nations." The word *beloved* may come from another servant text in Isaiah 44:2, "Jacob, my servant, the beloved I have chosen," or it may evoke Gen 22:2, where Isaac is called Abraham's beloved son who is to be offered in sacrifice. Another interesting text is Psalm 89, which sings of God's love and his covenant choice of David, his servant (vv. 4, 21). There is a reference to the anointing of David with holy oil to make him strong (vv. 21–22—compare the "stronger one" in Matthew). Then: "My faithfulness and my steadfast love shall be with him, and in my name shall his horn be exalted. I will set his hand on the sea and his right hand on the rivers. He shall cry to me, 'Thou art my Father, my God, and the Rock of my salvation.' And I will make him the first-born, the highest of the kings of the earth"

(vv. 25–27). Note the themes of exaltation, standing victorious over the waters, God as his father, the Messiah as God's son, the firstborn. To sum up, there is a melding here of OT texts portraying the Messiah king and the Servant of the Lord. Thus this terse voice identifies Jesus as the personal Messiah but also, as Matthew has been at pains to tell us in his infancy gospel, as the embodiment of Israel as a people. Another way of emphasizing that Jesus will save his people not as a *deus ex machina* but by identification with them, as God-with-us.

This identification of Jesus with the people of God can best be understood in terms of what the scholars have called *corporate personality*, a concept somewhat foreign to western thinking. The Bible's interest in persons like Adam, Abraham, Isaac, Jacob and Joseph, and women such as Eve, Sarah and Rachel, is not so much in their uniqueness as in the fact that their experiences embody and often forecast those of their descendants. Adam's fall and loss of integrity after a period of intimacy with God typifies the experience of the whole human race. The Lord's providential choice of Jacob despite or even because of his trickster character typifies the Lord's continuing choice of "Jacob" (used as a name for the people descended from him) despite their ambiguous virtue. And so on. Similarly, by evoking peak moments in Israel's history, Matthew sees Jesus as summing up and typifying that history in a purified form, of living that history as it should have been lived.

But more than that. The corporate personality of Jesus also looks forward. He embodies and models the new people of God, the church. We see *our* experience pre-lived and modeled in Jesus, beginning with baptism and continuing, as we shall see, in the temptation and public life of Jesus. Matthew does not have Paul's image of the church as the body of Christ, nor John's of the vine and the branches. But his ecclesiology is no less profoundly Christ-centered in the even more biblically rooted concept of corporate personality. He is God-with-us not only as *El-Gibor*, champion, but as *one of us*—or better, the One that *is us*. He has been through our spiritual journey before us and is now with us as we re-live his.

*Faithful Son (4:1–11)*

4 THEN JESUS was led up by the Spirit into the wilderness to be tempted by the devil. ²And he fasted forty days and forty nights, and afterward he was hungry. ³And the tempter came and said to him, "If you are the Son of God, command these stones to become loaves of bread." ⁴But he answered, "It is written,

'Man shall not live by bread alone,
but by every word that proceeds from the mouth of God.'"

⁵Then the devil took him to the holy city, and set him on the pinnacle of the temple, ⁶and said to him, "If you are the Son of God, throw yourself down; for it is written,

'He will give his angels charge of you,'

and

'On their hands they will bear you up,
lest you strike your foot against a stone.'"

⁷Jesus said to him, "Again it is written, 'You shall not tempt the Lord your God.'" ⁸Again, the devil took him to a very high mountain, and showed him all the kingdoms of the world and the glory of them; ⁹and he said to him, "All these I will give you, if you will fall down and worship me." ¹⁰Then Jesus said to him, "Begone, Satan! for it is written,

'You shall worship the Lord your God
and him only shall you serve.'"

¹¹Then the devil left him, and behold, angels came and ministered to him.

After the people of Israel passed through the waters to freedom in the Exodus, they were tested in the desert for forty years. A number of times they failed, complaining against the Lord and even worshipping a god made by their own hands. Jesus, the faithful Israel, has just passed through the waters of the new creation, and he is led into the desert by the Holy Spirit in order to face the evil spirit who will test the validity of the baptism and the voice that proclaimed Jesus God's son. The three temptations look backwards to Israel's history and forward to Jesus' ministry and the life of the church.

Is there any power in the title "son of God"? The proof would be—so argues the tempter—in Jesus' turning stones into bread to satisfy his hunger. Unspoken, of course, is the assumption that Jesus should use whatever divine power he might have in his own interest, and should he do so in the matter of food, he would in effect withdraw himself from solidarity with his people of old and the people of his day who do not have it in their power to do such things and must instead rely on the sweat of their brow and trust in God. Jesus' answer means that he will use the power of his divine sonship only in the service of others, not in his self-interest. Even on the cross he will not resort to a miraculous escape.

Jesus' choice of Deut 8:1–3 to parry the tempter contains another lesson. Bread for the stomach is not enough to feed the human person. Only God's word can satisfy the deepest longing of the human heart. Fasting expresses hunger for that food of the spirit. On the other hand, when people are starving, what God expects is that we give them food, not some pious palliative (25:35; James 2:15–17). Later in his ministry Jesus will fill his listeners with both kinds of bread. Here, in the temptation, Jesus reverses ancient Israel's failure in the desert by preferring to wait for the Father's word than to take the tempter's invitation to dinner.

Jesus has shown himself to be immune to the temptation to selfish indulgence. He is not a charlatan but a truly spiritual man. A spiritual man! Very well, muses the tempter. We will move our battlefield to religious grounds, the temple and the word of God—which, as Shakespeare said, the devil can quote brilliantly to his purpose. If the temptation to premature indulgence could be dismissed as not from God, the temptation induced by religious motives is most difficult to discern. How many crimes, wars, deaths, tortures and other forms of violence have been committed because the perpetrators were convinced "God wants it"! A spiritual, religious person may not be seduced in the flesh; but he may be all the more susceptible to seduction in the spirit. When the tempter cannot make us fall by our weaknesses, he will try to make us fall by our strengths. He is the cleverest of wrestlers. He tempts Jesus to do something that would glorify God and prove the truth of God's word!

The only problem is that Jesus, not the Father, would be setting the agenda. And that would mean trying to get control of
God's power and manipulating it in one's own interest. Another
word for black magic. Israel of old "tested" God in this way;
Jesus rejects this avenue both because he is faithful to Israel
and because his miracles will not be religious entertainment.
They will not be exercises in magic, glorifying only the magi-
cian, but works of compassion and healing, glorifying and revealing the Father.

Finally, bested in the realms both of the flesh and the
spirit, the devil is willing to throw all he has into a final assault.
So this man is God's son, sent to bring the kingdom of God on
earth. I will give him the prize he can't resist, the temptation
of the short-cut. Deal with the devil and you will get what you
want more quickly. If you are to be king, why not get your
kingdom the easy way? Why take the path of obedience to the
Father, which could lead to failure and death? But the price?
Giving to the devil what belongs to God alone. Israel of old
failed through idolatry. Jesus will not.

A number of consequences for today's Christians are apparent from Matthew's account of the temptations of Jesus. If
we are baptized in the Holy Spirit with Jesus, then the first
leading of the Spirit in us is to face clearly the demons which
will beset us on the journey. There will be many, no doubt,
certainly more than three. But it is important to face and name
the major ones at the start, lest the work of the Holy Spirit
be prematurely undone. We are warned first that we will be
tempted to gauge our life by its human comforts rather than
by our obedience to God's word. A culture of consumerism
might be all the tempter would need to fell us with one blow.
Secondly, we will be tempted even to misuse spiritual power
and spiritual gifts for our own glory or benefit rather than for
the service of others and the building of a kingdom of love.
Thirdly, we may be tempted to seize power by the short-cut,
to identify, for example, the political goals of a party as those
of the church or the kingdom. It goes without saying that if
we are to identify and dispel the demons that lurk in our path,
we shall periodically have to return with Jesus to the desert.

## To Galilee of the Gentiles (4:12–16)

12 Now when he heard that John had been arrested, he withdrew into Galilee; [13]and leaving Nazareth he went and dwelt in Caperna-um by the sea, in the territory of Zebulun and Naphtali, [14]that what was spoken by the prophet Isaiah might be fulfilled:
[15]"The land of Zebulun and the land of Naphtali,
  toward the sea, across the Jordan,
  Galilee of the Gentiles—
[16]the people who sat in darkness
  have seen a great light,
  and for those who sat in the region and shadow of
    death
  light has dawned."

After Herod arrests John the Baptist, Jesus withdraws from the desert, not to escape Herod, since Galilee was also part of his realm, but to illustrate a principle that will repeat itself often: rejection of the gospel in one place leads to the preaching of it in another (see Matthew's similar use of "withdrew" in 2:22; 12:15). John is "delivered up," a term Matthew will later use of Jesus (26:15). Jesus and John not only have the same message, they will suffer martyrdom during the reign of the same king. Whether Jesus returned to Nazareth only for a short stay or whether he simply transferred his residence to Capernaum is not clear. Capernaum "by the sea" (Matthew's way of connecting it clearly with the Scripture text) is in the old region of Naphtali, which with Zebulon and the other tribes of the northern kingdom was annexed by Assyria in 734 B.C. and thereafter flooded with pagan immigrants, giving the orthodox Jews in Jerusalem reason to suspect their doctrinal purity. Isaiah had foretold their deliverance, which Matthew, compressing Is 8:23–9:1, sees fulfilled when Jesus arrives there. Galilee, on the one hand, is the homeland of Jews, illustrating the principle that Jesus goes first to the lost sheep of the house of Israel (10:6; 15:4). But it is also the "district of the gentiles," giving Jesus much contact with non-Jews. Galilee thus typifies the mixed composition of Matthew's community.

*First Preaching and First Disciples (4:17–22)*

[17]From that time Jesus began to preach, saying, "Repent, for the kingdom of heaven is at hand."

18 As he walked by the Sea of Galilee, he saw two brothers, Simon who is called Peter and Andrew his brother, casting a net into the sea; for they were fishermen. [19]And he said to them, "Follow me, and I will make you fishers of men." [20]Immediately they left their nets and followed him. [21]And going on from there he saw two other brothers, James the son of Zebedee and John his brother, in the boat with Zebedee their father, mending their nets, and he called them. [22]Immediately they left the boat and their father, and followed him.

Verse 17 is a key link to the gospel. On the one hand, giving the same message as that of John the Baptist, it concludes the section beginning in chapter 3. On the other hand, the expression, "From that time onward Jesus began . . ." is the sign post of the first part of Jesus' public ministry, the second being at 16:21, where the same expression will be used.

From the earliest hour Jesus surrounds himself with disciples. Why? Because he realizes that his teaching will be lost if it is not embodied in the life of individuals and in the life of a community. This community, which today we call the church, will be light and salt for the world (5:13–16). Thus before Jesus teaches or works a single miracle, he must have witnesses. Witnesses not only in the sense of seeing and hearing what he does but witnesses willing to live the message. The preached word is quickly forgotten by the curious, the superficial, the uncommitted, the crowds. The written word may be the buried word if it is not alive in human hearts and proclaimed by a living voice.

But they are to be more than rabbinical students; they are to be more even than witnesses. Jesus' call includes a promise that he will make them fishers of men, a vocatio. They will begin to fulfill when Jesus sends them out on their first evangelizing mission in chapter 10.

So far we have met two of the key *dramatis personae* of Matthew's gospel, Jesus and the disciples. We will now meet the third, the crowds.

## The Crowds Gather (4:23–25)

23 And he went about all Galilee, teaching in their synagogues and preaching the gospel of the kingdom and healing every disease and every infirmity among the people. ²⁴So his fame spread throughout all Syria, and they brought him all the sick, those afflicted with various diseases and pains, demoniacs, epileptics and paralytics, and he healed them. ²⁵And great crowds followed him from Galilee and the Decapolis and Jerusalem and Judea and from beyond the Jordan.

This tiny section, a summary of Jesus' early Galilean ministry, is a key to Matthew's portrait of Jesus. Jesus *teaches*. No content of his teaching is given here, but we are prepared for the Sermon on the Mount soon to follow. For Matthew more than for any other evangelist, Jesus is teacher. He exploits a natural, weekly platform in the synagogues—which Matthew now classifies as *their* synagogues, since he considers the church no longer confined to its Jewish origins—and preaches the good news of the kingdom more frequently in the streets and countryside. He is also a *healer*, and thus we are prepared for the series of miracles to follow the Sermon on the Mount in chapters 8 and 9.

Why Matthew singles out Syria among the territories touched by Jesus' fame is a fascinating question. Many scholars think Matthew's community was situated in Syria, perhaps in or around Antioch, and if so Matthew would be rooting the apostolic evangelization of Syria in an earlier coming of Syrians to Jesus. Among them no doubt were also gentiles, like the Canaanite woman whose daughter Jesus heals in 15:21–28. Thus we have another forecast of the gentile mission and the mixed composition of Matthew's community.

The little section climaxes with a wide-angle view of the "great crowds" that come from all of Galilee and Judea, on both

sides of the Jordan. They have now taken their seats and the
stage is set for the Sermon on the Mount.

## DISCOURSE:
## THE NEW LAW-GIVER AND THE NEW LAW
## (5:1–7:28)

### The Setting (5:1–2)

5 SEEING THE crowds, he went up on the mountain, and
when he sat down his disciples came to him. [2]And he
opened his mouth and taught them, saying: . . .

This seemingly casual introduction is in fact a synthesis of
Matthew's understanding of church. There are three concentric
circles here. The outer circle is the *crowds*. They are attracted
to Jesus but as yet are uncommitted to him. They are curious,
they look for signs and miracles but otherwise remain passive.
In Matthew's day, they represent the masses yet to be evangelized. At the center is Jesus. Seeing the gathering crowds,
he wants to teach them because the teaching by which they
have been fed until now, even the teaching of Moses, is inadequate. To do this, like a new Moses, he "goes up the mountain"
to proclaim the new law. Between Jesus and the crowds are
the *disciples*. They leave the crowd and *come to him*. The disciples differ from the masses in their commitment to the person
of Jesus. They are willing to be publicly identified as his. They
"cross the line" by a decision which will prove costly. Thus in
this scene, often repeated no doubt in Jesus' public ministry,
Matthew sees a model for the church of his day. The church is
the gathering of Jesus' disciples *from* the masses to be taught
by him in the sight of the masses. For Matthew's community
of the eighties the disciples are the baptized, and the teaching
given to them and not directly to the crowds, is Christian ca-
techesis. The high expectations Jesus lays down in his teaching
are not for the crowd but for those who have committed themselves to him. The crowds hear the teaching but they also
watch the disciples to see how the teaching is received and how
it is lived.

For us today, there is a message. The high ideals Jesus will present will be nonsense or at most a quixotic dream if Jesus does not mean more to us than acceptability by the crowd and if we do not recognize that to be a Christian is a fundamental commitment entailing a willingness to be different and to be recognized as different because of our Christian faith and Christian values. It also means we are called to be listeners to his words and livers of his word before we try to preach or teach.

Jesus sits. The disciples stand as befits the rabbinic custom of the day. Then Matthew introduces the sermon with the solemnity of a fanfare: "And he opened his mouth" is redundant, but it recalls the solemn way wisdom teaching was introduced in the OT (Job 33:2; Ps 49:4; 78:2; Mt 13:35). Jesus, the new lawgiver, is also the new wisdom.

## God's Seesaw (5:3–12)

3 "Blessed are the poor in spirit, for theirs is the kingdom of heaven.

4 "Blessed are those who mourn, for they shall be comforted.

5 "Blessed are the meek, for they shall inherit the earth.

6 "Blessed are those who hunger and thirst for righteousness, for they shall be satisfied.

7 "Blessed are the merciful, for they shall obtain mercy.

8 "Blessed are the pure in heart, for they shall see God.

9 "Blessed are the peacemakers, for they shall be called sons of God.

10 "Blessed are those who are persecuted for righteousness' sake, for theirs is the kingdom of heaven.

11 "Blessed are you when men revile you and persecute you and utter all kinds of evil against you falsely on my account. 12Rejoice and be glad, for your reward is great in heaven, for so men persecuted the prophets who were before you.

In the beatitudes we touch the core of the original teaching of Jesus. Matthew's version differs considerably from Luke's (Lk 6:20–26). It is possible that both evangelists have drawn on an earlier version and adjusted it to their purpose.

"Beatitude," like "bliss," is an old word meaning happiness. "The beatitudes" might be more accurately translated "the blessings," since the series picks up a frequent OT phrase that begins with "Blessed is the one who . . ." In any case, the blessing or happiness meant here is neither an inner state of contentment nor an outer state of tranquility. It means some good or virtue one presently possesses which carries with it the promise of exaltation, fulfillment, fruitfulness, glory. In the context of Jesus' preaching of the kingdom, the meaning here is: what kind of attitude or action *now* assures access to the coming kingdom of God? To whom does God's kingdom belong?

The first meaning then is eschatological, that is, when God at last will put all things in order, rewarding the good and judging the wicked, who will stand where? Surprises there will be, since the judgments of who and what is important in this world will be reversed. The proud will be humbled, the lowly exalted (Lk 18:14). In this seesaw, the big names will vanish, the hidden saints acclaimed.

I once lived for three days in the New Jerusalem community in Cincinnati. In those days it was a charismatic community of mostly young people. But in the house in which I was staying there was an elderly Franciscan nun they called Sister Tony, who, after spending her life as a hospital laundress, had received permission from her superiors to spend a year with these young people. She made daily visits to needy people in the neighborhood. One morning she returned aglow, explaining to me in her heavy German accent that she had just visited a woman in her forties, mother of three children, who was dying of cancer. "Ach, what faith she had, what joy in the midst of this terrible cross! I went to bring her cheer, and it was she who blessed me!"

"People like that don't make the headlines, do they?" I remarked.

"Yah," she responded, "but dey make de headlines dat Gott reads!"

They make the headlines that God reads! What better description of the people of the beatitudes, the people who are
important to God. For this is precisely what Jesus is saying:
Who are the people important to God? Who are the people who
carry in their hearts the key to eternal happiness?

It is impossible, of course, for the joy of the final consummation not to spill over into the present, as happened with the
lady Sister Tony met. Joy, Paul will say, is one of the fruits of
the Holy Spirit visible already now (Gal 5:22). The source of
the bliss is not the suffering in itself—that would be masochism
and a justification of the oppressor, an interpretation used, unfortunately, by some so-called Christians in the past to keep
the oppressed "in their place." Rather the source of joy is faith
in the loving providence of the Father, who knows their plight
and will do something about it. The closest OT parallel to this
teaching of Jesus is Psalm 37, which promises that the Lord
will reverse the lots of the poor and their oppressors.

More specifically, this bliss is possible because it is the
bliss of Jesus, who is the first to have lived the spirit of the
beatitudes perfectly, who experienced the kingdom in his own
heart during his earthly life and the issue of his fidelity in the
resurrection. And since he is God-with-us, the power and the
joy of his resurrection are already possessed in an incipient but
real way by those disciples who walk in the spirit of the beatitudes. That is why the *ninth* beatitude is key to understanding the eight: "because of me" explains not only the reason for
the cross of persecution which Christians have to bear but the
joy of the resurrection which already floods their hearts.


## Blessed Are the Poor in Spirit

A Rolls-Royce passes by. We see a private yacht or a man-
sion with manicured lawns, and a voice within us says, "Don't
you wish you were rich like that? Wouldn't wealth solve all your
problems and for once make you happy?"

Jesus' first blessing flies in the face of such a desire. Yet
he does not proclaim destitution a blessing either. Those

blessed are the poor in spirit. To understand fully the meaning of this phrase, a brief sketch of the OT background is necessary. The covenant the Lord made with his people in the desert established among the Israelites a fraternity which proscribed inequities. When the people settled in the land, however, it was not long before landgrabbing became common and even a class of landless poor appeared. The latter were supposed to find a champion in judge and king, but often they found their only champion in the Lord (see Ps 40:18). Thus "the poor" came to stand not only for the materially poor but for any who were afflicted or oppressed and could look only to the Lord for justice. So on the first level this blessing of Jesus says that God, who cares for the oppressed even when no one else does, will reverse their lot, in the spirit of Psalm 37:14–17:

> A sword the wicked draw; they bend their
>      bow
>   to bring down the afflicted and the *poor,*
>   to slaughter *those whose path is right.* . . .
> Better is the scanty store of the *just*
>   than the great wealth of the wicked.
> For the power of the wicked shall be broken,
>   but the Lord supports the *just.* (NAB)

Notice the equation of "poor" and "just" in the passage just quoted. This leads us to a second level of meaning to "the poor" here. They are the interiorly, spiritually poor. This development of meaning began already in the OT. After the exile there was a movement of "the poor" in Judea. A number of our psalms were probably composed by poets or scribes belonging to this school. These are the "lowly" who rejoice to hear a brother or sister praise the Lord (Ps 34:3). At Qumran "the poor" was a title for members of the community.

Thus at this second level, the beatitude means "Blessed are they who know they need God." God can do little for those who don't know they need him. But those who feel their emptiness, even though they may not even know they need God to fill it, have experienced the first and foundational movement of grace. And this is true whether they have been that kind of

"poor" who are also "just," that is, faithful to the Lord despite
the blandishments of riches or oppression by the mighty, or
whether, on the other hand, their self-constructed world has
fallen apart and they have hit bottom. It can be a grace to hit
bottom, because there is nowhere to go but up. The pangs of
hunger that hit the prodigal son were the first stirrings of
grace. It was this attitude that made some people welcome
Jesus, and the lack of it made others resist him. Conversion
from alcoholism begins when the alcoholic confesses his or her
life is a shambles and that he or she needs help. But the world
is filled with smug self-contents who need nothing because they
*think* they are filled. It is the attitude condemned in Rev 3:17:
"You say, I am rich, I have prospered, and I need nothing; not
knowing that you are wretched, pitiable, poor, blind and naked."

To those graced with the attitude of need before God, Jesus makes a great promise: the kingdom of God is theirs. The
kingdom is still coming (6:10), but it has already broken
through in Jesus (12:28), and the reward that the poor now
enjoy is nothing else than the good news which they alone can
receive. The rich will find it hard to enter the kingdom (19:23),
but the child will find it easy (18:3–4).

At this level, then, to be poor in spirit means to be open,
receptive, willing to be changed by the word and the spirit of
God, an attitude that can be found in those of any economic
condition.

### Blessed Are the Grieving

Translations of this saying vary: "mourning," "weeping,"
"sorrowing." "Grieving" seems to be a more current word
which covers bereavement for the dead as well as other kinds
of painful loss.

What a paradox! Jesus proclaims blessed those who weep!
Is this masochism? Hardly. For one thing, the promise is that
their grieving will be removed, they will be consoled. But what
kind of mourning is spoken of here? The OT background is the
same as that for the poor in spirit. In fact, if we turn to the
Isaiah passage which Luke tells us Jesus used in the Nazareth

synagogue to open his public ministry, we will find striking parallels with the first two beatitudes with which Jesus begins his teaching in Matthew: both texts have to do with the poor, the lowly, and those who mourn:

> He has sent me to bring good news to the poor,
> to heal the broken-hearted . . .
> to comfort all who mourn,
> to place on those who mourn in Zion a diadem
> instead of ashes,
> to give them oil of gladness in place of mourning,
> a glorious mantle instead of a listless
> spirit (Is 61:1–3). (NAB)

Mourning over irreparable loss must normally take its course. There is value in simply weeping until one has no more tears to shed. But the prophets knew how to turn their tears into intercessory prayer: "Oh that my head were waters, and my eyes a fountain of tears, that I might weep day and night for the slain of the daughter of my people" (Jer 8:23). And today, those who lament the collapse of human and Christian values in their country, who grieve over what is happening to the family and to human brotherhood, who weep for the poor and the suffering, if this mourning is a pleading before God— these are assured their prayer will be heard.

The same holds for personal grief which is laid in the hands of the Lord. In my Bible, Psalm 56:9 is underlined and next to it is the date, July 29, 1980. I was grieving over a personal disappointment at that time. In prayer I sought the Lord and he gave me that most beautiful word of the Psalmist: "My tears are stored in your flask." That single word was consolation enough. The truth of faith is that if our loving Father knows every hair of our head, he knows every tear as well. And perhaps the reason he lets us weep is that only those who weep can laugh. Tears break open the heart to compassion and joy.

There is another kind of mourning envisioned here. It is the mourning for sin, the mourning of repentance, the mourning of which the Psalmist speaks when he says, "I acknowledge my guilt: I grieve over my sin" (Ps 38:19). This is a far cry from the false guilt that merely burdens, whether this be for something that was no sin in the first place or a sin confessed and forgiven. Paul calls such false guilt "worldly sorrow" and contrasts it with the sorrow that leads to repentance, the sorrow that is already the grace of God, the sorrow that leads to salvation (2 Cor 7:9–10). It was the kind of sorrow that moved the prodigal son to return to his father. It is also the sorrow of the lukewarm Christian who, having grown cold in the Lord's service, decides to return to his first love (Rev 2:4–5). It is the prelude to joy.

To this beatitude is attached a promise: "they shall be comforted." The passive form of the verb in Hebrew usage means, "God will comfort them." This is a promise of utter reliability when human comfort or forgiveness fails. The comfort of friends is one of the most cherished of gifts in times of sorrow. But even that comfort has its limits, and that is why the Christian who looks to that city where every tear will be wiped away and death and mourning will be no more (Rev 21:4) can experience a foretaste of God's satiating comfort even now.

That comfort is not a pain-killer. It is an inner strengthening, encouragement, emboldening—the chief meaning of the Greek verb *parakalein*—and it can be experienced in the midst of great suffering: "The God of all consolation comforts us in all our afflictions and thus enables us to comfort those who are in trouble, with the same consolation we have received from him. As we have shared much in the suffering of Christ, so through Christ do we share abundantly in his consolation" (2 Cor 1:3–5). (NAB)

## Blessed Are the Meek

This beatitude is a direct quotation from Psalm 37:11, and to understand its meaning, the psalm merits a careful hearing from its beginning:

> Fret not yourself because of the wicked,
> be not envious of wrong doers!
> For they will soon fade like the grass,
> and wither like the green herb.

Trust in the Lord, and do good;
  so you will dwell in the land, and enjoy security.
Take delight in the Lord,
  and he will give you the desires of your heart.
Commit your way to the Lord;
  trust in him, and he will act.
He will bring forth your vindication as the light,
  and your right as the noonday.
Be still before the Lord, and wait patiently for him;
  fret not yourself over him who prospers in his
    way,
  over the man who carries out evil devices!
Refrain from anger, and forsake wrath!
  Fret not yourself; it tends only to evil.
For the wicked shall be cut off;
  but those who wait for the Lord shall possess the
    land.
Yet a little while, and the wicked will be no more;
  though you look well at his place, he will not be
    there.
But the meek shall possess the land
  and delight themselves in abundant prosperity.
  (RSV)

Notice the twofold direction in the attitude that is blessed here. One looks to God, the other to the wicked and the persecutor. The Psalmist dissuades from revenge and the passion to retaliate, leaving to God the judgment of the wicked.

The meekness that is blessed here is not the groveling subservience of the oppressed to the power of the oppressor. True, this is a program for non-violence, but of the kind that perseveres in its fidelity to God and the cause of his justice. It is not a rejection of just anger and indignation at social evil, particularly if that evil is done to *others*. The Jesus who proclaims the meek blessed, who describes himself as meek and humble of heart (11:29) is the same Jesus whose eyes blaze with anger at the scribes and Pharisees who would forbid him to heal on the Sabbath (Mark 3:5), the same Jesus who drives the money changers from the temple (21:12–13). And the Jesus who pronounces this beatitude is the same Jesus who fires six woes at the scribes and Pharisees in a passionate speech of condemnation (chapter 23). Jesus is meek for those who labor and are heavily burdened (11:28) but merciless toward those who create the burdens and will do nothing to lift them (23:4).

There is surrender and submission here. But it is surrender and submission to God. That raises the question, of course, of how God is involved in what we suffer from others. We can understand rejection and persecution if we have been at fault. But what if we haven't? Why should we suffer, and why should God allow it, if we have tried to do what is right? We ask "Why me?"

A friend of mine, suffering it seemed without cause, asked a priest, "Father, why me?"

"Why not you?" he replied.

That simple response triggered a realization of my friend's solidarity with the world of innocent sufferers and ultimately of her solidarity with the holiest human being who ever lived and who, because of his holiness, ended his life on a cross, the one who had more reason than any to say, "Why me?" but who said instead, at the end of an agonizing prayer, "Father, let it be as you would have it, not as I. . . . Your will be done!" (26:39, 42)

What is the attitude of the Christian to his persecutor? If it is the Father's love for the poor and the oppressed that triggers Jesus' anger when, like Amos, he sees them trampled upon (Amos 2:7), it is also the Father's love that enables Jesus to endure his passion like a lamb (26:63; Acts 8:32–33). And he tells his disciples that when they experience personal rejection or persecution they should turn the other cheek (5:39), love their enemies and pray for their persecutors (5:44). A paradox indeed and easily misinterpreted unless we understand that Jesus expects his disciples to be so rooted in the Father's love that persecution only evokes pity for the persecutor and the hope that somehow he too may come to know the Father's love. In that case, revenge would only alienate and further justify the persecutor, while love, by absorbing the hatred, gives the only hope of exhausting it and healing its source. Paul puts it this way: "Bless those who persecute you; bless and do not curse them . . . Repay no one evil for evil . . . Never avenge yourselves, but leave it to the wrath of God; for it is written,

'Vengeance is mine, I will repay, says the Lord.' No, if your
enemy is hungry, feed him; if he is thirsty, give him drink . . .
Do not be overcome by evil, but overcome evil with good" (Rom
12:14–21).

This is Jesus' answer to the curse that has plagued the
human race since Lamech swore escalating violence in his revenge (Gen 4:23–24). There is a force more powerful than hate,
retaliation and revenge. It is the power of love, and it is Jesus'
expectation for his disciples, for it is available in him.

On Jesus' lips the "land" must mean the kingdom, that is,
the consummate bliss of union with God and the fulfillment of
all one's hopes and desires.

## Blessed Are Those Who Hunger and Thirst for Justice

The varying translations of the Greek *dikaiosune* ("justice," "righteousness," "holiness") reflect the richness of the
word as well as the difficulty of deciding in a given passage
which meaning is primary.

1. The most likely primary meaning here is God's justice,
that is, his saving action in favor of his people. When the Lord
says, "I am bringing on my *justice*, it is not far off, my *salvation* shall not tarry" (Is 46:13), or the psalmist cries, "In your
justice answer me" (Ps 143:1), justice means the Lord's intervention to save his people. Why is such an act not called mercy,
or simply salvation (with which it is often associated)? Because
when the Lord acts on behalf of his people, it is the fulfillment
of his promise sealed long ago in the covenant at Sinai, and
even before that in the covenant with Abraham. He is just to
his own word and faithful to his promise, because the people
he saves are his own.

We have already seen this meaning in 3:15, where Jesus
says John must baptize him in order to fulfill *all justice* (or
*righteousness*), that is, to accomplish God's plan of salvation.
Thus this beatitude parallels the others we have seen: those
who long for God's salvation, his kingdom, will see it. Those
who have no taste or desire for it will not. Jesus will encounter
both in his ministry, and so will the disciples in theirs. Matthew's community may well have understood justice here to

mean the Lord's vindication of them in the face of their persecutors, for their prayer may well have been similar to that
of the martyred spirits in Rev 6:10: "How long, O Lord, before
you do us justice and avenge our blood?"

2. Social justice is another closely allied meaning that we
find especially in the prophets. In Is 5:7 the Lord complains
that he "looked for judgment (*mishpat*), but see, bloodshed
(*mispat*), for justice (*sedaqah*), but hark, the outcry (*se'aqah*)."
Amos decried, "See the great disorders within her, the oppressor in her midst. For they know not how to do what is
right, says the Lord, storing up in their castles what they have
extorted and robbed . . ." (Am 3:10). "Woe to those who cast
justice to the ground" (5:1). "Let justice prevail at the gate"
(5:15). "If you would offer me holocausts, then let justice surge
like water, and goodness like an unfailing stream" (5:24) (NAB).
In this meaning, Jesus promises that those who long to see
inequities reversed, oppression replaced by liberation, the
needs of the poor met, will have their desires fulfilled.

3. Finally, justice can mean personal righteousness. In the
OT the just man was the man who lived according to God's law,
in relation to God himself and to his neighbor. By Jesus' time,
however, the Pharisees and their scribes had evolved a complex
legal system which they expected to give them a mathematical
certitude of their own righteousness before God. Paul will show
that true righteousness comes not from the works of the law
but from faith, that is, the acceptance of the gift of God in
Christ Jesus (Rom 1:17; Gal 2:16). In Matthew, Jesus will say
that his disciples' righteousness must go beyond that of the
scribes and the Pharisees (5:17). Clearly the word here means
personal holiness, and the Sermon on the Mount has for its
purpose to define and describe the kind of holiness Jesus expects.

Note, however, that the blessing is not said to fall on those
who have achieved righteousness. It falls on those who hunger
and thirst for it. Luke's version does not mention justice at all
but only the state of hunger, and there Jesus pronounces a woe
against those who are full (Lk 6:21,25). Few of us who live in
developed countries and have water at our finger tips have ever
experienced real thirst. But there are places in the world today

where water is such a precious commodity it is wealth itself. In 1987 the Indian state of Gujurat was in the grips of a long drought. Parents who were marrying off their daughters were hard pressed to pay the expected dowry. One family offered a gift that could not be refused—a tank of water! I never realized what a gift water is until I spent a full day traveling through the blazing Judean desert without it, to be satisfied finally at the spring of Ein Gedi.

As for hunger, few of us have ever experienced that either. But we have seen pictures of the starving peoples of Sudan and Ethiopia. Extreme hunger can drive a person to bizarre, insane behavior. Josephus tells us that during the Roman siege of Jerusalem in 70 A.D. mothers fell into cannibalism and ate their own children.

The meaning here then would be "Blessed are those who hunger or thirst for justice with the intensity of a person starving for food or dying of thirst." Thus the blessed are neither those who are righteous nor those who claim to be, but those who desire righteousness with their whole being. To be filled, one must be empty. The Christian practice of fasting is one way of giving this emptiness a practical outward expression.

## Blessed Are the Merciful

If the first four beatitudes describe a stance of waiting upon God, here there is a shift toward action. The word for mercy, *eleos*, is used most often in the Greek OT to translate *hesed*, often associated with *rahamim*. *Hesed* means mercy that proceeds from an identification with the other, either because of blood relationship or covenant. It can be translated therefore *loyal love*. It means we feel the other's burden as our own, and as a result we *do* something about it. The loosely related *rahamim* (Hos 2:21) means compassion with the stress on the feeling, the movement of the heart, literally the "bowels," the seat of compassion.

If one had to reduce the Bible's attributes of God to one, it would surely be mercy. One of the earliest creeds of Israel reads: "The Lord, the Lord, a God merciful and gracious, slow to anger, and abounding in steadfast love and faithfulness" (Ex

34:6). And if one had to reduce the Bible's attributes of the ideal Israelite to one, it would also be mercy: "It is mercy I desire, not sacrifice" (Hos 6:6). The mark of the degeneration of Israel is its loss of mercy: "There is no fidelity, no mercy, no knowledge of God in the land" (Hos 4:1). That is why, when the Lord promises to renew his people in their covenant love, he will endow them with *hesed* and *rahamim*, mercy and compassion (Hos 2:19).

The pagan world of Biblical times showed little concern for mercy. Two groups especially suffered—slaves and children. Slaves were considered tools, and masters had the right to kill them as they wished. Unwanted infants were left to die of exposure, particularly girls. And, as happens even today in some countries, unwanted children could be picked up for the "slave trade" or deliberately maimed and used by racketeers to beg. The modern world flinches at such accounts, then abets them by legalized abortion. Our mercy, like that of our pagan forebears, is selective.

A disciple shows mercy not only by acts of kindness toward the afflicted but also by forgiveness. The unforgiving debtor lost his master's forgiveness because he was not willing to show mercy, i.e., forgiveness, to his fellow servant (18:33; see also 6:14,15; 7:2). That parable also illustrates the meaning of the promise, "They shall obtain mercy." The mercy promised is not human favors received in response to practicing Christian mercy, as if mercy were good business. The mercy received is the mercy of God. We are being distantly prepared for the final judgment scene in 25:31–46, where those who have shown mercy to their fellows on earth are welcomed into the kingdom, and those who have not are excluded. James 2:13 puts it succinctly: "Judgment is without mercy to one who has shown no mercy; yet mercy triumphs over judgment."

## Blessed Are the Pure of Heart

Jesus is echoing here the teaching of Psalm 24:3–6:

> Who shall ascend the hill of the Lord?
> And who shall stand in his holy place?

He who has clean hands and a pure heart,
who does not lift up his soul to what is false,
and does not swear deceitfully.
He will receive blessing from the Lord,
and vindication from the God of his salvation.
Such is the generation of those who seek him,
who seek the face of the God of Jacob. (RSV)

This psalm, like Psalm 15, is remarkable in that the conditions of purity it lays down are not ritual (of which there were many in the OT) but ethical. And even more surprising, the ethical touches not only external conduct but inner desires of the heart. So Jesus is not innovating here. He is drawing from the deepest well of OT spirituality, a well that had, in Jesus' day, all but gone dry from lack of use. For the emphasis on ritual and external purity had become so dominant that it met some of Jesus' most stinging accusations (23:24–28).

Purity of heart here embraces chastity, of course, and prepares Jesus' statement that even lustful desires are adulterous (5:27–30), but it goes beyond that. Just as in the sphere of metals purity means to be without alloy, in the moral sphere it means to be not only without evil motives for good actions but without mixed motives as well. Thus some translations read "single-hearted." But how difficult that is! To have perfectly pure, perfectly disinterested motives! It must take the work of a lifetime, or the special cleansing power of the Holy Spirit, to attain that kind of purity.

Still, to the degree to which this is possible, one can *see* God. This is an astounding statement. In the OT it was believed that no one could see God and live (Ex 33:20). Manoah, who had received an angelic messenger foretelling of the birth of Samson, told his wife, "We will certainly die, for we have seen God" (Jgs 13:22). And Isaiah, terrified by his vision of the Lord in the temple, cried, "Woe is me, I am doomed!" (Is 6:5).

Short of that, the Psalmist spoke of seeing God by gazing on the sanctuary of the temple (Pss 42:3; 63:3; Ex 23:17). And it was for that kind of presence that the Psalmist taught that purity of heart and hand was necessary (Pss 15 and 24). But for Jesus, seeing God was more than visiting the temple, however worthily. If we must wait for Paul to use the expression, "face to face" (1 Cor 13:12), Jesus nonetheless promises that the pure of heart will, at the coming of the kingdom, *see* God. The meaning is the final, consummate union with God. But surely there is a spillover into the present, since in Jesus the good things of the world to come begin even now. The pure of heart will experience them and in this way already see God.

## Blessed Are the Peacemakers

The Hebrew *shalom* means more than the absence of war. The day the second World War ended, people said peace had come. But Europe and much of the Pacific was in rubble, families were separated, hunger and disease were widespread. That is not the biblical view of peace.

Nor does *shalom* mean the inner tranquillity, the *apatheia* of the Stoic immune to the chances and changes of the world. It has little affinity with the Buddhist ideal of the absence of desire. Rather *shalom* means fullness of life, prosperity, fruitfulness, the development of all resources and possibilities. That is why the biblical symbol of peace is a flowing river (Is 48:18; 66:12; Ps 46:5; Rev 22:1–5) or a lush garden (Gen 2:8–15). It is not surprising then that Jews, who greet one another with *shalom*, should also love the cheer, *lechaim*, "life!"

Those, then, who feed the hungry, house the homeless, clothe the naked, heal the sick—and particularly those who address themselves to developing social systems that will make the world a better place to live in—these are peacemakers. This is more than isolated acts of mercy. It is more clearly development, the making of a world more worthy of the children of God.

But *shalom* also means right relationships. Although the word peace is not used to describe the ideal state of Eden in Genesis 2, the life in the garden was a life of peace in a fourfold relationship. First, with God: the man and his wife walked with God in the cool of the evening. The breakdown of this relationship is symbolized by their hiding from the Lord (Gen 3:8). Then with the other: the two, originally one in Adam's side, become one flesh. This breaks down as the man flings blame on the woman and she in turn blames the serpent (Gen 2:20–24; 3:12–13) and further disintegrates as brother kills brother (Gen 4:1–12), revenge escalates into unlimited bloodshed (Gen 4:23–24), and peoples can no longer communicate or understand each other (Gen 11:1–9). Thirdly, with self: the original nakedness, symbolizing integrity, is replaced by shame and seeking cover (Gen 3:8–11). Here begins the struggle between flesh and spirit Paul so graphically describes in Romans 7 and 8, and on which William Barclay comments: "A man is a walking civil war." Finally, peace with creation, lost in the garden, gives way to thorns and thistles, and the creativity of gardening gives way to the toil and sweat of earning a living.

Jesus is the first peacemaker. "He is our peace" (Eph 2:14–18), "making peace by the blood of his cross" (Col 1:20), peace of humankind with God, revealing the face of a loving God to man and the first totally loving and faithful human face to God. In doing so he initiates a process of establishing peace among human beings, setting first the example of crossing barriers and making community with publicans and sinners—a path that led to his death—and, after the resurrection, commanding his Jewish disciples to do the same with the gentiles (28:19). He brought peace to the demoniac who had been legion (Mk 5:15). And finally, he taught that brotherhood with the lilies of the field and the birds of the air which would later captivate Francis of Assisi.

His disciples, who are listening to the Sermon on the Mount, are to be peacemakers. Not just lovers of peace, but makers of peace. There are those who love peace but are unwilling to pay the price to make it, as Jesus did. It takes initiative, risk of rejection, patience and perseverance to be a peacemaker. It means finding the good in the alienated and reaching out to them, as Barnabas did with Paul (Acts 9:26–27; 11:25–26). And it means willingness to "hang in there" in love and prayer until the other chooses to cross the bridge one has laid.

Those who make peace will be called children of God, because God is the God of peace (1 Thes 5:23). In the Wisdom of Solomon, God vindicates the just person after his death by giving him the glory of the angels, those heavenly beings to whom the title "sons of God" was originally given: "See how he is associated among the sons of God; how his lot is with the saints" (Wis 5:5). On the lips of Jesus, however—especially as interpreted to us by Matthew—the title does not mean angels. Nor does the "calling" mean a mere external labeling. A real filial relationship is created with the God whom Jesus knows as "Abba" and whom the disciples are to address as "Father." Here, among the beatitudes which look to the final inbreaking of God's kingdom, we probably have something similar to Paul's promise that at the end time the "children of God will be revealed" (Rom 8:23) or the promise of Rev 21:7 that the one who is faithful to the end will be God's son or daughter. Thus, those who make peace, though their efforts be unappreciated or rejected, though they be tramped on, as a bridge always is, have the firm assurance that, like Jesus who suffered the same lot, they are sons and daughters of God and in the end will be welcomed as such in the Father's arms.

## Blessed Are the Persecuted

Only those who have experienced persecution for their faith have the authority to explain this passage, the culminating paradox of discipleship, the bliss of the martyr. Having lived most of my life in the nominally Christian west, where priests, religious and ministers are generally held in high esteem, I have never known what it is to be persecuted for my faith. On the contrary, my faith and my priesthood have often been a source of privilege—exemption from military service and some forms of taxation, the respectful title "Father," a free lunch, sailing through customs, to name but a few. It was only when I began living in a country where it is a crime to preach, baptize, or become a Christian, that I began to feel the cost of my faith—not so much from what I suffered personally but from what I saw other Christians suffer—unwarranted arrest, beatings even of women, humiliations, detention in inhuman circumstances, and prolonged judicial processes. But those brothers and sisters also taught me more about this beatitude than I ever learned from books. They showed me the joy and the radiance of martyrs, the absolute truth of Jesus' words that those persecuted for their faith are blessed.

The eighth beatitude forms an inclusion with the first by repeating the promise, "theirs is the kingdom of heaven." Again the word *dikaiosune*, translated "justice" or "righteousness" or "holiness," appears. Here it means fidelity to one's faith. But since what causes the persecution is most often not the creedal content but rather its consequent life-style, which others find threatening to their values—"justice" must also embrace those Christian values which Jesus exemplifies and teaches in the rest of the Sermon on the Mount. In other words, though Christians would be persecuted for their belief that "Jesus is Lord," it was the consequences of that faith that enraged the powers. If "Jesus is Lord" then Caesar is not. If in Christ there is "neither Jew nor Greek, neither slave nor free, neither male nor female" (Gal 3:28), then the traditional walls of society, Jewish or gentile, are threatened. And just as Jesus' behavior of embracing the outcast was the real issue that got him into trouble, so would the "justice" of his disciples stir the opposition of the authorities and even the faceless masses easily swayed by rumor, false accusations and xenophobic panic.

To this last beatitude is attached a ninth, one Matthew shares with Luke (the so-called Q tradition). The persecuted are no longer the general "they" but "you." And Matthew's version adds, "and speak all kinds of evil against you falsely." This addition probably reflects the situation of Matthew's community now separated from the synagogue but still suffering the effects of the break. *Falsely* is a reminder that Christians should never by their behavior give their opponents grounds for true fault-finding: "If you are reproached for the name of Christ, you are blessed. . . But let none of you suffer as a murderer, or a thief, or a wrongdoer, or a mischief-maker; yet if one suffers as a Christian let him not be ashamed, but under that name let him glorify God" (1 Pet 4:14–16). *For the name of Christ* and, implicitly, *under that name*, is the equivalent of "on my account," the first time that Matthew reveals the Christ-centered base of the beatitudes. Matthew probably intends to have this focus on the person of Jesus reflect back on all the preceding beatitudes, for that is the setting he has cho-

sen—Jesus, surrounded by his disciples. It is indeed because
they have chosen to leave the crowds and approach Jesus that
they are ready to hear and to heed his ideals for living.

Living the beatitudes in fidelity to Jesus is sure to bring
persecution. But that is because Christian discipleship is a prophetic vocation, sharing the agony and the ecstasy of Israel's
ancient prophets. We are now prepared to hear Jesus proclaim
that prophetic vocation in the images of salt and light.

Before doing so, however, let us sum up the chief points
of the beatitudes.

1. For the Christian, true bliss is not due to some external
   boon like wealth or power or fame which may come by
   chance or achievement, and by chance or failure be lost.
   True happiness is an attitude of spirit, a *be*-attitude. The
   Christian can be happy in any *circum*stance because of his
   *inner* stance.

2. This inner stance is not a flaccid passivity, but a clinging to
   the Lord and his promises in the midst of the most adverse
   circumstances, even in persecution, and perseverance in
   good works, especially works of mercy and peace.

3. The fullness of the promised bliss is in the "kingdom of
   heaven," but it begins even now in the joy and radiance
   experienced in living the beatitudes.

4. The source of this bliss is Jesus, who embodies the beatitudes in his own life and teaching and who shares this bliss
   with his disciples as a permanent presence in their midst
   (1:23; 28:20).

5. Because this way of life clashes with the world's values, it
   will evoke the world's suspicion, fear and rejection. But that
   too is the joy of the prophetic vocation shared with Jesus.

6. Finally, we should note that the beatitudes are not in the
   form of laws but in the form of blessings, that is, the new
   law given by the new Moses is first of all *grace*. Matthew
   does not speak of "grace" as such. For him the person of
   Jesus abiding in the church *is* grace, for he alone makes the
   impossible dream possible. And that is why only the disciple

committed to Jesus is expected to understand and live as
Jesus lives.

## You Are Salt, You Are Light (5:13–16)

13 "You are the salt of the earth; but if salt has lost its
taste, how shall its saltness be restored? It is no longer good
for anything except to be thrown out and trodden under foot
by men.

14 "You are the light of the world. A city set on a hill
cannot be hid. ¹⁵Nor do men light a lamp and put it under
a bushel, but on a stand, and it gives light to all in the house.
¹⁶Let your light so shine before men, that they may see your
good works and give glory to your Father who is in heaven.

Jesus continues to address his disciples. The parallel saying
in Luke is only a general one: "Salt is good, but if it loses its
taste . . ." (Lk 14:34), but here, calling his disciples the salt of
the earth, Jesus focuses on their function for the whole world.
What is envisaged here is not their preaching but their mission
to live and witness to the message of the Sermon on the Mount.
How does salt symbolize this? It purifies and gives taste (Job
6:6). Sacrifices were salted (Ez 30:35; Lev 2:13; Mk 9:49) and
so were newborn children (Ez 16:4). Salt also is a preservative.
Before the advent of the deep-freeze, every farm family in the
United States had its crock of brine to cure and preserve pork.
. . The salt figure is especially meaningful in this respect: salt
brings out the flavor that is already there and preserves the
object salted. In missionary activity, there is a goodness already awaiting the arrival of the good news. The church comes
not to destroy or replace the good that is there but to call it
forth, to purify and preserve it. This is achieved in the first
place by the witness of a Christian life. Missionaries of past
centuries did not always understand this but often imported
and imposed their own cultural forms on their converts. Other
missionaries were able to respect and incorporate the local culture in such a way as to indigenize and incarnate the gospel in
the distinct forms of the local culture. The former thought of
themselves as angels of light banishing the darkness of the pa-

gan world. The latter were salt calling forth the goodness already there, preserving it and purifying it as a sacrifice pleasing to the Lord (see Mal 1:11). It is in this sense that the real
values of any culture, like the OT itself, can be prophetic. They
point beyond themselves and wait for fulfillment in Christ. It
was this approach that inspired Vatican II in its *Constitution
of the Church in the Modern World.*

The image ends with a warning that the disciples must
remain faithful to their call, otherwise their mission of witness
to the world will be useless and they themselves will be rejected (see 1 Cor 9:27).

The statement "You are the light of the world" is unique
in the gospel tradition. Mark and Luke use the example of the
lamp as a symbol of Jesus or the good news (Mk 4:21; Lk 8:16).
In John Jesus says he is the light of the world, and the disciples
at most have the light of life to walk by (Jn 8:12). But here the
disciples are the light of the world. In contrast to the Essenes
of Qumran, who called themselves "the sons of light" but hid
away under the bushel of their enclave, the disciples of Jesus
are to bring the light to the world. They are to fulfill the prophecy of the Servant of the Lord who was to bring the light of
salvation to the nations (Is 42:6; 49:6). How can Jesus say this,
and why does Matthew record it, since he knows Jesus himself
is the fulfillment of that prophecy? Because for Matthew Jesus
and the church are one. This is confirmed by the immediate
mention of the city set on a hill, an allusion to the new Jerusalem, city of light (Is 60:19-20; Rev 21:23-25), an image that
fits the disciples who are gathered on a hill at the feet of Jesus.
It is not the individual disciples but the community as such—
the city—which bears this light for the world, and this underlines the importance of mutual relationships among the disciples. It also means that if the world, represented here by the
crowds, finds the demands of the Sermon on the Mount too
high, it should be able to see them joyfully lived in this brotherhood and thus discover that Jesus' way of life is not an impossible dream.

The image of light here has to do not with preaching but
with good works. If the image of salt stresses witnessing and

discovering, affirming, purifying and preserving the good in others in the process of evangelization, the image of light stresses the evangelizing value of works of love. Later the disciples will be commissioned to preach (10:7) and teach (28:20). But before doing so, they are first of all to *be*—not statically but actively by loving and animating the world and showing, by the attraction of their community life and good works, the light of Christ. I once met a young Hindu who had become a Christian. Knowing the price of such a conversion in terms of family relationships and the rich religious culture out of which he came, I asked him what moved him to begin considering this costly step. "It was the example of the Missionaries of Charity in their selfless work for the poorest of the poor," he said. "No one preached to me, but I asked myself what power motivated these men and women to give up marriage, family, money and independence to spend the rest of their lives in this kind of service. If Christ was the power—and they said he was—I wanted to find him."

This passage on salt and light epitomizes Matthew's theology of church, grace, and law. The beatitudes stressed the primacy of grace, of God's action and the disciples surrendering to it in preparation for the inbreaking of the kingdom. What will now follow in the major part of Jesus' discourse concerns the specific ethic of the interim in which the importance of doing certain works and avoiding others, comes through loud and clear. As a bridge Matthew presents the church, gathered around Jesus and listening to his word as a community that has been given its savor and its light as pure gift to be shared with the world. In the new creation, between grace on the one hand and the new law on the other, stands the *witness* of the church, meeting point of grace and law, achievement of the humanly impossible because it is centered on Jesus, God-with-us.

The psalmist foretold that one day grace would look down from heaven and fidelity spring from the earth, and that the two would, for the first time in history, kiss and embrace (Ps 85:11). For Matthew, the church of Jesus is that kiss and that embrace.

*Fulfillment through Greater Righteousness (5:17–20)*

17 "Think not that I have come to abolish the law and
the prophets; I have come not to abolish them but to fulfil
them. [18]For truly, I say to you, till heaven and earth pass
away, not an iota, not a dot, will pass from the law until all
is accomplished. [19]Whoever then relaxes one of the least of
these commandments and teaches men so, shall be called
least in the kingdom of heaven; but he who does them and
teaches them shall be called great in the kingdom of heaven.
[20]For I tell you, unless your righteousness exceeds that of
the scribes and Pharisees, you will never enter the kingdom
of heaven.

In the beatitudes Jesus laid out a limitless ideal. Though
drawing his teaching from the Scriptures, especially the
Psalms, Jesus has so far left unanswered the question of how
his teaching is related to the Scriptures which have been the
life blood of his Jewish audience. He now addresses the question of continuity or discontinuity with the Old Testament.

There is continuity, first of all, he says, because he comes
to fulfill not only what the prophets foretold but also the law.
Everything hinges around the meaning of "fulfill" here. It can
mean "to do everything commanded by the law," but that could
hardly square with Jesus' revisions of the law soon to be ex-
pounded, nor with Jesus' own behavior which often disregarded
the law. "To fulfill" can also mean to live out a prophecy. Jesus
here has associated the law with prophecy, and he explicitly
says in 11:13 that the law, as well as the prophets, prophesied.
If this is so, then, like the prophets, everything in the law
pointed forward to a greater fulfillment. The law was more than
law; it was also promise. Jesus, then, fulfills the *meaning* of
the law, even by the changes he will introduce.

In this way "every iota and every dot" of the law will *happen*—for that is the most common meaning of the Greek verb
*genetai*, which the RSV translates "is accomplished" and the
NABR "have taken place." Notice that there are *two* "until"
clauses in verse 18: "till heaven and earth pass away" and "until

all is accomplished." Does this mean that the law, fulfilled in Jesus, will last till the end of time? But Jesus later says his words will last beyond the passing of heaven and earth (24:35). In 24:34 "till all these things take place (the same verb *genetai*)" is used for the fulfillment of a prophesied *event*. So we must be prepared to see the fulfillment of the law (itself prophetic, as we have seen) in an event. That event, as we shall see, is the death and resurrection of Jesus. See the *excursus* below on "How Jesus Fulfills the Law."

But Jesus also fulfills, that is, completes the law by his teaching. "These commandments," lacking any antecedent, must refer to what follows, i.e., Jesus' commandments. Proclaiming great the one who *does* and *teaches*, Jesus prepares Matthew's community to accept the teaching authority of the disciples and at the same time warns them that they must first of all practice what they preach.

Finally, Jesus compares the righteousness he proclaims with that of the scribes and the Pharisees. The Pharisees, a small minority of the people, sought to live the law, written and oral, in its most minute details, a project which eventually separated them from the common people unlearned in the law, earning them the title Pharisees, meaning *separated*. The scribes were learned in the law, the theologian-lawyers of the day. To see what practices of theirs were condemned by Jesus we need to read chapter 23. For the moment, the way Jesus' righteousness exceeds that of the scribes and Pharisees will be detailed in what follows, in which the comparison with two important contemporary Jewish groups explains much of the Jewish context of Jesus' teaching. Unlike the converted gentiles, the Jewish members of Matthew's community belonged to a rich religious and strict ethical tradition. Jesus' teaching presupposes that tradition and seeks to correct and transcend it.

Christians today in the west belong to a culture that still, despite its many attritions, retains many Christian elements. But religion for many is still a very external thing, a church-going on Sunday, a christening, a marriage, a funeral, a jewelry cross worn, because it's the thing to do or because one fears the consequences of not doing it. It is not something that grips and changes one's very being and daily life. Such persons, like

the scribes and Pharisees, have the law but have not yet found
Jesus.

W.D. Davies and others have pointed out that the outline
of the Sermon from this point onwards follows the pattern of
the rabbis who taught that there were three foundations for
the world: the law, temple worship, and good deeds. Jesus ex-
pounds the new law in 5:17–48, teaches about true worship in
6:1–18, and discusses good works from 6:19 to the end.

## EXCURSUS: HOW JESUS FULFILLS THE LAW

In Matthew 5:17 Jesus says he has come to fulfill the
law. This does not mean that he reaffirms as valid every
jot and tittle (or "iota" and "dot") of the old law, for his
actions and his teaching show that he often departed from
the old law.

### A. Jesus fulfills the old law in two ways:

1. *The law fulfilled as teaching.* In Matthew there is
a great respect for the law (5:17; 22:36; 23:23). Every letter and tiniest part of a letter finds its meaning in the
teaching of Jesus—that is, just as prophecy foretold a fulfillment, so the law, all of it, pointed beyond itself (11:13).
And the law is fulfilled *as Jesus interprets it, and only as
Jesus interprets it,* and his interpreting principle is *love*:
"Do to others whatever you would have them do to you.
*This is the law and the prophets*" (7:12 NABR). "You shall
love the Lord your God. . . . You shall love your neighbor
as yourself. *On these two commandments depend all the
law and the prophets*" (22:37–40). If love is the essence of
the law, then love supersedes any other consideration in
applying the law. For example, human need comes before
the sabbath commandment (12:12). The love commandment proceeds from the nature of God himself, who is merciful, gracious and loving (5:43–48; 9:13; 12:7). And the
obligation to show love is founded in the love one has re-

ceived from God (18:12–14, 21–35).

2. *The law fulfilled in event.* The law is prophetic (11:13). The event of Jesus' baptism "fulfills all justice" (3:15). This event itself points forward, however, to the central event which fulfills everything, the death and resurrection of Jesus. Matthew subtly shows this by the cosmic apocalyptic signs that happen when Jesus dies and rises from the tomb. The temple veil is rent in two (27:51), a sign that one of the three Jewish foundations of the world has crumbled. Apocalyptic darkness envelops the earth (27:45). An earthquake (27:51), repeated at the rising of Jesus (28:2), is followed by the dead rising from the tombs (27:52). These signs suggest that Jesus' prophecy that heaven and earth would pass away was indeed fulfilled in his death/resurrection, and now only the words of Jesus abide (24:35). Thus when Jesus dies and rises, the law's passing prophetic function has been achieved, and it passes away with "heaven and earth," remaining only as it is transformed in the teaching of Jesus.

## B. The New Law in the Church

The church continues the new law both as teaching and as event:

1. *As teaching.* Jesus commissions his disciples after the resurrection to make other disciples and to "teach them to observe all that I have commanded you" (28:19–20). "All" refers to the entire gospel, but especially to the Sermon on the Mount, evoked by the mountain of the Great Commission. Though commissioned earlier to preach, heal and deliver (10:1–8), the disciples receive the teaching authority only after the resurrection. Thus the *event* of the resurrection authorizes the teaching. Which leads to the next point.

2. *As event.* Baptism replaces circumcision, a cardinal event of the old law (28:19). And the *Eucharist* is the covenant sacrifice fulfilled in Jesus' death and resurrection and celebrated and proclaimed in the church (26:26–28).

*Anger (5:21–26)*

21 "You have heard that it was said to the men of old,
'You shall not kill; and whoever kills shall be liable to judgment.' ²²But I say to you that every one who is angry with
his brother shall be liable to judgment; whoever insults his
brother shall be liable to the council, and whoever says,
'You fool!' shall be liable to the hell of fire. ²³So if you are
offering your gift at the altar, and there remember that
your brother has something against you, ²⁴leave your gift
there before the altar and go; first be reconciled to your
brother, and then come and offer your gift. ²⁵Make friends
quickly with your accuser, while you are going with him to
court, lest your accuser hand you over to the judge, and the
judge to the guard, and you be put in prison; ²⁶truly, I say
to you, you will never get out till you have paid the last
penny.

The first of Jesus' six contrasts with the old law begins
with a quotation from Ex 20:13, repeated in Deut 5:17, forbidding murder. The second part of the statement, about judgment, is not a direct quotation from the OT but may be inferred
from Ex 21:12 and Deut 16:18. Jesus does not revoke the OT
law but deepens it. In his eyes, anger is murder in the heart.
This text has often been misinterpreted to create guilt for
any feeling of anger. Surely it is not aimed at the kind of indignation against social injustice we see often in Jesus and of
which Matthew himself give us an extended example in chapter
23. The key to understanding what anger means here lies in
the word *brother*. While the term could conceivably apply to
any other human being, the context here suggests that it
means another member of the Christian community, to whom
one is bound in the intimate covenant ties of the new family of
Jesus (12:46–50). This is the community whose mutual relationships are to be the light of the world (5:14). To allow anger
to wound or destroy those relationships is serious indeed, as
Jesus indicates by tightening the judgments. What to the
scribes was the most severe, the "judgment" or "little Sanhedrin" or local council, is with Jesus the first and most lenient

measure. Whoever goes further to verbal abuse, calling his brother *raka*, imbecile, is subject to the supreme court, the Sanhedrin. Whoever calls his brother fool is subject to the fire of Gehenna, symbol of final judgment and perdition.

Of course the anger envisaged here is anger that is unresolved and destructive, the anger that chooses either aggression or repression rather than confrontation and reconciliation (see 18:15–17). This is evident from the attached saying about reconciliation with a brother before worship, for there is no reconciliation with God (the purpose of sacrifice) without reconciliation with the neighbor.

In verses 25 and 26 we have a beautiful example of Matthean composition. What was originally a detached saying of Jesus about the wisdom of settling disputes out of court is attached here to the theme about reconciliation with the brother, and in so doing the fraternal reconciliation is placed in the context of the final judgment (as it is also in 18:21–35). For both parties are on their way to the court of God's final judgment, and it is much better to settle grievances with a brother here in this life than to leave it to God's final judgment, which will be painfully exacting. In Paul's words, "If we judged ourselves, we would not be judged" (1 Cor 11:31).

## Purity of Heart (5:27–30)

27 "You have heard that it was said, 'You shall not commit adultery.' 28 But I say to you that every one who looks at a woman lustfully has already committed adultery with her in his heart. 29 If your right eye causes you to sin, pluck it out and throw it away; it is better that you lose one of your members than that your whole body be thrown into hell. 30 And if your right hand causes you to sin, cut it off and throw it away; it is better that you lose one of your members than that your whole body go into hell.

Little commentary is needed here. As Jesus did for the murder commandment, so he does for the commandment about adultery. Sin begins in the heart, and if one wishes to avoid external sins of lust, the place to begin is the heart. The images of plucking out the eye or cutting off the hand Jesus did not mean in a physical sense. Origen, for all his brilliant writings as a Father of the church, was never venerated as a saint because he took this text with extreme literalism and castrated himself. Yet the image is a powerful reminder that without discipline of thoughts and desires and the willingness to forego the occasions of sin, purity and integrity of life is not possible. How often a tragedy, the breakup of a marriage and family, could have been averted if the person had made the painful sacrifice of an emotional involvement in its beginnings. The songs of our culture hail the irresistible power of romantic love and wail over broken relationships, but never sing of the love that, to be faithful, is willing to say a heroic "no."

## Divorce (5:31–32)

31 "It was also said, 'Whoever divorces his wife, let him give her a certificate of divorce.' [32]But I say to you that every one who divorces his wife, except on the ground of unchastity, makes her an adulteress; and whoever marries a divorced woman commits adultery.

Here Jesus actually revokes the letter of the old law. The teaching is clear, although it is not the only NT text on the matter. Paul will discuss various cases and even an exception (1 Cor 7:1–16). There is an exception here too, which the RSV translates, "except on the ground of unchastity" and the NAB "lewd conduct is a separate case." The same exceptive clause will appear in 19:19. Recent studies have made it virtually certain that the meaning is a marriage that was, according to Jewish law, within the illicit degree of kinship and therefore invalid from the beginning (Lev 18:16–18). Such incestuous marriages were occasional among the gentiles with whom the Christian Jews were now trying to form a faith community. The matter was settled at the council of Jerusalem by reaffirming the illicit nature of such marriages and requiring the gentiles to abstain from them (Acts 15:20,29). Hence the NABR translates correctly, "unless the marriage is unlawful." A gentile married to a brother or sister or other close relative, for example, was, on becoming a Christian, permitted and probably even required to dissolve the union. See the strong stand of Paul on such an incestuous marriage in 1 Cor 5:1–5. Jesus' teaching on the permanence of marriage is therefore clear, grounding the church's reluctance to permit divorce and remarriage unless, like the case envisaged in the exceptive clause here, there was a radical flaw from the beginning.

## Swearing (5:33–37)

33 "Again you have heard that it was said to the men of old, 'You shall not swear falsely, but shall perform to the Lord what you have sworn.' ³⁴But I say to you, Do not swear at all, either by heaven, for it is the throne of God, ³⁵or by the earth, for it is his footstool, or by Jerusalem, for it is the city of the great King. ³⁶And do not swear by your head, for you cannot make one hair white or black. ³⁷Let what you say be simply 'Yes' or 'No'; anything more than this comes from evil.

Here again Jesus revokes the letter of the old law, which permitted taking oaths and proscribed only perjury. But Jesus points out the underlying fallacy of oath taking. It implies a difference between the truth of ordinary language and the truth of an oath. Today people are careful not to put into writing what they would not hesitate to say orally. And even more careful to check what they say under oath, whereas they might purvey the grossest lies if not. Again we must remember Jesus addresses this word to committed disciples. Though the Christian may have no control on the requirements of secular courts, no recourse to oaths should be necessary among Christians.

## Retaliation (5:38–42)

38 "You have heard that it was said, 'An eye for an eye and a tooth for a tooth.' ³⁹But I say to you, Do not resist one who is evil. But if any one strikes you on the right cheek, turn to him the other also; ⁴⁰and if any one would sue you and take your coat, let him have your cloak as well; ⁴¹and if any one forces you to go one mile, go with him two miles.

⁴²Give to him who begs from you, and do not refuse him who would borrow from you.

The law of talion (Ex 21:24; Lev 24:20; Deut 19:21) had for its purpose to limit violence and blood feuds through the fear of retaliation. It also sought to limit revenge to equity (*only an eye for an eye*. . .), against Lamech's program of unlimited revenge (Gen 4:23–24), repeated so often in the modern world's one-upmanship in settling scores. Gandhi, who lived and died to bring feuding factions together, loved to refer to this saying of Jesus, rephrasing it thus: "If we all lived by the principle of an eye for an eye, soon the whole world would be blind." Here Jesus again revokes the old law—no revenge at all!

How can Jesus possibly expect his disciples to live this way in the real world? John P. Meier comments:

> What Jesus does is to prohibit any court action to obtain retribution or compensation. All human legal systems, which are necessarily based on a need to balance rights and redress injuries, are undermined by this antithesis. The "otherness" of the kingdom and its justice could not be clearer. In the sermon on the mount Jesus is not presenting a new program for human society; he is announcing the end of human society, the end of the world. That is what *eschatological* morality is all about. It is possible only for the believing disciple who through Jesus already lives in the end time (*Matthew*, p. 54).

But what does this mean to the parent who, to defend his children's rights and future security, has no alternative but to take a crook to court? To make the spirit of this saying of Jesus livable, we should observe:

1. The saying has to do with personal injury, not with defending the rights of *others*. One may choose to turn the other cheek when by doing so no one else would be harmed, but should doing so involve harm to the innocent, then it would be a travesty of the disinterested love Jesus preaches not to take action if one can do so.

2. The inner spirit of non-violence and turning the other cheek is always possible. When someone does me an injustice, it is, morally speaking, not my problem but his. To yield to resentment, hatred, the desire to make the other pay, and pay more, for what he has done, to tighten my heart into a clenched fist, is to become part of the problem, not the solution. If I cannot forgive, perhaps I can at least realize the offender needs healing, and I can, if truly a disciple of Jesus, pray that he may find it. This leads naturally to the final and climactic antithesis.

## Love of Enemies (5:43–48)

43 "You have heard that it was said, 'You shall love your neighbor and hate your enemy.' ⁴⁴But I say to you, Love your enemies and pray for those who persecute you, ⁴⁵so that you may be sons of your Father who is in heaven; for he makes his sun rise on the evil and on the good, and sends rain on the just and on the unjust. ⁴⁶For if you love those who love you, what reward have you? Do not even the tax collectors do the same? ⁴⁷And if you salute only your brethren, what more are you doing than others? Do not even the Gentiles do the same? ⁴⁸You, therefore, must be perfect, as your heavenly Father is perfect.

The command to love one's neighbor comes from Leviticus 19:2. "You shall hate your enemy" is not found in the OT but is something "you have heard." Where did Israel "hear" this limitation of the love of neighbor? Perhaps it had been inferred from the old stories of the battles of Israel against their enemies, of the persecuting Babylonians and Greeks, and the rejoicing over their downfall and punishment such as we find in Ps 137:8–9: "O daughter of Babylon, you devastator! Happy shall he be who requites you what you have done to us! Happy shall he be who takes your little ones and dashes them against the rock!" Or in Psalm 139:21–22: "Do I not hate them that hate thee, O Lord? And do I not loathe them that rise up against thee? I hate them with perfect hatred; I count them my enemies." The disciples at Qumran were commanded by their rule to hate those outside the community, whom they called "sons of darkness." It has always seemed part of loyalty to God to hate and destroy those whom we are convinced are thwarting his purposes in the world—and ours!

But here Jesus strikes at what is undoubtedly the most "understandable" of human hatreds—and source of all its bloodshed. He commands us to love not only the stranger and the foreigner, for whom after all, a modicum of compassion would lead us at least to pity, but our enemies. And who are our enemies? Are they those faceless foreign powers we know only by their flags and emblems? Yes, but those who have really hurt us—and whom we want to hate—are those we have loved. The loved one *becomes* enemy when for any cause *we* withdraw the love once given. It is not the *hurt* that makes the other our enemy. It is *our* withdrawal of love. The prodigal son, for all the hurt he caused his father, never became the father's enemy, because the father never withdrew his love. So it is with God, who continues to shower sinners with his blessings, and if he ever withdraws them, it is only the better to reach the sinner's heart, whom he continues to love.

It may not be possible even to communicate with our enemy, however much we may wish to. But there is one way always open to express our love for him: prayer. When we begin to pray for our enemies, suddenly things begin to change— sometimes in the other, but always in ourselves.

Earlier, in discussing the ninth beatitude, "blessed are the persecuted," I told of my first experience of persecution—new for me because until then I had only experienced privilege and support for my Christian faith. This new experience really depressed me. I felt a ton of darkness weighing on me. Knowing that such feelings are an invitation to find the Lord more deeply, I took my depression to prayer. And the word I heard was, "Pray for your persecutors." I didn't feel like praying for them, but I began to do so. Suddenly the depression vanished and I stood above the situation, victorious over it and actually tasting some of the joy Jesus promised in the beatitude—which is a change in *attitude* about *being,* as Jesus says here, "Pray for your persecutors," not that *they* change (though that may well happen) but "that *you* may *be* children of your Father in heaven." When I began to pray for my enemies, the change happened in *me*. I experienced myself as a son of this Father of universal love, this Father who realizes that those who oppose him are hurting themselves most of all, and for that reason deserve all the more love and compassion.

The *more* of verse 47 is the *more* of 5:20, the way in which the righteousness of Jesus surpasses that of the scribes and Pharisees, and now of the publicans and gentiles as well. To love one's enemies, to pray for one's persecutors, is to love beyond the normal limits of the human heart. It is to love as God loves, to be perfect with the perfection of God.

### The Anonymous Donor (6:1-4)

6 "BEWARE OF practicing your piety before men in order to be seen by them; for then you will have no reward from your Father who is in heaven.

2 "Thus, when you give alms, sound no trumpet before you, as the hypocrites do in the synagogues and in the streets, that they may be praised by men. Truly, I say to you, they have received their reward. ³But when you give alms, do not let your left hand know what your right hand is doing, ⁴so that your alms may be in secret; and your Father who sees in secret will reward you.

Having concluded the six antitheses, Matthew's portrait of Jesus shows him dealing with the three practices pious Jews like the Pharisees considered chief: almsgiving, prayer and fasting. Because the original Jewish element in Matthew's community were already accustomed to these practices, it was not a question of recommending them (compare Luke's catechism of prayer for gentile Christians, Lk 11:1-13), but only of insisting on the interior dispositions that should accompany them—dispositions that Jesus repeatedly found lacking in the external piety of the Pharisees he knew.

Jesus, who told his disciples in 5:16 to let their light shine so that people could see their good works, now warns them not to do these works to be seen. The key to this paradox lies in the words *in order to* here. The disciple is to do good works that are visible in the world for the Father's glory (5:16). But if one acts *in order to* win human approval rather than God's, there will be no reward with the Father. It is a trap into which religious people can easily fall—beginning with good intentions and, having done some good work, to derive one's subsequent energy and motivation from the adulation received. One then ends up following the call of adulation rather than doing the will of the Father. One becomes a stage-actor (the basic meaning of *hypocrite*), in which the galleries give the cues and ultimately one's identity. A trap indeed, the trap of the role-player, and all the more seductive when the role is religious, for the outer role more easily masks growing inconsistencies in covert behavior. The fear of rejection is simply the flip-side of role-playing. One avoids being true to one's faith and convictions because one fears what others might say or do. The "pleaser" syndrome also ends in fragmenting one's identity, because one no longer belongs to self or to God but to anyone whose esteem one fears to lose at the moment.

This "hypocrite" is the polar opposite of the one Jesus blesses for enduring persecutions for his sake (5:11–12), and that is why he addresses all his woes in chapter 23 to the "hypocrites."

Jesus applies this principle first of all to almsgiving.

## Simple, Secret Prayer (6:5–6)

5 "And when you pray, you must not be like the hypocrites; for they love to stand and pray in the synagogues and at the street corners, that they may be seen by men. Truly, I say to you, they have received their reward. ⁶But when you pray, go into your room and shut the door and pray to your Father who is in secret; and your Father who sees in secret will reward you.

Prayer, too, is a matter of the heart. The hypocrites who pray to be seen already have their reward in the ambiguous esteem they have sought. Men have heard them pray, God has not. In contrast, God hears the secret prayer of his children. Even if one does not pray in order to be seen by others, it is possible to pray in order to be seen by oneself. Basil Pennington in his book on centering prayer describes a favorite distraction of those who earnestly try to pray: watching oneself pray. A very understandable diversion of energy, but genuine prayer must break through such "role-playing" and focus directly on the Lord.

Does this saying of Jesus proscribe common prayer? Hardly. For while it uses "you" in the singular, it prepares us for the next teaching in which "you" becomes plural, and the disciples are to address God as *our* Father.

## The Lord's Prayer (6:7–13)

7 "And in praying do not heap up empty phrases as the Gentiles do; for they think that they will be heard for their many words. ⁸Do not be like them, for your Father knows what you need before you ask him. ⁹Pray then like this:
Our Father who art in heaven,
Hallowed be thy name.
¹⁰Thy kingdom come,
Thy will be done,
On earth as it is in heaven.
¹¹Give us this day our daily bread;
¹²And forgive us our debts,
As we also have forgiven our debtors;
¹³And lead us not into temptation,
But deliver us from evil.

Separating the Christian community from both gentiles and Jews, Jesus here presents a model formula for brief, heartfelt prayer. The gentiles *think* they will be heard by trying every possible formula in a kind of prayer-roulette to gain his attention. A magical notion of God! But even before we ask, God *knows what we need*. He is a better judge of our needs than we are, and his priorities may not be the same as ours. This is why our prayer should first of all be for God's plans to come about. Our needs can be reduced to the simplest. This, in fact, is the spirit of the prayer Jesus teaches.

Already several times up to this point Jesus has referred to God as "your Father" (5:45,48; 6:1,4,6). We now come to the centerpiece of the Sermon on the Mount, the prayer that contains the essence of Jesus' revelation and teaching, the prayer in which we dare to call God Father. It deserves careful and extended study.

## Our Father

From his Jewish childhood, Jesus had learned many names for God—Lord, King, Shepherd, Rock, Fortress—and, yes, Father. Used hardly more than a dozen times in the OT, it was always the formal address, and it was not frequently used in the prayers Jesus had learned as a boy. But there was something else going on in Jesus' childhood that would have a determining impact on his understanding of God, and it did not happen in the synagogue. The Talmud says that when a baby first begins to speak, his first words are *Imma* and *Abba*, both the titles of intimacy by which he addresses his "mummy" and "daddy." The first person, therefore, whom Jesus addressed as *Abba* was not God but Joseph. And, in the mysterious development of his human religious consciousness, when Jesus came to the moment of choosing his name for God, the title was none other than the one he had first given to his foster father Joseph.

It was a word never used in the OT for God, nor in the prayer literature of late Judaism, for it was no doubt considered much too familiar, but it stuck with Jesus into his adult life until the very end, for Mark tells us that was precisely the name Jesus used in his prayer in the garden of Gethsemane (Mk 14:36). And the Aramaic *Abba* could hardly have passed unchanged into vocabulary of the Greek-speaking Christians, as we know from its use by St. Paul (Gal 4:6; Rom 8:15), had it not originated with Jesus. Parenthetically, the greatest title to honor for Joseph in the church is the fact that his relationship with Jesus was so marvelously unique that it would inspire Jesus to transfer to God the name he had first given to Joseph.

What *Abba* conveys then is essentially the ultimate in intimacy and with that intimacy the correlative attitude of a child completely surrendered in trust. This point is crucial in the discussion of language in the church today. In searching for alternatives to sexually exclusive language, some have proposed eliminating "Father" from our liturgical vocabulary, replacing it with "creator" or simply "God." The price to be paid for such a change is, however, not minimal. For the apparent gain of being fair to women and true to the fact that the Supreme Being transcends all sexual differences, such terms reverse and negate what was most new and unique about the revelation of Jesus—the intimacy of God. This topic is too complex to develop in detail here. Suffice it to say that tampering with the basic title of God given us by Jesus is to touch the very foundations of the Christian faith and the Christian experience.

The modifier *our* does not appear in Luke's version of the Lord's prayer (Lk 11:2). If the *Abba* experience is so intimate and personal, one might conclude that it is too precious to share. But Matthew's version reflects a theme that runs through his gospel like a mighty river: who God is determines how we relate with others. And in this gospel Jesus is constantly referring all his teaching about relationships to "your Father in heaven." Because God is Father, Jesus sees everyone as a brother or sister—at least a potential one—cutting across every barrier of class and caste. And this sociological conclusion of his relationship to the Father led ultimately to his own death at the hands of those who could not accept to make community with the unclean and sinners. To say *"our* Father" then is not an idle word. It involves an acceptance and a welcoming of others (18:5) in a shared cry of *"Abba!"* That is why so much of Christian worship is community worship, climaxing in the Eucharist and why, from the first century onwards, the Christian community has said the Lord's prayer just before receiving the body and blood of the Lord.

## Who Art in Heaven

During a shared prayer session one of my novices said, "When I was a little child, barely learning how to speak, my mother had a terrible time trying to teach me the Lord's prayer. I kept saying, 'Our Father is not in heaven,' and I refused to say it any differently, because I knew our father lived in the same house with us."

This story illustrates how the word "Father" makes a child naturally think of the only father he has experienced, his own human father. If our earthly father was very much like Joseph, perhaps we had little difficulty in making the transfer to the heavenly Father. But if our father was a drunkard, if he had fits of anger and beat mother and children, then we must surely have had a real problem in calling God "Father." Either we said, "But God could not possibly be like that," or, worse, we expected God to act and be like our human father and thus we developed a slavish fear or distrust of him. For most of us, our fathers were neither the holiest of saints nor the worst of sinners, but a mixture of goodness and weakness. It is a great step forward in our human and spiritual growth, to accept our parents as they are or were—a mixture. If somehow we have expected them to be God, we must consciously relieve them, and ourselves, of that expectation. And, equally important, we must relieve God of any limitation we may have put on him because of our experience of our human father's weaknesses and limitations. We need to let our father be our father and let God be God. And when we call God "Father" we must realize that he has all the goodness we have experienced in our human father without the shortcomings. That is what it means to say "Our Father *who art in heaven.*"

But what of the orphan who never knew his earthly father? Is it possible for him to have the *Abba* experience of God? Or what about the person whose experience of his earthly father was entirely negative? God can, of course, extraordinarily supply, by the gift of the Holy Spirit, the direct experience of himself as *Abba*. Normally, though, there are other human persons from whom we can learn what it is to be fathered. Parents are not the only ones who love us into life.

## Hallowed Be Thy Name

One rainy night outside our house in St. Louis a young driver side-swiped one car, hit another parked car, sending it crashing into another across the street, and finally ended by crashing into a tree. The driver was unhurt but badly shaken.

Arriving on the scene, the police officer began filling in his report. "What is your name?" he asked the trembling driver. "Smith," came the answer. "Hallowed B. Smith."

"I've heard of Smith, but never a name like Hallowed B. How do you spell it?"

"Just like you pray it. When I was born, my mamma looked at me and said, 'Hallowed B. thy name,' and that's what I've been called ever since."

*Hallowed* is an old English word reserved today for ancient liturgical texts like the Lord's prayer. No wonder it is misunderstood! "Hallow" means to make holy or to declare holy. If God's name is already holy, then we can hardly be asking that the name *be* holy. And so the usual understanding is that we are asking that the name and person of God the Father may be acknowledged and proclaimed as holy by the entire world. This first of the "thou" petitions puts God and his glory first— an instruction for those who think of prayer as bringing God a shopping list of needs.

There is, however, another meaning rooted in the word's biblical background. The passive form is often used in Hebrew as a way of asking God to act. Thus the meaning would be "Sanctify your name." Since the Lord has chosen Israel as his own people and made a covenant with them, his holy name is upon this people and somehow involved with their history. Thus when Israel sins and brings upon itself the disgrace of the exile, the holy name of the Lord is defiled. When the prophet foretells the restoration of his people, he says that the Lord will sanctify his name, that is, he will clean up the bad image his people have given him by acting once again in their behalf, saving them and bringing them home to their land (Ez 36:20–24). In this meaning, then, we are asking the Father to come to the aid of his people, to champion the cause of the oppressed, to act in time and history and to set things right. It is an aggressive, missionary prayer. And its meaning is very closely related to the next petition.

## Thy Kingdom Come

For most countries today kings and kingdoms belong to history or romance. Even if we were closer to the experience of royalty, what would the kingdom of *God* mean? And, even more obscure, what would it mean for that kingdom to *come?* Here a little background will help.

One of the prayers that Jesus learned from childhood days in the synagogue was the following:

> Exalted and hallowed be his great name
> in the world which he created according to his will.
> May he rule his kingdom
> in your lifetime and in your days and in the
> lifetime of the whole house of Israel, speedily and soon.

Notice how closely are joined the prayer the Lord's name be hailed as holy and that his kingdom come. This prayer, called the *Qaddish* ("Holy"), reflects the ancient Jewish idea of the Lord as king, which goes back to the exodus and the Mosaic covenant. When a king is enthroned, two things happen. First, the people hail him as king, they "proclaim his name" with great pomp and splendor. Second, once the new king has taken his throne, he puts down all opposition, all political chaos. For an interregnum is a classic time of unrest—neighboring kings may seize the moment of weakness in the country to invade, or malcontents within the kingdom may plot a coup. The first priority of the new king is to assure order and stability in his kingdom.

In Jesus' day Israel had no king as in the distant past. And for hundreds of years she had been under the domination of foreigners—first the Babylonians, then the Persians, then the Greeks, and now the Romans. Still they believed that the Lord was their true king and that one day soon he would come in a very visible way to take over the rule of his people, either directly by some miraculous act, or indirectly through the Messiah, the human king, descendant of David, who would be God's instrument for establishing his peace and justice on earth. When that would happen, people would hail his name (shout that it was holy), and the Lord would settle all chaos and disturbance in nature and in the political world. This hope was fanned by those Psalms which celebrated the kingship of the Lord, a rule imperfect now but soon to come in its perfection (see Pss 93:1–3; 96:9–13; 97:1–6; 99:1–5; 29:10).

As Christians we too believe that our Abba God is a king and that this world is meant to be his kingdom. Jesus is the Messiah, Son of David whom the Father has sent to establish his kingdom. Like the Jews we live in a world where God's plan of peace and love and justice has not been fully realized. So we pray that his kingdom will come—that is, we pray that he will take up his rule on earth. Of course we are praying for the final victory at the end of world history (see Rev 12:10; 19:6–8). But we are also praying for the smaller comings each day, and for such immediate things as justice, peace and the joy of the Holy Spirit, which Paul tells us are the real elements of God's kingdom (Rom 14:17). In one early manuscript instead of "Thy kingdom come" we read "Thy Holy Spirit come upon us and cleanse us." Coming probably from a baptismal liturgy, this text reflects the thought of Luke that the Holy Spirit is the interim gift empowering the church until God's kingdom is fully established.

The Jews of Jesus' day thought of God primarily as king. But for Jesus God is also *Abba*, the loving Father. By combining the traditional image of king with that of the Father, Jesus creates something new. On the one hand, the kingdom image prevents the prayer from becoming self-centered and escapist. The kingdom prayer is essentially missionary, and whoever prays it seriously commits himself to work to bring God's kingdom about on earth. But since the king is also *Abba*, his kingdom is above all a matter of love and compassion. This fusing of "father" and "king" is exactly what we find in the parables. In Mt 18:21–35, the king who forgives without measure is the father who expects his children to do the same. And in Mt 25:31–46, where the kingdom belongs to those who practice love on earth, the kingly Son of Man says, "Come, O blessed of my *Father*, inherit the *kingdom* . . ." (25:34).

## *Thy Will Be Done on Earth as It Is in Heaven*

Some would interpret this petition, absent from Luke's version (Lk 11:2), to mean that they should accept whatever they find in the world with resignation, as if there is nothing

to be done about the evil and injustice they meet every day—
Stoic resignation to fate. Some Christians, alas, have used this
verse to tell the poor to accept their situation, even to accept
oppression by the rich and powerful, telling them that God will
reward them in the next life. This would be little different from
the Hindu notion that into whatever situation one is born in
this life one must work out one's *karma* and hope to be re-
incarnated in a better life after this one.

Jesus could hardly have meant that. He came to challenge
that idea. Through his healings and exorcisms he changed people's lives and lifted their burden of suffering. And he preached
justice and equality of all men and women as children of the
Father. The primary meaning, then, seems to be essentially
the same as "thy kingdom come": May your will, your plan of
justice, love and peace be realized as perfectly on earth as it
is in heaven! It is an aggressive, revolutionary kind of prayer.
And to say it from the heart means also that we commit ourselves to work to bring that will, that plan about.

But if "thy will be done" means the same as "thy kingdom
come," why say it? Because the words recall for us how this
prayer was lived out in the life and especially the passion and
death of Jesus. It recalls the crisis and change in Jesus' own
life when, in the Father's mysterious will, the cross replaced
Jesus' preaching and miracles as the way to the kingdom.

If we take the parable of the wicked tenants seriously (it
appears in all three gospels, Mt 21:33–46; Mk 12:1–12; Lk 20:9–
19), then it is not exactly true to say that God sent his son to
die for us. The Father sent Jesus, just as he sent the prophets,
to call his people to conversion and to give signs that he was
truly God's messenger and more: he was God's son—"They will
respect my son." Jesus began his mission preaching the kingdom and setting people free from their burdens and oppression.
He also proclaimed a new order of love and gave the example
by calling people from all walks of life to form a new community
with him. Had things gone according to the Father's original
plan, Jesus would not have had to suffer. But in fact Jesus was
too true and too good for the people in power to accept. They
determined to get rid of him, and they found a way. That way
involved betrayal by one of his own disciples and the most

shameful and painful death known at the time, crucifixion.

At some point in his ministry Jesus must have become aware of the dark future ahead of him if he remained faithful to the mission the Father had given him. There must have been a great struggle in his soul. It reached its climax in the agony in the garden. Jesus prayed to his *Abba* over and over again to take the cup away. In his human heart he could not understand why he had to die for the kingdom to be established. For that matter, according to the parable, the Father could not understand either! Yet the Father, who knows how to make all things work together unto good (Rom 8:28), would use even the rejection and execution of Jesus to bring about his saving plan. Without understanding this plan, Jesus surrendered to it in the words, "Your will, not mine be done." We might say that the Father did not answer Jesus' prayer. But that is not the way the epistle to the Hebrews understands the situation: "In the days when he was in the flesh, [Jesus] offered prayers and supplications with loud cries and tears to the one who was able to save him from death, *and he was heard because of his reverence*" (Heb 5:7 NABR). How did the Father hear him? Not by sparing Jesus the cross his enemies had chosen for him, but by responding to Jesus' surrender (his *reverence*) by the resurrection and making him the head of the new people of God. Or, as Jesus interprets the parable of the wicked tenants, the stone rejected by the builders becomes the cornerstone (21:42).

What power in those few words, "Thy will be done"! They put us in touch with the mystery of the cross—and its victory. The cross: The two mysteries the disciples found so hard to understand—that God should be *Abba* and that Jesus should suffer—are part of our lives as Christians. It is the greatest of paradoxes: that God loves us as his dearest children, and yet he allows us to suffer as Jesus, his beloved, did. Of course, unlike Jesus, we suffer some things because of our sinfulness, our attachments to things or values which are not from God. And in this the cross is a blessing inasmuch as it purifies us from sin and the effects of sin. But when we too, like Jesus, wrestle with the Father concerning his plan for us and say in the end, as he did, "Thy will be done!" we know in faith that our cross will somehow be turned to life. We know that, no matter how much the original blueprint may be revised, his kingdom will come and his victory will be won.

## Give Us This Day Our Daily Bread

After addressing the Father for the things concerning him (the "thou" petitions), we now turn to the things that concern us, the "we" petitions. Aside from the title *Abba*, Jesus' originality appears most in this part of the prayer. For while the "thou" petitions were similar to the *Qaddish*, the "we" petitions here have no similarities to that prayer.

The common understanding of the first petition here is that we are asking for the food we need today. That indeed seems to be the meaning in Luke's version which reads, "Give us each day our daily bread." But Matthew's version raises some questions. The Greek work *epiousion*, which most translations render "daily," has many possible meanings, and it would be hard to decide which was the meaning of Matthew, and before him the meaning of Jesus, if it were not for St. Jerome. In the fourth century, Jerome was able to find a copy of "The gospel according to the Hebrews," written in Aramaic, the language Jesus spoke. He says the Aramaic word he found there for the Greek *epiousion* was *mahar*, which means "tomorrow." The meaning would not be "our daily bread" but "the bread of tomorrow." In the Judaism of Jesus' day, "tomorrow" was often used for the Great Tomorrow, the tomorrow of the kingdom, when God would begin his reign. From elsewhere in the NT we know that another image for the kingdom was the heavenly banquet (26:29; Lk 12:37; 14:15; 22:30). Combining these two images, the meaning would be: "Give us today the bread from your heavenly table." Or: "If your kingdom isn't coming today, at least give us a taste of the bread we will eat there. Let us experience a foretaste of the kingdom today." That foretaste could be experienced in many ways—healings, miracles, the gift of the Holy Spirit, reconciliation, strength in trial and persecution. But most of all, "bread" would make the early Christians think immediately of the Eucharist, the "bread from heaven," Jesus himself coming not in glory but very really in

the simple sign of a meal he told his disciples to celebrate until
he would return (see John 6 and 1 Cor 11:26). This would be
particularly meaningful when the prayer was said just before
receiving the Eucharist, the bread of the "Great Tomorrow"
which we are privileged to receive today.

Luke's version has a different thrust. Throughout his gospel he hammers home the danger of riches, particularly riches
that are not shared. The compulsion to stockpile betrays the
trust that the Christian should have in the Father's care. Thus
in Luke the petition seems to mean, "Give us each day just the
bread we need for that day."

## Forgive . . . as We Forgive

Like the other petitions we have examined, this one is
colored by Jesus' concern for the coming of the kingdom. His
teaching on forgiveness is often set within the framework of
the final judgment. In 5:23–26 we saw that not only is it important to be reconciled with one's brother before offering our
gift at the altar, but if our brother is our "opponent," we must
remember that the common-sense advice about "settling out of
court" applies even more to our relationship to him before God.
For we are both on our way to the final judgment, and it is
infinitely better to be reconciled on the way than to wait for
God to settle the accounts. The best Matthean commentary on
this petition, however, will come in 18:21–35: We have been
forgiven, but if we refuse to forgive our neighbor we lose the
forgiveness of God. And so in this petition we pray to be forgiven, and in the same breath we pledge to forgive anyone who
has hurt us. This is the only petition to which Jesus adds a
commentary at the end of the prayer (6:14–15).

## Lead Us Not into Temptation

Newer translations of this petition are generally an im-
provement, for our older translation seems to assume that the
Father *could* lead us into temptation. That is not possible, says
St. James: "Let no one say when he is tempted, 'I am tempted

by God'; for God cannot be tempted with evil and he himself tempts no one" (James 1:13). Actually the Greek word here means *testing*, and it refers to the final trial of our faith, whether this be martyrdom or any severe, ultimate testing that might make us fall away. In that testing we ask the grace to persevere. "He who perseveres to the end will be saved" (24:13). St. Thomas More was very afraid of being disemboweled while alive—a way many enemies of the English king were tortured and put to death. He prayed to be spared that, because he was afraid his faith might fail him. He was spared that suffering, but he went cheerfully to his death by beheading.

## Deliver Us from Evil

This petition, which appears only in Matthew's version, is parallel in form and meaning with the preceding one. The "evil" from which we wish to be delivered is not so much the evil we might do, nor is it the evil we might suffer in persecution—it would be legitimate to pray for that, but Jesus promised persecutions. Like the preceding request, it is a prayer to be delivered and to be victorious *in* our struggle with evil—or, better, with the evil *one*, the devil.

That means that the Christian life all the way to its last moment, is a spiritual combat. Jesus was tempted by the devil. He said his death and resurrection would cast out the Prince of this world. And we are reminded, "Be sober, be watchful. Your adversary the devil prowls around like a roaring lion, seeking someone to devour. Resist him, firm in your faith" (1 Pet 5:8–9). An extensive description of the Christian's armor needed for this combat is given in Ephesians 6:10–18, where we are told: "We are not contending against flesh and blood, but against the principalities, against the powers, against the world rulers of this present darkness, against the spiritual hosts of wickedness" (Eph 6:12).

Today, other models of the Christian life seem to be more fashionable. It is a journey, a following of Jesus, a continual growth. The image of the spiritual combat, however, is equally biblical. It is a reminder of the need for decisiveness, discernment, and grace to negotiate the pitfalls and snares on the journey. It is not spiritual paranoia to believe that there is an enemy out to destroy us. Whether we understand that enemy as the Prince of Darkness or self-centered desire (as James 1:14 does) or the tragic flaw that could lead us, like Hamlet or Judas, to our destruction, it is important to know the ultimate consequences of little decisions we make—or fail to make—along the way and that even final perseverance is a grace to be sought in prayer.

In conclusion we note that there are actually three "we" petitions which match the three "thou" petitions. All are examples of simple, short prayer. If we can speak of God having needs, they are simple: his glory, his kingdom, his will. For us the real needs of our lives are incredibly simple: bread, forgiveness and perseverance. These petitions tell us in very concrete ways what it is to seek first the kingdom of God and his righteousness, knowing that everything else will be given us besides (6:33).

## What Happened to the Kingdom, the Power and the Glory?

When I was a child, my aunt used to tell me that one of the main differences between Protestants and Catholics was the concluding line of the Lord's Prayer. The Protestants added, "For thine is the kingdom and the power and the glory," whereas the Catholics stopped at "evil." Though neither Luke nor Matthew carries these words, the addition is very ancient. It is found already in a first-century document called the *Didache*, the "Teaching of the Twelve Apostles." In Jewish prayer practice it was customary, after reciting a traditional formula of prayer, for the leader to add a spontaneous original conclusion. This conclusion was called the "seal" of the prayer. Obviously it would vary from prayer-leader to prayer-leader. This conclusion was not part of the formula but it was always expected as a way of giving a "grand finale" to the prayer. Jesus himself may have done so at the end of the prayer he gave his disciples, for it is unlikely that he would have ended either with "temptation" or "evil." If so, the tradition did not consider the

conclusion he used to be mandatory but rather, in keeping with
the practice of the "seal," left the formulation to the creativity
of the one praying. Hence it seems that the conclusion we are
discussing was composed by someone spontaneously, then became popular and widely used in the early church, and this is
the "doxology" that has come down to us.

## Forgiveness Again (6:14–15)

[14]For if you forgive men their trespasses, your heavenly
Father also will forgive you; [15]but if you do not forgive men
their trespasses, neither will your Father forgive your trespasses.

It is remarkable, as we have already pointed out, that the
only commentary Jesus offers to this prayer concerns forgiveness. Matthew's addition of his saying, which may well have
been an isolated saying of Jesus (it is found in a different context in Mk 11:25–26), shows how central is the theme of forgiveness and reconciliation in this gospel. We have already met
it in 5:21–26, the first of the contrasts with the old law, and
we will meet it again in 18:21–35. The essence of Christian
discipleship is the ability to forgive.

## Fasting (6:16–18)

16 "And when you fast, do not look dismal, like the
hypocrites, for they disfigure their faces that their fasting
may be seen by men. Truly, I say to you, they have received
their reward. [17]But when you fast, anoint your head and
wash your face, [18]that your fasting may not be seen by men
but by your Father who is in secret; and your Father who
sees in secret will reward you.

Again Jesus is speaking to Jewish disciples for whom fasting is a practice taken for granted. And again Jesus insists it
be done in a way as unostentatious as possible. Anointing the
head and washing the face were signs of life and joy normally

omitted when fasting. But Jesus' disciples are to radiate the life and joy of union with the Father, which would be compromised by anything calling attention to their fasting.

In 9:14–15 it appears that Jesus' disciples did not fast at all because of the joy of having him, the bridegroom, with them. So this saying here must refer to the time "when the bridegroom is taken away from them." Fasting was, in fact, practiced by the early church (Acts 13:2).

## The Treasure of the Heart (6:19–24)

19. "Do not lay up for yourselves treasures on earth, where moth and rust consume and where thieves break in and steal, ²⁰but lay up for yourselves treasures in heaven, where neither moth nor rust consumes and where thieves do not break in and steal. ²¹For where your treasure is, there will your heart be also.

22 "The eye is the lamp of the body. So, if your eye is sound, your whole body will be full of light; ²³but if your eye is not sound, your whole body will be full of darkness. If then the light in you is darkness, how great is the darkness!

24 "No one can serve two masters; for either he will hate the one and love the other, or he will be devoted to the one and despise the other. You cannot serve God and mammon.

Having completed the Christian counterpart of the Jewish traditions on almsgiving, prayer and fasting, Matthew now assembles a number of sayings of Jesus, all of which are practical consequences of the fatherhood of God proclaimed in the Lord's prayer. If there is one theme in all that follows now to the end of the Sermon, it is this: If God is your Father, trust him and show that trust by the way you live.

The first enemy of that trust is the passion for wealth and property. The irony is that earthly wardrobes and fixtures and even money are perishable, no matter what precautions one may take to secure them. In undeveloped nations today, it is still widespread practice to bury one's treasures outside or in the floor of one's house, or to put them all into jewelry worn on the body. Are today's banks and stock-markets any safer? The point is that no matter how great the treasure or how safe the hiding or the investment, anxiety about them claims the heart. Jesus is not condemning earning an honest living. He is warning against accumulating wealth, which takes energy away from accumulating the spiritual treasures which will not perish.

It is in this context that Matthew places the parable of the eye, lamp of the body. As the eye provides the light that directs the entire person, so faith in the teaching of Jesus about trust and detachment fills the disciple with light and guides his every action. To be without it is to grope in a world of darkness.

The third saying about two masters is the climactic point. Accumulation of wealth is not freedom but slavery. Wealth is made to serve man, not to be his god. In greed we are serving a god, and a false one at that—mammon, a Semitic word for wealth or property. However much we might like to combine the service of God with the service of mammon, it is impossible. Love of God and love of wealth don't mix.

## Worry and Priorities (6:25–34)

25 "Therefore I tell you, do not be anxious about your life, what you shall eat or what you shall drink, nor about your body, what you shall put on. Is not life more than food, and the body more than clothing? [26]Look at the birds of the air: they neither sow nor reap nor gather into barns, and yet your heavenly Father feeds them. Are you not of more value than they? [27]And which of you by being anxious can add one cubit to his span of life? [28]And why are you anxious about clothing? Consider the lilies of the field, how they grow; they neither toil nor spin; [29]yet I tell you, even Solomon in all his glory was not arrayed like one of these. [30]But if God so clothes the grass of the field, which today is alive and tomorrow is thrown into the oven, will he not much more clothe you, O men of little faith? [31]Therefore do not be anxious, saying, 'What shall we eat?' or 'What shall we drink?' or 'What shall we wear?' [32]For the Gentiles seek all these things; and your heavenly Father knows that you need them all. [33]But seek first his kingdom and his righ-

teousness, and all these things shall be yours as well.
34 "Therefore do not be anxious about tomorrow, for
tomorrow will be anxious for itself. Let the day's own trouble be sufficient for the day.

Another enemy of trust: worry. It is probably the most
common waste of energy, because it is where energy goes when
there is nothing—or nothing more—we can *do* about a problem. Yet it can be the raw material for trust, if we learn how
to put our worries in the Father's hands.

Jesus applies his teaching about trust to three most fundamental areas: food, drink, and clothing. To these he will add
a fourth toward the end of the passage, the future.

Isn't life more than eating and the body more than the
clothes you wear? I remember seeing a poster on the door of
a confrere who was struggling with obesity: "When all else
fails, eat!" It was a humorous reminder to him that food should
not be a refuge from life's challenges, nor an admission that
even God has failed. Jesus put it another way when in the first
temptation he told Satan, "One does not live by bread alone"
(4:4). When poor health forced me to return from the third
world, American food was a gastric paradise, but I soon realized it could control my life as much as the amoebas had done
if I let it. And the challenge was not discipline. The challenge
was whether I could trust the Father's care enough not to let
worry about health turn me into a compulsive eater. Anxiety
is really fear. And what we do out of fear can outrival what
we do out of love. Excessive concern about food and drink and
clothes is really fear that we will be nothing without them. That
is what Jesus means by *little faith*. The disciple who follows
Jesus has another, unfailing source of his security—the Father's love. And this enables him to receive with gratitude and
hold with a relaxed grasp all the Father's gifts.

*Seek first the kingdom of God.* Each word here is dynamite. *Seek.* For some spiritual gurus, perfection is the absence
of desire. For Jesus perfection is not the absence of desire but
the ordering of it. And the ruling desire, the ruling passion
should be hunger for God. It is the seeker who finds (7:8).
Before healing the blind man Jesus asks, "What do you *want*

me to do for you?" (20:32). He who has no hunger will never be filled. A corpse has no desires. Those who hunger and thirst for righteousness will be satisfied (5:6). The kingdom is yours for the asking.

*Seek first.* Jesus does not say, "Seek nothing else" but "seek first." He tells us to pray for our daily bread. He answers those who beg him for healing. Such petitions for personal or family needs may come easily. But it is not so easy to put "God's kingdom and his righteousness" before all other seeking. Yet that is what Jesus teaches in the Lord's prayer: "Thy kingdom come, thy will be done" comes before anything else.

Now what does that mean in practice?

It means: *prioritize.* In the OT God told his people to keep holy one day of the week, to give him the first fruits of the harvest, to consecrate the firstborn. For us in the modern world there are analogs. We can prioritize our *time.* Stop to examine your time management. How much of it do you spend each day reading the newspaper, watching TV? Of that time, could you spend ten minutes reading the word of God? And could you reorder your week so as to pay a visit to the sick or prisoners, or do some work to build up the community of your parish?

We can prioritize our *money.* A budget is just common sense. But if everything we have is God's gift, we ought to think first of what percentage we can return to the Lord and his work—and *then* consider our other needs.

We can prioritize our *appointments* and *commitments.* We can arrange a time each week for prayer and Scripture sharing with one or more friends.

We can look at all the facets of our life and prioritize. To do so is not to lose but to gain: "All these things shall be yours as well."

Including tomorrow.

## Judging (7:1-6)

7 "JUDGE NOT, that you be not judged. ²For with the judgment you pronounce you will be judged, and the measure you give will be the measure you get. ³Why do you

see the speck that is in your brother's eye, but do not notice the log that is in your own eye? ⁴Or how can you say to your brother, 'Let me take the speck out of your eye,' when there is the log in your own eye? ⁵You hypocrite, first take the log out of your own eye, and then you will see clearly to take the speck out of your brother's eye.

6 "Do not give dogs what is holy; and do not throw your pearls before swine, lest they trample them under foot and turn to attack you.

From here on the structure of the Sermon becomes less clear. Matthew has assembled sayings of Jesus that may have some connection with the Lord's prayer. The first, on judging, echoes the teaching that forgiveness of others is a condition for God's forgiveness (6:12, 14–15). What Jesus commands here is not a blind indifference to evil. The judgment of which he speaks is a definitive condemnation of the person, which of course involves unforgiveness. The way we treat others is the way God will treat us. In v. 3 the word "brothers" makes it obvious we are in the context of the Christian community. Instead of condemning, we are to correct the failing brother (18:15–17) in such a way that we begin with ourself, as Paul says, "Brothers, even if a person is caught in some transgression, you who are spiritual should correct that one in a gentle spirit, so that you also may not be tempted" (Gal 6:1 NABR).

In Matthew's community there were doubtless rigorists who had a program for everyone else without first looking into their own hearts. Such people are *hypocrites*. Elsewhere Jesus has applied this title to the scribes and Pharisees, but here for the first time he applies it to those of his own disciples who would correct others without correcting themselves.

Verse 6 about pearls and swine is puzzling. It was originally an isolated saying of Jesus for which the context is lost. The meaning we are interested in is the meaning Matthew intended by inserting it here. Scholars have suggested many possibilities. Some say "what is holy," in parallelism with "pearls," means the gospel, which is compared to a pearl in 13:45. Since the rabbis called gentiles dogs or swine, some say this saying originally forbade mission to the gentiles (Jesus so limited his own disciples on their first mission, 10:5). Others say the reference is to apostate or unrepentant Christians (18:17) or those who refuse to hear the gospel (10:14–15). But none of these meanings have anything to do with the context here, and so I believe a better meaning is that Christians should do their correcting of each other within the privacy of the community itself and not take their disputes to outsiders, as Paul teaches in 1 Cor 6:1–11. If so, then "what is holy" is the process of fraternal correction and reconciliation in the community—and Christians should not let that precious dynamic be subjected to the judgment of outsiders who are not committed to the community.

## Prayer of Petition (7:7–11)

7 "Ask, and it will be given you; seek, and you will find; knock, and it will be opened to you. [8]For every one who asks receives, and he who seeks finds, and to him who knocks it will be opened. [9]Or what man of you, if his son asks him for bread, will give him a stone? [10]Or if he asks for a fish, will give him a serpent? [11]If you then, who are evil, know how to give good gifts to your children, how much more will your Father who is in heaven give good things to those who ask him!

This little section is best understood as a commentary on the Lord's prayer given above, a context in which it also appears in Luke (11:9–13). If the disciples are first to seek the kingdom (6:10, 33), they are also to ask for their daily bread (6:11), knowing that the Father will not give them a stone. "Bread" here echoes the fourth petition of the prayer. But there is no object indicated for the asking, seeking and knocking. Thus there is no limitation placed on what we might ask for. But neither is there promised an exact *quid pro quo* response. The Father's response will always be something good— though it might not be exactly what we had in mind. There is important teaching here: 1) Never fear to ask your Father for anything you need or want. 2) Believe and trust that he will always answer your prayer, no matter what you have asked. 3) If what he gives is not what you expected, it will be something better. 4) The reason is that he is Father, and he can only give good things to his children.

## The Golden Rule (7:12)

[12]So whatever you wish that men would do to you, do so to them; for this is the law and the prophets.

This rule was a commonplace among the gentiles and the rabbis as well and therefore certainly is not original with Jesus. But it is a piece of common sense and enlightened self-interest which Jesus shared. Rabbi Hillel said that the rule in its negative form (Do *not* do unto others . . .) was the essence of the law. Jesus too says that it sums up the law and the prophets, an identification he will later make of the commandments to love God and neighbor (22:34–40).

## Conclusion of the Sermon: Be Authentic! (7:13–28)

13 "Enter by the narrow gate; for the gate is wide and the way is easy, that leads to destruction, and those who enter by it are many. [14]For the gate is narrow and the way is hard, that leads to life, and those who find it are few.

15 "Beware of false prophets, who come to you in sheep's clothing but inwardly are ravenous wolves. [16]You will know them by their fruits. Are grapes gathered from thorns, or figs from thistles? [17]So, every sound tree bears good fruit, but the bad tree bears evil fruit. [18]A sound tree cannot bear evil fruit, nor can a bad tree bear good fruit. [19]Every tree that does not bear good fruit is cut down and thrown into the fire. [20]Thus you will know them by their fruits.

21 "Not every one who says to me, 'Lord, Lord,' shall enter the kingdom of heaven, but he who does the will of my Father who is in heaven. [22]On that day many will say to me, 'Lord, Lord, did we not prophesy in your name, and cast out demons in your name, and do many mighty works in your name?' [23]And then will I declare to them, 'I never knew you;

depart from me, you evildoers.'

24 "Every one then who hears these words of mine and does them will be like a wise man who built his house upon the rock; ²⁵and the rain fell, and the floods came, and the winds blew and beat upon that house, but it did not fall, because it had been founded on the rock. ²⁶And every one who hears these words of mine and does not do them will be like a foolish man who built his house upon the sand; ²⁷and the rain fell, and the floods came, and the winds blew and beat against that house, and it fell; and great was the fall of it."

28 And when Jesus finished these sayings, the crowds were astonished at his teaching.

This section, unlike the one we have just seen, has a single binding theme, as the Sermon moves swiftly to its end: Be authentic disciples! By the time he wrote his gospel, Matthew's community was a mixture not only of Jews and gentiles but of rigorists and laxists, of false and true prophets, of unrepentant sinners on the one hand and, on the other, those who could not forgive—a mixture that will help us understand the parables of the weeds among the wheat (13:24–30, 36–43) and the net which hauls in all kinds of fish (13:47–50). So Matthew gathers sayings of Jesus which present contrasts—two kinds of gates, two kinds of roads, two kinds of trees, two kinds of foundations. And the implied challenge Jesus is giving as he concludes his revelation of the new law is the challenge with which Moses concluded his promulgation of the old law in Deuteronomy 30:15–20: Choose!

The choice, however, is not between the extremes in Matthew's community. Throughout the Sermon Jesus has contrasted the life-style he expects of his disciples with that of both the scribes and Pharisees on the one hand and the gentiles on the other. The authentic disciple is to be neither playboy nor Pharisee. He must choose the new way of Jesus and live it.

Jesus never said following him would be easy. On the contrary, it is a narrow gate through which only those free of baggage can enter. It is a hard road not made for vacationers. It is neither legalism nor license. The difficulty of Jesus' path is not some kind of ascetic self-flagellation either. It is simply the difficulty of choosing and persevering in the distinctive way of life just outlined by Jesus, which is basically a love fruitful in good works.

The contrast of trees applies this principle to prophets in the community. Matthew's community, like others of the early church, was animated by the gift of prophecy. This gift was exercised in a wide variety of ways—by exhortation, or reading of hearts, or predicting future events, or revealing an insight into Scripture. Gradually it became associated with certain persons who were given the title "prophets" and were highly esteemed in the communities (as we see in Acts and in the first century *Didache*). But as time went on, some prophets no longer used their gifts or status for the upbuilding of the community in love, as Paul said they should (1 Cor 14:3,5,12,26) but for their own gratification. In some cases their teaching was false, but it was the example of their lax and self-centered lives that most disturbed Matthew and the fact that they claimed to be Christians. They are wolves in sheep's clothing. The enemy outside is easily identified and tends even to unite the community. The enemy within weakens and divides. The false prophets, though attractive to many because of their charismatic power, can be known by their fruits. And so may the authentic prophets. Jesus does not specify what the fruits are, but we can easily infer from the preceding teaching that the good fruits are the works of love, the bad those that minimize the demands of Jesus and weaken and divide the community.

In his teaching Jesus has revealed "the will of my Father who is in heaven" (v. 21). Not only the prophets but any disciple who outwardly confesses the Lordship of Jesus, even though he be a worker of miracles, will be judged on whether he has actually *done* the Father's will. The final judgment is never far from Matthew's mind. In the panoramic scene of the sheep and goats in 25:31–46 recurs the same expression we have here, "Depart from me," said to the accursed. And there the distinguishing principle between the judged is whether or not they have done the works of mercy and love.

The climax of Jesus' address to his disciples comes in the image of the two foundations. The contrast is not that Jesus' words are rock and other teachers' are sand. The contrast lies in the hearers of the same word. Those who hear and *do* are founded on unshakable rock. Those who hear and *do not* are built on sand. The same contrast is found in James 1:22–25: "Be doers of the word and not hearers only, deceiving yourselves. For if any one is a hearer of the word and not a doer, he is like a man who observes his natural face in a mirror; for he observes himself and goes away and at once forgets what he was like. But he who looks into the perfect law, the law of liberty, and perseveres, being no hearer that forgets but a doer that acts, he shall be blessed in his doing." (RSV) The point was also made repeatedly in the rabbinical tradition: "The one who learns in order not to do would better have not been created" (*Sipra Behuqqotai parasha* 1.5 to Lev 26:3).

The flood is the judgment of God. In it only the doer will stand.

In his peroration Jesus does not cajole or exhort or invite. Telling his disciples what they may expect of their response to his demands, he speaks with divine authority. It is this that amazes the crowds. The scribes in their interpretations of the law would run for support to a list of rabbis or cross references to Scripture. Jesus speaks on his own authority and revises even Moses: "Moses said . . . but I say . . ." The crowd which has been listening all along now reappears in Matthew's wide-angle lens, as a preparation for the next chapter. ■

# Book Two:

## Mission in Galilee
## (8:1–11:1)

Here we meet the first long narrative section of Matthew's gospel, the bulk of which Matthew has drawn from Mark but so arranged and edited that we not only see Jesus the wonder-worker, the Messiah of deed as he has been the Messiah of word, but we find important examples of faith and lessons about discipleship. The nine healing stories are interlarded by five discipleship stories, and one of the stories, the stilling of the storm, combines miracle and discipleship themes. Matthew's arrangement is intentional: the disciples who are with Jesus in his ministry are being prepared for their mission in chapter 10 to do the same works they witness Jesus doing.

### Jesus, the Burden-Lifter (8:1–17)

8 WHEN HE came down from the mountain, great crowds followed him; ²and behold, a leper came to him and knelt before him, saying, "Lord, if you will, you can make me clean." ³And he stretched out his hand and touched him, saying, "I will; be clean." And immediately his leprosy was cleansed. ⁴And Jesus said to him, "See that you say nothing to any one; but go, show yourself to the priest, and offer the gift that Moses commanded, for a proof to the people."

5 As he entered Caperna-um, a centurion came forward to him, beseeching him ⁶and saying, "Lord, my servant is lying paralyzed at home, in terrible distress." ⁷And he said to him, "I will come and heal him." But the centurion answered him, "Lord, I am not worth  ⟩ have you come under my roof; but only say the word, an⟨ my servant will

be healed. [9]For I am a man under authority, with soldiers under me; and I say to one, 'Go,' and he goes, and to another, 'Come,' and he comes, and to my slave, 'Do this,' and he does it." [10]When Jesus heard him, he marveled, and said to those who followed him, "Truly, I say to you, not even in Israel have I found such faith. [11]I tell you, many will come from east and west and sit at table with Abraham, Isaac, and Jacob in the kingdom of heaven, [12]while the sons of the kingdom will be thrown into the outer darkness; there men will weep and gnash their teeth." [13]And to the centurion Jesus said, "Go; be it done for you as you have believed." And the servant was healed at that very moment.

14 And when Jesus entered Peter's house, he saw his mother-in-law lying sick with a fever; [15]he touched her hand, and the fever left her, and she rose and served him. [16]That evening they brought to him many who were possessed with demons; and he cast out the spirits with a word, and healed all who were sick. [17]This was to fulfil what was spoken by the prophet Isaiah, "He took our infirmities and bore our diseases."

The first three healing stories are bound tightly together and illustrate Isaiah's description of the Servant of the Lord given in verse 17. They happen on one day. Both the leper and the centurion address Jesus as *kyrie* (translated "Sir" or "Lord," depending on whether we see the beneficiaries in their original historical setting or with Matthew as types of the Christian who knows Jesus as Lord). The leper and Peter's mother-in-law are both healed by touch—important because Matthew generally prefers to show Jesus healing by his word alone, as he does for the centurion in anticipation of v. 16, where Jesus casts out spirits "with a word."

Note the contrast between the fervent petitions by the leper and the centurion and the absence of any petition in favor of Peter's mother-in-law (Matthew actually omits Mark's detail that on entering the house "immediately they told him of her"). Jesus blesses petitioning faith, but his compassion is not limited thereto. Jesus takes the initiative in an obvious need.

The three beneficiaries are all marginalized people. The leper was an outcast by law. He was required to live outside the city and to cry "Unclean! Unclean!" (Lev 13:45–46) whenever anyone approached him. In third world countries today families often reject the leper as cursed by God for some sin, and the leper's greatest suffering is his alienation from family and society. It is all the more surprising, then, that Jesus should touch the leper. He does not fear what others fear. He wants the leper to know God's love *touches* the untouchable.

In India, where the caste system is still prevalent, Louis, one of our candidates, was in a minor seminary when their water supply failed. He went to the well of a high-class Hindu and begged water. The man refused and told him to go away. Two years later Louis was sent to work at a leprosy center. There the greatest suffering of most of the patients was not the dreaded disease but total rejection by their families. Making his rounds, Louis suddenly stopped in his tracks. There before him, stricken with leprosy, was the man who had refused him water two years previously. Louis spoke to him, befriended him, did not fear to touch him. The man was humbled and changed.

The centurion is a gentile, one whom the Jews referred to as "dogs." Yet he shows more faith than Jesus has found in Israel. He is a type of those gentiles pouring into Matthew's originally Jewish community with more fervor than any of the chosen of Israel. Finally, Peter's mother-in-law is a woman, a second-class citizen by contemporary standards. Yet, healed by Jesus, she rises and serves *him* (Mark and Luke have *them*), becoming thus a type of the Christian disciple who serves and modeling the attitude which the chosen twelve in their ambition still do not have (20:20–28).

When Matthew climaxes this section with the quotation from Isaiah 53:4, "He took our infirmities and bore our diseases," he means that Jesus fulfills this OT promise not by becoming sick himself but by identifying himself in compassion with the sick and outcast and carrying the sicknesses *away*. But the burdens he lifts are more than that. They are also the burdens of rejection by society, the burdens of the outcast, the burdens of the oppressed, the burdens of those at the bottom of the heap, suffering the weight of all those on top. On Jesus' shoulders these burdens will be experienced not as sickness but as persecution and ultimately crucifixion, for that is the price he will have to pay for championing the outcast and oppressed and making community with them. For in this Jesus is living out his conviction that all are children of one Father, whose name he has revealed.

Today this gospel challenges us to inquire in our own lives who are the outcast and the oppressed. Surely the victims of AIDS are the lepers of today. But each of us needs to ask who are the people we have written off, consciously or unconsciously as outside the pale of "respectable people." Who are the people we label? Who are the people we consider "gentiles" today? Hindus, Buddhists, Moslems? Blacks, browns, whites? Alcoholics, drug addicts, prostitutes? And who are the Christians whose ministry to us we would find hard to accept? I remember once asking the members of a prayer group to pray over me. One of those who prayed for me was a clinical psychologist, another had a Ph.D. in math. Their prayers were easy to accept because they were "respectable" people. But a few of those praying were people I and others thought of as "kooks." Could I believe God would hear *their* prayers? Perhaps the greatest grace of that moment was to accept them as channels of God's love to me.

Every Christian community needs to ask itself whether it is a *petite chapelle*, a closed group of self-contented people or whether it is faithful to the challenge of Jesus to reach out to those beyond its doors and seek to make community with them.

## The Cost of Discipleship (8:18–27)

18 Now when Jesus saw great crowds around him, he gave orders to go over to the other side. [19]And a scribe came up and said to him, "Teacher, I will follow you wherever you go." [20]And Jesus said to him, "Foxes have holes, and birds of the air have nests; but the Son of man has nowhere to lay his head." [21]Another of the disciples said to him, "Lord, let me first go and bury my father." [22]But Jesus said to him,

"Follow me, and leave the dead to bury their own dead."
23 And when he got into the boat, his disciples followed him. [24]And behold, there arose a great storm on the sea, so that the boat was being swamped by the waves; but he was asleep. [25]And they went and woke him, saying, "Save, Lord; we are perishing." [26]And he said to them, "Why are you afraid, O men of little faith?" Then he rose and rebuked the winds and the sea; and there was a great calm. [27]And the men marveled, saying, "What sort of man is this, that even winds and sea obey him?".

Again Jesus observes the great crowds. And again there is the narrowing of the scene to the disciples. This time, however, the crowds will be left on the shore and only the disciples will follow Jesus. Still, it is not yet clear who belongs to the disciples and who to the crowds—and that is precisely the point of this section. In the opening v. 18, Jesus, seeing the crowds, gives orders to cross to the other side. It is not said to whom he gives orders, and Matthew lets us infer that the crowds themselves hear the orders, with the possibility that they, or some of them, may obey the orders. Jesus stands as a new Moses ready to cross the sea. But who will follow him?

The first is a theologian who lets his heart speak for once. For him, Jesus is not *kyrie*, Lord, but *teacher*. He admires Jesus as a great scribe or theologian, and would love to bask in his shadow. But he is quite unaware that following Jesus is not an invitation to the lecture circuit. It will mean at the very least a constant pilgrimage without a place to call home—and, as we shall soon see, entrance into a storm and ultimately the way of the cross. The first obstacle any would-be disciple must overcome is his attachment to security, whatever that may be in his life. Did this man follow Jesus? Matthew doesn't tell us, because the scribe is you and me, and each of us has to calculate the cost and decide.

The second one to step forward is already a disciple—the best translation here being, "Another, one of his disciples, said . . . ." Using the title *Lord* distinguishes him from the insufficiently enlightened and committed scribe. Martin Hengel holds that this verse sets Jesus totally apart from his Jewish environment and confirms that he thought of himself as ushering in the final kingdom of God, with an urgency that suspends even the most normal of family relationships. However, in the context of Matthew's gospel, Jesus' answer could hardly negate the commandment to honor father and mother, which he elsewhere upholds (19:19). His word to the disciple here, then, must be intended to teach in a dramatic way that commitment to Jesus must be placed above family ties. Many of the Jewish members in Matthew's community were constantly under pressure from their families to leave Jesus and return to the old synagogue practices. Converts often experience the same tension when their families do not understand how they could leave the traditional family religion because of their newfound faith. But any relationship that stands in the way of following Jesus must yield to him as our first love.

In v. 23, Matthew significantly changes a detail in Mark's account. For Mark, the disciples get into the boat and take Jesus with them. For Matthew, Jesus gets into the boat first, and the disciples follow. Matthew sees the catechetical value of this story. Jesus is taking the risk of a sea voyage with its ensuing storm. Only those who are disciples follow him. If any of the crowd who have heard the crossing order have decided to follow, they are no longer part of the faceless mass. They have become disciples. The point: More is demanded of a disciple than merely hearing Jesus' word and witnessing his miracles. A disciple must be willing to share Jesus' life-style, to put Jesus above family ties, to enter into a community with other disciples who share Jesus' lot (the boat is the church) and brave the storm with him.

The storm is one of apocalyptic dimensions. *Seismos megas* (a *great storm*) is the same expression Matthew uses to describe the earthquake at Jesus' resurrection (28:2). The disciples cry out with the cry the church will later make its own, "Save us, Lord!" (compare Mark: "*Teacher*, do you not care?" and Luke: "*Master, Master*, we are perishing!"). Now one would think that such a fervent prayer would win praise from Jesus or at least the instantaneous stilling of the storm, as indeed happens in Mark. But in Matthew there is not only a rebuke of their little faith, but the rebuke *precedes* the stilling of the storm. Matthew's point: the church needs to show its trust of Jesus *in* the storm, before it sees the miracle. Jesus himself sleeps in the storm because of his perfect trust in the Father. So should the church's trust be when it endures the tempest of trials and persecutions. Again the Emmanuel theme: God is with us not only in the moment of deliverance but in the very storm itself.

## Anticipating the Gentile Mission (8:28–34)

28 And when he came to the other side, to the country of the Gadarenes, two demoniacs met him, coming out of the tombs, so fierce that no one could pass that way. ²⁹And behold, they cried out, "What have you to do with us, O Son of God? Have you come here to torment us before the time?" ³⁰Now a herd of many swine was feeding at some distance from them. ³¹And the demons begged him, "If you cast us out, send us away into the herd of swine." ³²And he said to them, "Go." So they came out and went into the swine; and behold, the whole herd rushed down the steep bank into the sea, and perished in the waters. ³³The herdsmen fled, and going into the city they told everything, and what had happened to the demoniacs. ³⁴And behold, all the city came out to meet Jesus; and when they saw him, they begged him to leave their neighborhood.

It is enlightening to compare this story with Mark's account (Mk 5:1–20). Where Mark has one possessed man, Matthew has two. This is not the only place Matthew sees double when he reads Mark. He has two blind men where Mark has one (Mk 10:46–52), and he even uses the story itself twice—in 9:27–31 and 20:29–34. What is Matthew up to? Of course, it is conceivable he is reporting a separate but similar incident. But the details are so alike, and since the bulk of Matthew's narrative material is drawn straight from Mark, it is much more probable that the doubling of characters is intentional. Some scholars have sought an explanation in the tendency of oral tradition to use the generalized plural "they" when relating a story—as we in English use the expression "they say"—or, as is becoming common parlance today, "Everyone does what *they* think best." Perhaps Matthew, who is using these stories catechetically and for whom the church as community is so important, wants to suggest that Jesus does his wonders not just for individuals but for the community, for those who unite their voices to request his favors, as Jesus expressly teaches in 18:19–20: "If two of you join your voices on earth to pray for anything whatever, it shall be granted you by my Father in heaven. Where two or three are gathered in my name, there am I in their midst." Or perhaps for the rabbinic-oriented Matthew, it is important for the validity of any testimony that there be two witnesses (Deut 19:15). None of the scholars has come up with a convincing demonstration of any of these alternatives. All simply admit it is a trait of Matthew's style.

The second thing we note when we compare with Mark is how Matthew has cut Mark's graphic details to the bone, with the result that emphasis falls on the dialogue. And here we find a surprising question by the demons, "Have you come here to torment us before the time?" (v. 29). What is *here* and what is the *time*? *Here* is the region of Gadara, gentile territory. The *time* is the time of the gentile mission which Jesus will give his disciples after the resurrection (28:19). The demons are reminding Jesus that he has been sent only to the lost sheep of the house of Israel (15:24) and that it is too early to be disturbing the demonic grip on the pagans.

Jesus of course ignores this ploy and proceeds to deliver the possessed men of their bondage, forecasting thus the disciples' later mission to the gentiles. He permits the demons to enter the swine, still considered unclean animals by the Jewish disciples, and the loss of the swine so fills the people with fear that they beg Jesus to leave their territory. They too, like the demons, are not ready for the release of Jesus' power in gentile territory, perhaps because the loss of their pigs is more important to them than the recovery of their lost and alienated brother. Like the lost son in Luke's parable, these men who lived in the tombs were as good as dead. They have come back to life, they were lost and have been found (see Lk 15:11–32). But not everyone is prepared to see the miracle that way. For some, pigs are more important than people or family or friends.

## Healing the Paralytic (9:1–8)

**9** AND GETTING into a boat he crossed over and came to his own city. ²And behold, they brought to him a paralytic, lying on his bed; and when Jesus saw their faith he said to the paralytic, "Take heart, my son; your sins are forgiven." ³And behold, some of the scribes said to themselves, "This man is blaspheming." ⁴But Jesus, knowing their thoughts, said, "Why do you think evil in your hearts? ⁵For which is easier, to say, 'Your sins are forgiven,' or to say, 'Rise and walk'? ⁶But that you may know that the Son of man has authority on earth to forgive sins"—he then said to the paralytic —"Rise, take up your bed and go home." ⁷And he rose and went home. ⁸When the crowds saw it, they were afraid, and they glorified God, who had given such authority to men.

There are several teachings, explicit and implicit, in this story.

1) The relationship of sickness to sin. In Jesus' day it was commonly thought that every sickness was due to sin. In John 9:3 Jesus denies this in the case of the man born blind. But neither does Jesus teach that sickness is never related to sin, and in this case it appears that he accepts at least the possibility that the man's paralysis is due to sin. It is obvious to the modern world too that many diseases are emotionally related to say the least (e.g., anger abets cancer), and certain diseases can easily be brought on by dissolute living or by addictions.

2) What wins the intervention of Jesus is the faith of the men who bring their friend for healing. Matthew's abbreviation of Mark obscures this point a bit, but it is nonetheless there. There are situations where the state of one member of the community is such that he finds little strength or faith to take the necessary initiative, like a patient who has to be cajoled to take his medicine. The faith of others then is a saving grace. Here we have an early demonstration that Jesus answers the prayers of two or more who unite to seek

his favor (18:19–20). The Orthodox and Catholic traditions apply this principle in the baptism of infants, taking the parents' faith and pledge as sufficient for the child's sacramental incorporation into the community.

3) Jesus here clearly claims the authority to forgive sins, as the scribes correctly interpret, accusing him of blasphemy, since, as Mark has it, God alone can forgive sins (Mk 2:7). Like his revision and revoking of the Mosaic law, here is another instance of Jesus acting with divine authority.

4) This is the first public collision of Jesus with the scribes. At this point they are only saying this accusation to themselves, but their opposition will become progressively more open.

5) Notice the surprising conclusion, "they glorified God, who had given such authority to *men.*" Why the plural? We have seen only Jesus forgiving sin in the story. But Matthew has another point for his readers of the second and third generations. Jesus' power to forgive sins continues and is available in the church (16:19; 18:18).

## The Call of Matthew and the Mission of Mercy (9:9–13)

9 As Jesus passed on from there, he saw a man called Matthew sitting at the tax office; and he said to him, "Follow me." And he rose and followed him.

10 And as he sat at table in the house, behold, many tax collectors and sinners came and sat down with Jesus and his disciples. ¹¹And when the Pharisees saw this, they said to his disciples, "Why does your teacher eat with tax collectors and sinners?" ¹²But when he heard it, he said, "Those who are well have no need of a physician, but those who are sick. ¹³Go and learn what this means, 'I desire mercy, and not sacrifice.' For I came not to call the righteous, but sinners."

Again intertwined with miracles we have a story about discipleship, one which illustrates both who Jesus is and the kind of community he is establishing. There is first, however, the question of who this Matthew is, since both Mark and Luke

1 — ̶ ̶ ̶ ̶

$$28 \overline{)330} \quad \begin{array}{r} 12 \\ \hline \end{array}$$

28
50

Horizontal
- Narvabuertra
- C
Vertical
Narralina

identify the tax-collector-become-disciple as Levi, son of Alphaeus. It has been a long and popular tradition that Matthew is simply another name for Levi, and that the Matthew called here is the apostle Matthew and the writer of this gospel. There are problems, however, with this conflation of names and persons. While occasionally Jews also had gentile names (John Mark, for example, or "Saul, also known as Paul," Acts 13:9), it was not usual practice to have two *Jewish* names. Since Levi is not mentioned in any of the lists of the apostles, whereas Matthew is, some scholars have suggested that our evangelist wanted to make sure this important disciple is one of the twelve and changed his name to do so. Another possibility, however, is that Jesus changed his name just as he did that of Simon to Kephas (Peter, Jn 1:42), though the meaning of Matthew's name as "Gift of the Lord" is nowhere exploited as Peter's (Rock) is. A more recent suggestion is that the evangelist himself chose from among the apostles' names the one that came closest to *mathetes*, meaning *disciple.* The fact is that no scholar has adequately explained the change, and we remain in the area of conjecture here. As for the relation of the evangelist to the apostle Matthew, see our Introduction.

That Jesus should call a tax-collector must have been a shock not only to the Pharisees but to the first-called disciples as well. The tax-collectors were universally despised by the Jews for their venal interests and their collusion with gentile Rome at the expense of their own people. They were forbidden entrance to the synagogue. We can imagine the conversion which this call demanded not only of Matthew but of the other disciples who had to accept him and create community with him—a challenge repeated every time Christians try to live or work together. This theme will return in 18:5. None of the evangelists gives us any psychological preparation for Matthew's call and response. The compelling attraction of Jesus is sufficient.

Then comes the party. "The house" may be Matthew's or Peter's or Jesus'. "Sinners" were the common and unlearned people who, largely because of their ignorance, frequently transgressed the finer points of the law. By eating with them Jesus incurs ritual defilement, which the Pharisees are quick to point out to the disciples.

In answer Jesus not only quotes the proverb about the sick needing the doctor, but in Matthew's version, using a rabbinic formula of introduction, "Go and learn," he quotes Hos 6:6, "I desire mercy, not sacrifice." This verse, unique to Matthew, is the key not only to the meaning of Matthew's call but to the surrounding passages as well and therefore to the whole mission of Jesus. In Hosea the text means, "I prefer mercy (i.e., deeds of loving kindness) to sacrifice," a theme often repeated in the prophets and the psalms. When the Jews could no longer offer sacrifice in the temple after the Romans destroyed it in A.D. 70, the rabbis quoted this text and others to show that they could still please God through good works which took the place of the temple sacrifices. Here Jesus understands "sacrifice" to mean the caste divisions and legalism which the Pharisees regarded as making them pleasing to God, and "mercy" the kind of reaching out which Jesus does to those alienated or otherwise in need. Each of the following stories echoes so clearly this theme of mercy over the constraints of ritual and legalism that we can be sure Matthew has introduced the OT text here as the keystone to interpreting the whole narrative section. Embracing tax-collectors is more important than ritual purity (9:11–13). Rejoicing at the gift of the Messiah is more important than fasting (9:14–17). Touching a corpse defiled a person for a week, but Jesus will do it to give life (9:25). Being touched by a bleeding woman also defiles Jesus, but he praises her faith and heals her (9:20–22). The blind, marginalized in Jewish society, cry "Mercy!" Jesus touches and heals them (9:27–31). He risks being accused of collusion with Satan to bring deliverance to a demoniac (9:32–34). Even the preceding story of the healing of the paralytic fits the theme, for forgiveness of sins (9:5) *is* the meaning of sacrifice.

Thus the call of Matthew with the tax-collectors' party keynotes the theme of the nine miracle stories in this section, which is to show Jesus in action as the revelation of the healing, reconciling and unifying mercy of God. Matthew chose this story as the point for inserting the Hosea text not merely because the doctor-proverb provided a convenient slot but because the call of Matthew illustrated the text better than any of the other stories. It was one thing for Jesus to show his mercy to outsiders, as he does in the other stories. It was quite another, and supreme exposure of vulnerability, for him to call and welcome a tax-collector as one of his own.

## Fasting (9:14–17)

14 Then the disciples of John came to him, saying, "Why do we and the Pharisees fast, but your disciples do not fast?" ¹⁵And Jesus said to them, "Can the wedding guests mourn as long as the bridegroom is with them? The days will come, when the bridegroom is taken away from them, and then they will fast. ¹⁶And no one puts a piece of unshrunk cloth on an old garment, for the patch tears away from the garment, and a worse tear is made. ¹⁷Neither is new wine put into old wineskins; if it is, the skins burst, and the wine is spilled, and the skins are destroyed; but new wine is put into fresh wineskins, and so both are preserved."

Some of the practices of Jesus clash not only with those of the scribes and the Pharisees but with those of John the Baptist as well. Originally this passage may have been a complaint that the disciples of Jesus do not mourn for John, for Jesus' response focuses on fasting as a sign of mourning. But in its present state, including a reference to the Pharisees fasting, the question is more general. Only one fast was prescribed by the written law, that on the day of Atonement (Lev 16:29). But pious Jews fasted on other occasions, and the Pharisees fasted twice a week (Lk 18:12). Jesus fasted during his time in the desert (4:2). But during his public ministry he did not fast, probably because, isolating him from others, it would have conflicted with his inclusive mission. At any rate, fasting as an expression of mourning would be inappropriate while Jesus the bridegroom is present. His ministry is a wedding celebration, for he has come to claim the people as his bride. The time will come, however, when the groom is taken away (Jesus' first prophecy of his passion—or an addition by the post-resurrection church to explain its resumption of fasting?). And then it will be appropriate to fast. The church after the resurrection fasts as a longing for her groom's return.

One of the problems every reformer has faced comes from those who would see the proposed newness as window-dressing and are willing to go along with it as long as the change is not radical. That is the problem Jesus now addresses in the cloth and wineskins images. The change he proposes is radical! It won't do to try to compromise by mixing old with new. But note: Matthew's version of this saying has an important addition: "and so both are preserved" (v. 17). Matthew is a pastor concerned to move his community into the radical newness of Jesus. Yet he realizes that the Jewish element has many riches which should not be lost in the wholesale pursuit of the new life-style of Jesus (see 13:52). Perhaps had he lived after Vatican II, he would have written the same line!

## Faith and New Life (9:18–26)

18 While he was thus speaking to them, behold, a ruler came in and knelt before him, saying, "My daughter has just died; but come and lay your hand on her, and she will live." [19]And Jesus rose and followed him, with his disciples. [20]And behold, a woman who had suffered from a hemorrhage for twelve years came up behind him and touched the fringe of his garment; [21]for she said to herself, "If I only touch his garment, I shall be made well." [22]Jesus turned, and seeing her he said, "Take heart, daughter; your faith has made you well." And instantly the woman was made well. [23]And when Jesus came to the ruler's house, and saw the flute players, and the crowd making a tumult, [24]he said, "Depart; for the girl is not dead but sleeping." And they laughed at him. [25]But when the crowd had been put outside, he went in and took her by the hand, and the girl arose. [26]And the report of this went through all that district.

Compare this two-in-one story with Mark's version (Mk 5:21–43) and you will be amazed at what Matthew does with it. He cuts Mark's 375 Greek words to 138. He pares out graphic but non-essential details, especially those which might reduce the reverence due Jesus, and focuses on the words of the characters. Whereas in Mark, the ruler's daughter is at the point of death and the father hopes Jesus will keep her alive, here the daughter has just died and the father asks Jesus to return her to life. Matthew's camera eliminates the crowds and zooms in on the disciples who follow Jesus. The woman with the hemorrhage touches Jesus' garment and is healed (literally, *saved*) not at that moment (as in Mark) but at the word of Jesus, "Your faith has made you well." Though Mark completes the healing story with the same word of Jesus, Matthew wishes to avoid any magical interpretation of a pushbutton God. Nonetheless, the woman has risked contaminating Jesus with ritual uncleanness, and Jesus welcomes the faith that does so.

The element of suspense caused by the girl's critical condition and the heightened tension caused by the news of her death is missing from Matthew. Jesus simply says the girl is sleeping. But the crowd is certainly convinced they have read the death signs accurately. The point which Matthew would make for his Christian readers is that it is as easy for Jesus to raise the dead as to awaken a living person from slumber. Whence the frequent Christian use of "sleep" for death. The gentile world used the figure for the everlasting sleep that followed life. Christians used it of the temporary sleep that precedes the resurrection and everlasting life.

Strangely, Matthew omits the word of command, "Little girl, I say to you, arise." He simply takes her hand and she rises. The element of touch is thus emphasized, as it was with the leper (8:1-4) and the woman with the flow of blood. Matthew generally prefers to have Jesus heal by word. The exceptions all have to do with the outcast or ritually unclean, where Jesus' touch shows him breaking the barriers of ritualistic Judaism. Here, when Jesus touches the dead girl's body, he becomes unclean for a week.

In South Asia I remember seeing people afraid to touch a person who had just died in the street. Corpses would often lie untouched till nightfall, when special low-caste people would take them away. Once I saw our Hindu neighbor returning from a funeral. As he entered the yard, his wife came out with a pot of burning incense and circled him with it several times.

Then, not entering the house, he bathed at the outside water
tap, then washed all his clothes there, hanging them on a line.
His wife then brought him clean clothes, which he donned before entering the house. I thought at once of the OT requirements of purification and scenes like this one. The touch which
"contaminates" Jesus gives life to the girl.

Matthew is not bound by Mark's concern to keep the "Messianic Secret," so there is no forbidding to tell the good news.

### Two Blind Men (9:27–31)

27 And as Jesus passed on from there, two blind men
followed him, crying aloud, "Have mercy on us, Son of
David." [28]When he entered the house, the blind men came
to him; and Jesus said to them, "Do you believe that I am
able to do this?" They said to him, "Yes, Lord." [29]Then he
touched their eyes, saying, "According to your faith be it
done to you." [30]And their eyes were opened. And Jesus
sternly charged them, "See that no one knows it." [31]But they
went away and spread his fame through all that district.

This story raises many questions. Put side by side with
the healing of two blind men in 20:29–34, it looks like the same
story in skeletal form. In verse 28 Jesus asks the men, "Do
you believe that I am able to do *this*?", but there is no antecedent to *this*. So it seems to many scholars that Matthew has
reused the same story for a catechetical purpose here, trim-
ming it drastically, with the result that the *this* is left dangling.
Scholars call this a *doublet*, i.e., a use of the same story or
expression twice in the same gospel. Matthew has probably
done so to complete his illustrations of the variety of works of
mercy Jesus has done. There is one important difference in this
story, however. The men follow Jesus before they are healed,
not afterwards as in 20:34. They tag along, crying for Jesus'
mercy, but Jesus tests their perseverance by waiting till he is
inside the house to cure them. They illustrate the asking-seek-
ing-knocking faith Jesus had promised to reward in the Sermon
on the Mount (7:7–8).

There is another curious element: Why did Matthew, who eliminated Mark's command of secrecy in the previous story (Mk 5:43), introduce it here where Mark does not have it at all (v. 30; Mk 10:52)? Did Matthew simply withhold the Markan detail from the Jairus story in order to place it here, where the secrecy might be more possible (no crowds, after all, are apparent here as they were at Jairus' house)?

A final matter of curiosity is the fact that there are two blind men in the story. The story most closely resembling this one in Mark has only one blind man (Mk 10:46–52). But Matthew in 10:29–34, obviously the parallel to Mark, has two, just as he has here. We discussed this Matthean tendency already in the story of the demoniacs (8:28–34). Here there may be another reason for it. Matthew knows Mark has two stories of Jesus healing a blind man—the one at Bethsaida (Mk 8:22–26), the other at Jericho (10:46–52). More concerned to illustrate categories of healings than to relate different details, yet not wanting to lose the essence of Mark's two stories, Matthew may have simply dealt with two beneficiaries in the same story.

At any rate, the point Matthew would have us retain is the variety of healings Jesus did. Here, by answering the cry of the blind for mercy, Jesus shows in still another way his preference of mercy over sacrifice (9:13). For the blind in Jesus' day were not given the special consideration the handicapped enjoy in today's developed countries. Unable to work and considered sinners by many (see John 9:2), they were often condemned to beggary. Unable to leave an inheritance, they were classified by the Talmud (*Ned. 64b*) along with the leper, the childless and the pauper as virtually dead. They could not serve as priests to offer sacrifice in the temple. Physically at least their condition put them on the fringe of society. In answering the cry of the two blind men for mercy Jesus shows in still another way his preference for mercy over sacrifice (9:13).

## The Dumb Demoniac (9:32–34)

32 As they were going away, behold, a dumb demoniac was brought to him. ³³And when the demon had been cast out, the dumb man spoke; and the crowds marveled, saying,

"Never was anything like this seen in Israel." ³⁴But the
Pharisees said, "He casts out demons by the prince of demons."

Here is another doublet, the second member of which appears in 12:22–24. Matthew uses the story here for two reasons. (1) It completes his picture of the mercy of Jesus (9:13).
The man is *kophos*, which can mean deaf as well as mute (see
11:5). Deaf-mutes were considered sub-normal by Jewish law.
(2) It prepares us for the favorable reaction of the crowd but
more particularly for the accusation of the Pharisees. It is not
just a healing but an exorcism, and from this springs the blasphemous accusation that Jesus' power is demonic. The rejection
theme has been brewing ever since the healing of the paralytic
(9:3). It forecasts more rejection to come, climaxing in Jesus'
passion and death.

## The Harvest Is Great (9:35–38)

35 And Jesus went about all the cities and villages,
teaching in their synagogues and preaching the gospel of the
kingdom, and healing every disease and every infirmity.
³⁶When he saw the crowds, he had compassion for them,
because they were harassed and helpless, like sheep without a shepherd. ³⁷Then he said to his disciples, "The harvest
is plentiful, but the laborers are few; ³⁸pray therefore the
Lord of the harvest to send out laborers into his harvest."

This passage is a bridge. It looks backwards to 4:23, sum-
marizing in the same words Jesus' ministry of word and deed.
It tells us that the healings we have just witnessed were mere
samples of the more extended ministry of Jesus. But just as
the presence of the crowds in 4:25 occasioned the Sermon on
the Mount, given to the disciples as the crowds looked on, now
the needs of the crowds occasion the mission of the disciples.
But again the discourse is not aimed at the crowds but at the
disciples who are being sent. Although Jesus' training of his
disciples is unfinished, he judges them ready for a missionary
experience. The disciples need not be perfect before they can

share the good news. And perhaps their attempts to share it will make them more eager to learn upon returning. In any case, Jesus' decision to send his disciples springs from the same mercy and compassion that has prompted his own ministry. In Lk 6:12–16 Jesus himself spends the whole night in prayer before selecting the twelve. Here Jesus tells the disciples themselves to pray to the "Lord of the harvest" (the Father? Jesus?) to send laborers into his harvest. Matthew's version envisages a later, ongoing church situation where the needs of the harvest are a permanent call to pray for harvesters.

The image of the harvest does not evoke to the modern reader the finality and urgency it has in the Bible, where it is practically equivalent to God's judgment (Joel 4:13; Hos 6:11; Rev 14:15). The twelve are reapers for the harvest of the elect, and their gathering in for the kingdom is part of the closing chapter of world history, as Matthew underscores by incorporating here large sections of Mark's eschatological discourse (Mk 13:9–13) and other sayings about decisiveness.

## DISCOURSE: MISSION (10:1–11:1)

*The Twelve and their Mission (10:1–16)*

**10** AND HE called to him his twelve disciples and gave them authority over unclean spirits, to cast them out, and to heal every disease and every infirmity. ²The names of the twelve apostles are these: first, Simon, who is called Peter, and Andrew his brother; James the son of Zebedee, and John his brother; ³Philip and Bartholomew; Thomas and Matthew the tax collector; James the son of Alphaeus, and Thaddaeus; ⁴Simon the Cananaean, and Judas Iscariot, who betrayed him.

5 These twelve Jesus sent out, charging them, "Go nowhere among the Gentiles, and enter no town of the Samaritans, ⁶but go rather to the lost sheep of the house of Israel. ⁷And preach as you go, saying, 'The kingdom of heaven is at hand.' ⁸Heal the sick, raise the dead, cleanse lepers, cast out demons. You received without paying, give without pay. ⁹Take no gold, nor silver, nor copper in your

belts, [10]no bag for your journey, nor two tunics, nor sandals, nor a staff; for the laborer deserves his food. [11]And whatever town or village you enter, find out who is worthy in it, and stay with him until you depart. [12]As you enter the house, salute it. [13]And if the house is worthy, let your peace come upon it; but if it is not worthy, let your peace return to you. [14]And if any one will not receive you or listen to your words, shake off the dust from your feet as you leave that house or town. [15]Truly, I say to you, it shall be more tolerable on the day of judgment for the land of Sodom and Gomorrah than for that town.

16 "Behold, I send you out as sheep in the midst of wolves; so be wise as serpents and innocent as doves.

Until now we have met only five of the disciples by name— Peter, Andrew, James, John and Matthew. We were given the impression, though, of a larger number surrounding Jesus. Now suddenly there are twelve, and Matthew has not obliged us, as Mark did, with a story of their selection (Mk 3:13–19). Here they are, for once, called apostles ("ones sent"), though Matthew will quickly return to his preferred title, *disciples*, because they represent all future disciples of Jesus. At the same time, bearing the titles "twelve" and "apostles" they are representative of the twelve tribes of the new Israel (19:28) and the pillars on which the church leaders of Matthew's day stand, over against false teachers and false prophets.

Matthew reworks slightly the list in Mark. Matthew is identified as "the tax-collector" whose call was recorded earlier. And Peter is not only placed first, as he is in Mark and Luke, but Matthew even puts the word *first* in front of his name, clearly underlining his leading role among the twelve and preparing us for his special commission in 16:17–19.

Verses 1 and 5 are both introductory, having been split by the list of the twelve. The authority Jesus gives them is to do everything he did, with the exception of teaching, a function reserved for their solemn commissioning after the resurrection (28:19). Matthew does not say Jesus sends them out two by two (as Luke does with the seventy-two, Lk 10:1), but this could be inferred from the list in which they are paired. They are to go only to the Jews, for Jesus' own public ministry was limited to them (15:24, the same expression, "the lost sheep of the house of Israel"). From Matthew's perspective, there was a time when Jesus and his disciples devoted themselves only to the Jews. That time has now passed, and the risen Christ has sent his disciples to evangelize all the nations (28:19).

This brief, limited mission to their own countrymen explains perhaps why the packing-list in Matthew is even more spartan than in Mark, not even sandals or a bag or a walking stick. They are to be weaponless, vulnerable, and dependent on the hospitality of the people whom they visit. The laws of hospitality in the East were such that it would be offensive to bring one's own food to eat. When my novices would go on mission to villages in India, they would follow this rule, except in those houses where the people themselves were starving. And eating the food offered, however prepared, was an important element of the evangelization process, because to share food is to share life. In some villages it was appropriate for the guest to leave a little food uneaten. The host would then consider it an honor to eat the remains from the plate of his guest. One priest, not knowing this, and feeling obliged to finish whatever was set before him, finished two full plates of food and gorged himself as far as he could on the third, only to discover the host was waiting for him to leave a little unfinished.

The evangelist is not to move from house to house to accept better lodging or food. I was once caught unwittingly in violating this protocol. Brother Tony and I were guests of a tribal family. We had been welcomed with the washing and anointing of our feet after a hot and dusty day's travel. The next morning there was a wedding in the village church. We accompanied our guests to the wedding Mass, after which the parish priest invited Tony and me to breakfast. We accepted. Meantime, a few houses away, some of the villagers were still in the week-long process of celebrating a wedding that had taken place a few days earlier. We were prevailed upon to pay them a visit—which meant eating again. On our return, the sisters whom we visited at the convent fed us again. As we left them, I told Tony, "I hope I don't see any more food for six hours." It was noon by the time we got back to our host's house. The father of the family met us at the door and said, "You lost your way! Come and have breakfast!"

"But we've had three breakfasts already!" I protested.

"But not here," he insisted. And we had no choice but to eat again, in the knowledge that after an only too brief respite we would be served lunch.

The worthy house is simply the one open to receive the disciples and their message. There is no prior requirement. The disciples' *peace* is never lost when it is given away. If it is not received, it returns undiminished. The only ones diminished are those who refuse the gospel of peace. Violating the sacred canons of hospitality and rejecting divine messengers as did the people of Sodom, they will have to face an even more severe judgment, though that is left in God's hands, not the disciples'. Shaking off the dust, a Jewish practice when leaving gentile territory, can be understood as a refusal to be contaminated, discouraged, or diminished in fervor by the rejection they have experienced. Thus while using all prudent means to achieve their goals and avoid harm to themselves (Paul's revelation of his Roman citizenship and his later appeal to Caesar would be an example, Acts 16:37; 25:11), they are to avoid betraying by their conduct the very gospel they are proclaiming. Sheep that they are, they are not to become wolves among wolves but, armed with the cleverness of serpents, they must retain the innocence of doves.

## Persecution of the Disciples (10:17–25)

[17]Beware of men; for they will deliver you up to councils, and flog you in their synagogues, [18]and you will be dragged before governors and kings for my sake, to bear testimony before them and the Gentiles. [19]When they deliver you up, do not be anxious how you are to speak or what you are to say; for what you are to say will be given to you in that hour; [20]for it is not you who speak, but the Spirit of your Father speaking through you. [21]Brother will deliver up brother to death, and the father his child, and children will rise against parents and have them put to death; [22]and you will be hated by all for my name's sake. But he who endures to the end

will be saved. ²³When they persecute you in one town, flee to the next; for truly, I say to you, you will not have gone through all the towns of Israel, before the Son of man comes.

24 "A disciple is not above his teacher, nor a servant above his master; ²⁵it is enough for the disciple to be like his teacher, and the servant like his master. If they have called the master of the house Be-elzebul, how much more will they malign those of his household.

What the wolves are now appears. They are "men" who will "deliver you up." The choice of the word "deliver up," repeated in v. 19 and 21, means the disciples will experience the same fate as Jesus. We are already beyond the perspective of the limited tour of the twelve during Jesus' public life. The sermon from here on envisages the later mission to the Jews first and then to the gentiles, and it will end without any report of the return of the twelve. Clearly, the sending of the twelve in 10:5 is for Matthew merely the occasion for presenting a full teaching on the mission of the church applicable to his day.

Persecution by Jews and gentiles has its positive aspect: it will be an opportunity for the disciples to witness to the good news about Jesus Christ. For that, they can rely on the Spirit "of your Father" to give them the words to say. They can expect betrayal and persecution even by closest relatives. "But he who endures to the end will be saved." The meaning of "the end" is not clear, and the meaning of "saved" depends on it. If it means the coming of the Son of Man (v. 23), then "saved" means "rescued." But the "end" may equally refer to death, since that is a possibility envisaged by v. 21, and then "saved" would refer to entrance into eternal life. Since by the time of Matthew's gospel, a number of Christian missionaries have died, the latter meaning is more likely the one Matthew sees in the saying.

The same problem emerges with v. 24. The first part is clear—there is no need to stay in a hostile town until one is martyred. But what is this coming of the Son of Man? The early Christians who carried on a mission to the Jews may well have thought of it as a promise that the parousia, the second, glorious coming of Jesus, would occur before they completed their difficult and dangerous work. But that could hardly be the interpretation of Matthew in the year 90, unless, like Paul, he thought a mass conversion of the Jews would precede the Lord's return. In the light of 28:16-20, it is likely that Matthew sees the coming of the Son of Man here to be that "little parousia" after the resurrection when Jesus came to his disciples and directed them to go to the gentiles.

The passage concludes with a warning that the disciples should not expect their lot to be any different from that of their master (compare John 13:16 and 15:20).

### Reasons Not To Fear (10:26-33)

26 "So have no fear of them; for nothing is covered that will not be revealed, or hidden that will not be known. 27What I tell you in the dark, utter in the light; and what you hear whispered, proclaim upon the housetops. 28And do not fear those who kill the body but cannot kill the soul; rather fear him who can destroy both soul and body in hell. 29Are not two sparrows sold for a penny? And not one of them will fall to the ground without your Father's will. 30But even the hairs of your head are all numbered. 31Fear not, therefore; you are of more value than many sparrows. 32So every one who acknowledges me before men, I also will acknowledge before my Father who is in heaven; 33but whoever denies me before men, I also will deny before my Father who is in heaven.

The greatest obstacle to be faced by a missionary or a martyr, or any disciple who tries to share his faith, is fear. In this section, aimed not only at the twelve for their brief mission but for the disciples of all ages, Jesus gives four reasons for his repeated counsel "Do not fear." 1) The revelation they carry will not be suppressed by their witness, even should they suffer in the process. It will only be enhanced. In countries today where Christianity is outlawed, more people learn about the gospel in the courtroom than on the street. 2) The persecutor may kill the body; he cannot kill the soul—unless the disciple surrenders to the evil one. 3) The Father knows what is happening to them and he cares. If they are called to suffer, even to die, they are called like Jesus to accept the Father's will, knowing that they mean infinitely more to him than the sparrows which do not escape his providence, and he will prove his love and care in the end. 4) If they witness faithfully to Jesus before the human court, Jesus will champion their cause at the only court that counts, that of the Father at the final judgment.

Jesus' words do not excuse us from witnessing. He will not allow us to be closet Christians. Few of us, perhaps, have been or will be in situations where our lives are endangered because of our faith or our witness. Alas, we are felled by fears far less traumatic. It doesn't matter how small the fear is. If it paralyzes us, it is bigger than we are. The fear of the suffering is worse than the suffering. My first memory of a spanking by my father convinces me of this. My father, a huge man of 280 pounds, wore a size 55 belt. I had done something wrong, and my father came after me with his belt. I ran and crawled under the kitchen table—to no avail, of course. But to this day, I have no recollection of the actual spanking, though I'm sure it happened. My most vivid memory is of myself shivering with fear under the table, not knowing what to do. And that is the power of fear. Once plunged into the suffering, we are in touch, physically or emotionally, with the object of our fear and thus are beginning to go through it. Fear is the paralysis of the unknown, the yet untouched over which we have no control.

The first time I introduced a talk on fears at my retreats I was overwhelmed by the response. I invited the participants to call out their fears while I would write them on the chalkboard. They came too fast for me to write, but with a helper we listed over a hundred. I learned that everyone has a "favorite" fear. But these biggest blocks to growth and authenticity can become the occasion of meeting him who has won the victory and hearing his voice, "Fear not!"

## Jesus' New Family (10:34–39)

34 "Do not think that I have come to bring peace on earth; I have not come to bring peace, but a sword. [35]For

I have come to set a man against his father, and a daughter against her mother, and a daughter-in-law against her mother-in-law; [36]and a man's foes will be those of his own household. [37]He who loves father or mother more than me is not worthy of me; and he who loves son or daughter more than me is not worthy of me; [38]and he who does not take his cross and follow me is not worthy of me. [39]He who finds his life will lose it, and he who loses his life for my sake will find it.

How can Jesus, who proclaims peacemakers blessed (5:9), who heals and preaches forgiveness and reconciliation, now say that he has come to bring not peace on earth (contrast Lk 2:14, "on earth peace") but a sword? The answer from the context is clear. The new way of life Jesus brings will not be accepted by all. Scribes and Pharisees may not be so bad; but when the disciples are rejected by their own families, they will know the cost of being a follower of Jesus. Jews, Hindus, Buddhists or Moslems who convert to Jesus today often find themselves ostracized. A young Hindu who found Jesus was told by his father never to enter his parents' home again, and he was disinherited. A Jewish girl who was already a Christian in heart hesitated a long time because of the response she feared her family would have to her baptism. Finally one day she was praying before a statue of Mary and found herself saying, "Well, you were just a Jewish girl too. And you must have had to go through all this. I guess I can too." And she did.

It may be difficult for cradle Christians to appreciate what such persons go through. There are two things the Christian community can do to help the passage. First, it can work at truly becoming the new family of Jesus, that is, a loving, interacting community which reaches out, welcomes and supports its new members. A convert is a transplant, and the new environment must help him grow or he will die. Secondly, in foreign cultures in particular, it can work at inculturation, that is, incorporating symbols and gestures familiar to the local people, so that the converts will not also be required to convert to a foreign culture when they become Christians.

Jesus is clear that family loyalties are not to be put above faith in him. For the first time in Matthew Jesus mentions taking up one's cross to follow him, though he has not yet forecast his own passion. In the context this refers to taking all the unpleasant consequences of commitment to Jesus. A tribal native in Bihar one day reached the Archbishop's house in Ranchi. "They burned my crops and my home, they kidnapped me and beat me, and I may have died had I not escaped. But they will never take away my faith."

Jesus concludes with a saying applicable to disciples of all ages: "Try to find your life, and you will lose it; lose it for me, and you will find it." The catechist in Sasaram who was tied to a tree and burned alive may have found the truth of this saying in eternal life. But it applies in less drastic situations whenever the Christian abandons the cult of self, measuring the value of life by "what I get out of it" and discovers the joy of total commitment and surrender to the Lord. This is not masochism nor the self-chosen martyrdom of co-dependency, which is simply addictive behavior. One cannot love one's neighbor as oneself if there is not a proper love of self. But neither can one love the Lord with one's whole self if one cannot accept his spiritual family and help build it. And that requires a forgetfulness of self, a losing one's life after the pattern of Jesus who, like a grain of wheat, laid down his life for his friends and found it again in abundance (John 12:25; 15:13).

## Receiving the Messengers (10:40–11:1)

40 "He who receives you receives me, and he who receives me receives him who sent me. ⁴¹He who receives a prophet because he is a prophet shall receive a prophet's reward, and he who receives a righteous man because he is a righteous man shall receive a righteous man's reward. ⁴²And whoever gives to one of these little ones even a cup of cold water because he is a disciple, truly, I say to you, he shall not lose his reward."

11 AND WHEN Jesus had finished instructing his twelve disciples, he went on from there to teach and preach in their cities.

From the bleak assurance of persecution Jesus now concludes his instructions with the blessing upon those who will receive his messengers. It is not only Jesus whom they receive but also the Father. The receiver will have the same reward as the one sent! This is because the reward is the message itself, and the message bearer, who himself was a receiver, expects no pay other than the joy of sharing the message (10:8), which is, in effect, Jesus and the Father in person. Repeating "just man" after "prophet" may well be Matthew's hint that the true prophet must also be a just man (compare 7:15-20). The welcome may not be equal from everyone. But even those who offer the missionaries ("these little ones") a cup of cold water will be rewarded.

The instruction concludes with no report of the success or failure of the mission, nor even of the disciples' return. Obviously, therefore, for Matthew the important element is the discourse itself, which, as we have seen, goes quite beyond the early mission to Israel and is meant for the church of all times. With 11:1 we are back to narrative, as Matthew repeats the formula he used at the end of the Sermon on the Mount (7:28). ■

*Book Three:*

# The Gathering Storm
## (11:2-13:53)

*STORY:* INVITATION AND RESPONSE (11:2-12:50)

The bright halcyon days of the Galilean ministry are over. Jesus will continue to heal, preach and teach, but the miracles are fewer and the critical question becomes response. Opposition from his enemies mounts, and Jesus devotes more attention to the formation of his disciples.

### What Kind of Messiah? (11:2-6)

2 Now when John heard in prison about the deeds of the Christ, he sent word by his disciples ³and said to him, "Are you he who is to come, or shall we look for another?" ⁴And Jesus answered them, "Go and tell John what you hear and see: ⁵the blind receive their sight and the lame walk, lepers are cleansed and the deaf hear, and the dead are raised up, and the poor have good news preached to them. ⁶And blessed is he who takes no offense at me."

Just before beginning his public ministry Jesus encountered Satan offering three Messianic role-definitions, all of which Jesus rejected. Now he meets another role-definition, that given by John the Baptist. John has been a reformer and a preacher of judgment, and the Messiah he heralded was to be the instrument of that judgment—by fire (3:7-12). Jesus did not correct that role definition at the time, but he did shock John by asking for baptism (3:13-17). Now Jesus has a track record, one shared by his disciples, since he sent them to do the same works he did (chapter 10), works not of judgment but of mercy. Puzzled, perhaps even disappointed, John sends disciples to inquire about the "deeds of Christ," that is, what kind of activity befits the Messiah. How is the OT script to be read? If Jesus and his disciples have not fulfilled John's expectations, "shall we (i.e. John and his disciples) look for someone else" who will? Jesus does not answer theoretically nor even by quoting OT passages like Is 35:5-6, which foretold the preaching of good news to the poor. Instead, he points to what has actually been happening in his ministry, events which Matthew has carefully reported for his readers: the blind see (9:27-31), the lame walk (9:1-8), lepers are cleansed (8:1-4), the deaf hear (9:32-34), the dead are raised (9:18-26), and the poor have the good news preached to them (5:3). For Matthew, the last item is as important as the miracles, perhaps even intentionally climactic, or he would not have given so much space in his gospel to the teaching of Jesus.

Then Jesus adds a challenge to John put in the gentlest, most prayerful form: "Blessed is the one who takes no offense at me for doing these things." Jesus is asking John to rethink his definition of the Messiah. We do not know the effect of the report on John. But the saying does set the stage for those who do and those who don't take offense at Jesus.

## The Role of John the Baptist (11:7-19)

7 As they went away, Jesus began to speak to the crowds concerning John: "What did you go out into the wilderness to behold? A reed shaken by the wind? ⁸Why then did you go out? To see a man clothed in soft raiment? Behold, those who wear soft raiment are in kings' houses. ⁹Why then did you go out? To see a prophet? Yes, I tell you, and more than a prophet. ¹⁰This is he of whom it is written,
'Behold, I send my messenger before thy face,
who shall prepare thy way before thee.'
¹¹Truly, I say to you, among those born of women there has risen no one greater than John the Baptist; yet he who is least in the kingdom of heaven is greater than he. ¹²From the days of John the Baptist until now the kingdom of heaven has suffered violence, and men of violence take it by force. ¹³For all the prophets and the law prophesied until

John; ¹⁴and if you are willing to accept it, he is Elijah who is to come. ¹⁵He who has ears to hear, let him hear.

16 "But to what shall I compare this generation? It is like children sitting in the market places and calling to their playmates,

¹⁷'We piped to you, and you did not dance;
we wailed, and you did not mourn.'

¹⁸For John came neither eating nor drinking, and they say, 'He has a demon'; ¹⁹the Son of man came eating and drinking, and they say, 'Behold, a glutton and a drunkard, a friend of tax collectors and sinners!' Yet wisdom is justified by her deeds."

Though Jesus has challenged John, he now holds him up for admiration to the crowds. Inasmuch as the voice of prophecy had been silent for nearly two centuries, Jesus' hailing of John as a prophet means that a new age has dawned on Israel. John spoke out clearly, condemning Herod's marriage and paying the price by landing in Herod's prison (14:3–4). But he was more than a prophet. He was the messenger of the covenant (Mal 3:1), the immediate forerunner of the Messiah, and therefore he stands at the turning point of the ages. He announces the arrival of the kingdom (3:2). Yet any disciple of Jesus is more fortunate than John, for being in possession of what John only promised.

Scholars are not agreed on the exact meaning of verse 12. It could mean that those who are honestly seeking the kingdom are willing to use violence on themselves to get it, to storm the castle, as it were. It could also mean that from the earliest preaching of the kingdom by John, the opponents of the good news have tried to prevent people from entering it. In v. 12, Matthew reverses the Jewish order of "the law and the prophets" and says that the law itself was prophecy, that is, all of it pointed to a fulfillment which has now happened in Jesus (5:17—and see our discussion on pp. 72–73). The text of Mal 3:23, "Lo, I will send you Elijah the prophet before the day of the Lord comes," was interpreted literally in Jewish tradition as a return to earth of the prophet who was taken heavenward in the fiery chariot (2 Kgs 2:11). Jesus here, as in 17:10–13, declares this prophecy fulfilled in John the Baptist, who resembled Elijah in many ways, including his clothing. Whether Jesus understands John to be actually in the kingdom or just at its threshold depends on whether the "until" of v. 13 includes John or excludes him. Verse 11 would seem to put him at the threshold of the kingdom looking in. But if so, this refers only to his ministry, for he too, like the prophets of old, surely benefitted in a supreme way from the fulfillment of what he had promised and longed for.

Whatever the fine tuning of this question, John's response stands in contrast to "this generation," the majority of whom have rejected both John and Jesus. Those who are set in their ways refuse to change, no matter what kind of invitation is offered them. John was sent by God as an ascetic prophet proclaiming God's imminent judgment. Jesus was sent as the hand of God's mercy, joyfully inviting all to join him in table-fellowship with the outcast. Neither way moves the scribes and the Pharisees.

But whose way is the way of God's wisdom? The one which proves by *deeds* its divine origin. The way of the scribes and Pharisees is fruitless legalism. The way of Jesus is deeds of healing and reaching out to the poor (11:2), showing him to be the wisdom of God. It is another way of saying, "By their fruits you will know them" (7:16,20).

## The Price of Rejection (11:20–24)

20 Then he began to upbraid the cities where most of his mighty works had been done, because they did not repent. [21]"Woe to you, Chorazin! woe to you, Beth-saida! for if the mighty works done in you had been done in Tyre and Sidon, they would have repented long ago in sackcloth and ashes. [22]But I tell you, it shall be more tolerable on the day of judgment for Tyre and Sidon than for you. [23]And you, Caperna-um, will you be exalted to heaven? You shall be brought down to Hades. For if the mighty works done in you had been done in Sodom, it would have remained until this day. [24]But I tell you that it shall be more tolerable on the day of judgment for the land of Sodom than for you."

Examples of the negative response of "this generation" are the Galilean cities of Corozain, Bethsaida and Capernaum, cities where Jesus had exercised his chief ministry. Nazareth is not mentioned in this tradition, but it will come in for its share in 13:53–58. Though Jesus' most successful ministry was in Galilee, it is evident from these passages that the response was not universal even there and that in fact these cities as a whole rejected Jesus. Matthew does not have the account of Jesus' weeping over Jerusalem (Lk 19:41–44) nor does Jesus weep here. Instead, speaking like an OT prophet, and using the "woe" form as he will again in chapter 23, he threatens a judgment more severe than upon those cities considered most wicked in the OT. Tyre, Sidon and Sodom were gentile cities, and Jesus' saying that they would have repented at Jesus' preaching is a forecast of those gentile communities that will turn enthusiastically to the good news the Jewish cities have rejected. For that reason, the judgment will be more severe where grace has abounded.

Today we might ask, what is it in our culture and in ourselves that resists the light of Jesus Christ? What is it that enables the young churches of the third world to evangelize so rapidly while so many churches of the developed world are shells with empty pews? What is it that makes their Christian faith part of their conscious identity, while for so many others it is simply cultural baggage?

## The Grace of Response (11:25–30)

25 At that time Jesus declared, "I thank thee, Father, Lord of heaven and earth, that thou hast hidden these things from the wise and understanding and revealed them to babes; [26]yea, Father, for such was thy gracious will. [27]All things have been delivered to me by my Father; and no one knows the Son except the Father, and no one knows the Father except the Son and any one to whom the Son chooses to reveal him. [28]Come to me, all who labor and are heavy laden, and I will give you rest. [29]Take my yoke upon you, and learn from me; for I am gentle and lowly in heart, and

you will find rest for your souls. ³⁰For my yoke is easy, and my burden is light."

"At that time"—that is, in the very midst of widespread rejection and even questioning by John the Baptist, Jesus turns to the reception being given to his message by the disciples. It would be natural for them, after hearing the judgment upon the cities, to congratulate themselves on the fact that they at least had chosen Jesus and thus would expect him to reward them with an expression of gratitude. But there is a surprising shift in this climactic and doctrinally programmatic passage. Jesus' praise is not for the disciples but for the Father, whom he addresses in prayer, the first example of Jesus' own prayer in Matthew. The only other will be in Gethsemane. To the Jewish title, "Lord of heaven and earth," Jesus prefixes "Father," which in the Aramaic was probably the intimate *Abba* which we discussed above (6:9).

Jewish tradition did not distinguish between God's direct and permissive will, so both the hiding and the revealing is attributed to the Father, though in fact it was their own refusal that hid the good news from the scribes and Pharisees. They were the "wise and understanding" because, knowing the law and the 613 precepts by which it was applied to daily life, they could observe it, unlike the simple and unlearned "people of the land," who in their ignorance no doubt transgressed these fine points and thus incurred the epithet "sinners." To these, whom Jesus here calls "babes" or "little children," the Father has revealed "these things"—that is, the meaning of all that Jesus preaches and teaches, including his own identity. (Lacking an antecedent, "these things" must refer to what follows, particularly Jesus and his relationship to the Father.) The revelation spoken of here is not the external words but the internal acceptance by faith and the understanding which that acceptance gives. For this Jesus chooses the image of children, because in the spiritual realm, one must have the openness and receptivity of a child to enter the kingdom (18:3) and to truly experience the fatherhood of God.

That some should reject and others receive is the mystery of God's grace: "such was your gracious will." "No one can come to me unless the Father who sent me draw him" (Jn 6:44). But here, mysteriously, it is also Jesus who chooses those to whom he wishes to reveal the Father. "All things" (v. 27) are doubtless the same as "these things" (v. 25) and refer to the totality of revelation given to Jesus for the world. "My Father" is Jesus' daring title for God. Though he teaches his disciples to say "Our" Father, he never includes himself with the disciples in saying "our." Limiting the use to "my Father" and "your Father," Jesus suggests there is a qualitative difference between his relationship to the Father and the relationship of the disciples to the Father, though the disciples are brought adoptively into a share in that relationship. This distinction is confirmed by the statement that "no one knows the Son except the Father, and no one knows the Father except the Son." That relationship is mutual and absolutely unique (it is *the* Son and *the* Father). The knowledge here is clearly a personal knowledge of supreme intimacy. But the good news is that Jesus does share his own knowledge of the Father with his disciples.

And this sharing is a gift. If one knows the Father in Jesus, it is only because of a prior elective love on Jesus' part. And here Jesus cuts from under the disciples any ground for boasting about their response to Jesus in contrast to the doomed Galilean cities. Even their choice of Jesus has been God's gift, for it was, at the deepest level of the mystery, Jesus' choice of them.

This section climaxes now with Jesus addressing his invitation to all. In crying out "Come to me . . ." Jesus is departing from the role of prophet, preacher, wonder-worker or rabbi. He is speaking as God's personified Wisdom spoke in the OT (Prov 8:1,4; 9:5; Sir 24:18). Those who "labor and are heavy laden" are especially the people burdened by the yoke of the scribes and the Pharisees whom Jesus condemns because "they tie up heavy burdens and lay them on people's shoulders but will not lift a finger to move them" (23:4), but the text is addressed to anyone burdened by expectations or guilt or hurts or addictions of any kind. Jesus promises rest. In the OT the promised rest was the holy land (Ps 95:11), but in the NT this is spiritualized to mean the blessings of the kingdom, the heavenly sabbath rest (Heb 4:1–11). Jesus here means an interim gift of rest in the present life, available whenever one turns to him.

In the OT the yoke was the way of life prescribed by the law (Sir 6:25; 24:22; 51:26; Bar 4:1). Though it promised joy after difficult beginnings, at the hands of the scribes and the Pharisees it had been turned into an insufferable burden. The yoke of Jesus is different. His teaching changes the old law, rejecting its legalistic interpretations and reducing it to mercy and love. It is true that his high expectations could be called the new law, but in the end the yoke is not laws but the person of Jesus himself. The disciple is not to study laws; he is to study Jesus, imitate him, follow him. And that makes the burden light because not only is he meek and humble of heart (5:5; 21:5); he is companion for the journey (28:20).

### Jesus' Authority Liberates (12:1–8)

12 AT THAT time Jesus went through the grainfields on the sabbath; his disciples were hungry, and they began to pluck heads of grain and to eat. ²But when the Pharisees saw it, they said to him, "Look, your disciples are doing what is not lawful to do on the sabbath." ³He said to them, "Have you not read what David did, when he was hungry, and those who were with him: ⁴how he entered the house of God and ate the bread of the Presence, which it was not lawful for him to eat nor for those who were with him, but only for the priests? ⁵Or have you not read in the law how on the sabbath the priests in the temple profane the sabbath, and are guiltless? ⁶I tell you, something greater than the temple is here. ⁷And if you had known what this means, 'I desire mercy, and not sacrifice,' you would not have condemned the guiltless. ⁸For the Son of man is lord of the sabbath."

Here we begin a new section of the narrative which parallels in several ways chapter 11. (1) The question of Jesus' identity is resumed, to be answered in the oblique way that Jesus is greater than the temple, the sabbath, Jonah and Solomon, and in the direct Scriptural way that he is the Servant who will bring salvation to the gentiles. (2) The theme of rejection by this generation returns in the specific guise of the scribes and Pharisees who protest Jesus' sabbath works and accuse him of collusion with Satan. (3) The section ends, as did the first, with the disciples who have accepted Jesus and become his family.

Jesus has just spoken of the rest which he will give (12:28–30), of which the sabbath was prophetic. Now the Pharisees, in their slavery to the letter of the sabbath, accuse the disciples of violating the sabbath by "harvesting," one of the thirty-nine activities forbidden on this day of "rest." The disciples, of course, are simply meeting a human need, pulling off enough grains to satisfy their hunger. Jesus answers by a progression of arguments. (1) David and his men ate the sacred loaves when hungry (1 Sam 21:1–6; Lev 24:9). (2) If the priests are allowed to perform their duties in the temple on the sabbath and are "guiltless" (*anaitioi*, Num 28:9–11), how much more the disciples who are in the company of one who is greater than the temple! This latter phrase, reported only by Matthew, was a startling claim. There was nothing in Israel greater than the temple, yet Jesus claims to be that greater reality—and he is *here*. This claim prepares for the claim in the concluding line, that he is Lord of the sabbath as well. (3) Finally, Jesus again quotes Hosea about the superiority of mercy to sacrifice, "sacrifice" here being the inflexible observance of sabbath ritual and "mercy" standing for human need. The disciples then are as guiltless as the priests in the temple (same word, *anaitioi*). As for Jesus, he is Lord of the sabbath, which means, in Matthew, that, just as he had authority to interpret and revise the Mosaic law (5–7), he has authority to interpret and legislate concerning the sabbath.

Thus the authority of Jesus, as he said in the previous passage, means liberation. For Matthew's community, subject to the pressures of the Pharisaic leadership in the wider Jewish community after the fall of the temple, passages such as these served to reconfirm the Jewish Christians in the authority and the liberation of Jesus. For us, too, they are an invitation to accept that same authority and that same liberation.

## The Sabbath: Life and Death (12:9–14)

9 And he went on from there, and entered their synagogue. [10]And behold, there was a man with a withered hand.
And they asked him, "Is it lawful to heal on the sabbath?"
so that they might accuse him. [11]He said to them, "What
man of you, if he has one sheep and it falls into a pit on the
sabbath, will not lay hold of it and lift it out? [12]Of how much
more value is a man than a sheep! So it is lawful to do good
on the sabbath." [13]Then he said to the man, "Stretch out
your hand." And the man stretched it out, and it was restored, whole like the other. [14]But the Pharisees went out
and took counsel against him, how to destroy him.

A second conflict over the sabbath. From Matthew's point
of view the Jewish synagogue is *theirs*, i.e., no longer the
Christian place of worship (see also 4:23; 9:35). Whereas in
Mark, Jesus' opponents watch to see if Jesus will cure and Jesus poses the question, here it is the Pharisees themselves who
throw the challenge at Jesus, with the only purpose to accuse
him. According to the rabbis, physicians were allowed to heal
on the sabbath only in danger of death. Such was surely not
the case of the man with the withered hand. But Jesus counters
with an *ad hominem* argument: if you had only one sheep and
it fell into a pit on the sabbath, would you not get it out? A
man is of more value than the sabbath restriction. And Jesus
twists his barb ironically, "It is *lawful* to do good on the sabbath!"

In Matthew as in Mark, it is this incident that leads the
Pharisees to plot the death of Jesus. Additional irony: They
who accuse Jesus of breaking the sabbath by healing a man,
decide to kill a man—on the sabbath! The restoring of life will
lead to the death of the life-giver. The same irony appears in
John 11, where the raising of Lazarus determines the authorities to kill Jesus. Here Matthew leaves out Mark's mention of
the Herodians, since they were not a group to be reckoned with
at the time of the writing of the gospel. But the Pharisees
were!

## Mission to the Gentiles (12:15–21)

15 Jesus, aware of this, withdrew from there. And many followed him, and he healed them all, [16]and ordered them not to make him known. [17]This was to fulfil what was spoken by the prophet Isaiah:
>     [18]"Behold, my servant whom I have chosen,
>     my beloved with whom my soul is well pleased.
> I will put my Spirit upon him,
>     and he shall proclaim justice to the Gentiles.
> [19]He will not wrangle or cry aloud,
>     nor will any one hear his voice in the streets;
> [20]he will not break a bruised reed
>     or quench a smoldering wick,
>     till he brings justice to victory;
> [21]and in his name will the Gentiles hope."

Hostility of the enemy leads Jesus, as elsewhere, to withdraw (a favorite Matthean word and theme, 12:22; 4:12; 14:13; 15:21), but crowds follow him. Here Matthew drastically abbreviates Mark 3:7–12 in order to focus on two points: (1) Jesus heals *all*. He is not cowed by the Pharisees' plots. He continues and even multiplies his miracles. (2) He orders the healed not to make him known. This point, impossible to fulfill, is the hook Matthew finds convenient for introducing his typical mid-point commentary, a Scripture quotation that illumines the surrounding passages. The command of silence connects with that part of the Isaian passage that speaks of not wrangling or crying aloud or letting his voice be heard in the streets. But the full text introduces much more than that. It is the text underlying the voice of God at Jesus' baptism (3:17), where Jesus is "Son" instead of Servant. The bruised reed and smoldering wick suggest sick and marginalized people Jesus continues to defend and heal, despite opposition, until God's saving plan is achieved (v. 20). But the major item which the text imports here, in a way that is awkward to the context, is the gentiles, mentioned twice. The last line shows special evidence of editing. The original Hebrew text reads, "the coastlands will wait (= hope) for his teaching." Now "coastlands," the lands of the Mediterranean, in the OT often referred to the pagan lands of the west, and so Matthew's substitution of "gentiles" is a legitimate equivalent. But Matthew also has "in his name" instead of "for his teaching."

Both these changes are significant. Matthew is affirming that the rejection of Jesus by the Jewish villages and the Pharisees will lead to the mission to the gentiles. He is perfectly aware that neither Jesus nor his disciples went to the gentiles during the time of his public ministry. He is also aware of how awkward this mention of the gentiles is at this point in the gospel. But that awkwardness is clearly intentional. The prophecy that the Servant will bring salvation ("justice") to the gentiles will be fulfilled after the resurrection through the ministry of those disciples who are with Jesus now.

The other change is the expression "in his name." It is not merely his teaching but the person of Jesus who is the ground of the gentiles' hope.

## Jesus and Beelzebul; the Tree and Its Fruits (12:22–37)

22 Then a blind and dumb demoniac was brought to him, and he healed him, so that the dumb man spoke and saw. ²³And all the people were amazed, and said, "Can this be the Son of David?" ²⁴But when the Pharisees heard it they said, "It is only by Be-elzebul, the prince of demons, that this man casts out demons." ²⁵Knowing their thoughts, he said to them, "Every kingdom divided against itself is laid waste, and no city or house divided against itself will stand; ²⁶and if Satan casts out Satan, he is divided against himself; how then will his kingdom stand? ²⁷And if I cast out demons by Be-elzebul, by whom do your sons cast them out? Therefore they shall be your judges. ²⁸But if it is by the Spirit of God that I cast out demons, then the kingdom of God has come upon you. ²⁹Or how can one enter a strong man's house and plunder his goods, unless he first binds the strong man? Then indeed he may plunder his house. ³⁰He who is not with me is against me, and he who does not gather with me scatters. ³¹Therefore I tell you, every sin

and blasphemy will be forgiven men, but the blasphemy against the Spirit will not be forgiven. [32]And whoever says a word against the Son of man will be forgiven; but whoever speaks against the Holy Spirit will not be forgiven, either in this age or in the age to come.

33. "Either make the tree good, and its fruit good; or make the tree bad, and its fruit bad; for the tree is known by its fruit. [34]You brood of vipers! how can you speak good, when you are evil? For out of the abundance of the heart the mouth speaks. [35]The good man out of his good treasure brings forth good, and the evil man out of his evil treasure brings forth evil. [36]I tell you, on the day of judgment men will render account for every careless word they utter; [37]for by your words you will be justified, and by your words you will be condemned."

To read this section fruitfully, it will be helpful to be aware that Matthew is passing on the traditions that come to him largely from the Q source, and that his use of those traditions serves a number of purposes here: (1) In terms of Matthew's plot, the conflict with the Pharisees intensifies in the public forum, as they accuse him of being the instrument of Satan. This also prepares for another contrast with the disciples who are Jesus' new family. (2) Matthew's community of the eighties is being warned that the Pharisaic leadership may be expected to continue its accusations against Jesus and his disciples. But the Pharisees' abuse of speech is also a counter-example from which the disciples must learn. Words can be used to spell one's own salvation or damnation. (3) The text continues to speak today of the effect of our words on others and upon ourselves.

Matthew has actually used a form of this story earlier, with the same reaction by the Pharisees (9:32–34), but he has waited until this point to record Jesus' full response to the accusation. This time the man is not only dumb but blind, and this is perhaps Matthew's way of ironically contrasting the light and speech which Jesus empowers with the spiritual blindness of the Pharisees who abuse their power of speech. Fearing the people's possible hailing of Jesus as Messiah—they are "astounded" and think of the title "Son of David"—the Pharisees accuse Jesus of using the power of Beelzebul ("lord of the house," an epithet for Satan) to cast out demons. Whether Jesus overheard the accusation is irrelevant to Matthew. Jesus knows their *thoughts*, the poisoned source of their words. Meek and gentle Messiah that he is, he nevertheless takes on these hypocrites and fires three arguments back at them. (1) Logic: if Satan is doing this, he is destroying his own empire. (2) *Ad hominem*: Does Jesus' method of casting out the demons by a simple word look more magical or demonic than the long and complicated rituals used by the Pharisees' exorcists? (3) That Jesus has, in fact, been casting out demons by the Spirit of God, a sign that the kingdom has already broken into human life, is shown by the binding of the strong man (Satan), which is the first step in despoiling his kingdom.

"He who is not with me is against me" is so obvious in the case of the Pharisees that we may suspect Matthew has some other purpose in passing on this tradition. His *Christian* audience should hear that one cannot fence-straddle with Jesus. There is no possibility of combining the Pharisaic teaching and example with those of Jesus. The response to Jesus must be total.

Jesus next takes the offensive, saying that the sin against the Spirit is the unforgivable sin. At the time of Matthew's writing, the forgivable sin against the Son of Man probably was understood to be the disbelief of many during Jesus' public life, when his divine power was veiled in humility and suffering, whereas the unforgivable sin against the Spirit was taken to refer to the time of the post-resurrection Church, when the Spirit had been given. To resist that Spirit is to sin against the light, and this sin is unforgivable, because as long as one sins against the light he never asks forgiveness. Jesus intuited that it was the same sin against the light to call the Spirit of his exorcisms the evil spirit.

Jesus and his works are to be judged like a tree. If the fruits are good, the tree must be good. But the Pharisees, seeing good fruits in Jesus' exorcisms, have declared their source bad. This saying may also look forward to what follows.

For the blasphemous words of the Pharisees are also like fruits, rotten fruits that reveal a rotten tree. The section ends with a saying proper to Matthew, which applies to everyone. On judgment day people will have to render an account not merely for every evil word they speak, but even every careless word— that is, every word that is thoughtless, insensitive, inaccurate, hurtful—all those shades of gray short of "evil."

Severity of judgment on the misuse of words goes back to the wisdom literature of the OT. "Death and life are in the power of the tongue" (Prov 18:21). "The fruit of a tree shows the care it has had; so too does a man's speech disclose the bent of his mind" (Sir 27:6). The tongue slays more victims than the sword (Prov 12:18; Sir 28:18). In the NT James gives a long instruction on the power of the tongue, not only in its external effects but, following the teaching of Jesus, in what it reveals of the heart of the speaker (James 3:2-12). For that reason, used well, words are a joy and a treasure (Prov 15:23; 25:11), with power to build up and minister grace to the listener (Eph 4:29). Matthew's community has no doubt suffered from misuse of the tongue by its own members, for no gospel hammers so persistently on the importance of fraternal relations, forgiveness and reconciliation. And any pastor can testify how much the unity of his community depends on the tongues of its members.

## The Sign of the Son of Man (12:38-42)

38 Then some of the scribes and Pharisees said to him, "Teacher, we wish to see a sign from you." [39]But he answered them, "An evil and adulterous generation seeks for a sign; but no sign shall be given to it except the sign of the prophet Jonah. [40]For as Jonah was three days and three nights in the belly of the whale, so will the Son of man be three days and three nights in the heart of the earth. [41]The men of Nineveh will arise at the judgment with this generation and condemn it; for they repented at the preaching of Jonah, and behold, something greater than Jonah is here. [42]The queen of the South will arise at the judgment with this

generation and condemn it; for she came from the ends of the earth to hear the wisdom of Solomon, and behold, something greater than Solomon is here.

The scribes now join the Pharisees and, addressing Jesus as "teacher" (a title used in Matthew by non-believers or half-believers), they ask for a sign. The miracles and exorcisms have not been enough. They would like a sign so compelling that they would no longer need faith, which means *they* would not have to surrender *their* lights to the revealing, converting light of God. Jesus refuses to give that kind of sign and offers them instead the sign of Jonah. In the Q tradition witnessed also by Luke 11:29–32, the sign is the faith and repentance of the gentiles of Nineveh at Jonah's preaching (to which a reference to the queen of Sheba is attached), contrasted with the disbelief of Jesus' own people. But Matthew inserts another allegorizing application—like Jonah, Jesus will be enclosed in the tomb for a short while prior to his resurrection. Thus for Matthew the sign is both the resurrection of Jesus and the conversion of the gentiles. The disbelief of his opponents is all the more grave, for Jesus is greater than Jonah and Solomon, just as he is greater than Moses (the Sermon on the Mount) and the temple itself (12:6).

## The Return of the Evil Spirit (12:43–45)

43 "When the unclean spirit has gone out of a man, he passes through waterless places seeking rest, but he finds none. 44Then he says, 'I will return to my house from which I came.' And when he comes he finds it empty, swept, and put in order. 45Then he goes and brings with him seven other spirits more evil than himself, and they enter and dwell there; and the last state of that man becomes worse than the first. So shall it be also with this evil generation."

This pericope, taken from Q with no significant change, could be a general wisdom teaching, but it is tied by Matthew to the preceding units by its reference to exorcism (v. 22) and the addition of the last sentence about "this evil generation"

(11:16; 12:39). Jesus' exorcisms show that he is driving Satan out of Israel. But if there is nothing to replace the evil spirit and guard the liberated house (i.e., faith and the Holy Spirit), the return of Satan will make the last state worse than the first. Matthew probably understands this to have been fulfilled in those whose disbelief persisted after the resurrection.

## Jesus' New Family (12:46–50)

46 While he was still speaking to the people, behold, his mother and his brothers stood outside, asking to speak to him. ⁴⁸But he replied to the men who told him, "Who is my mother, and who are my brothers?" ⁴⁹And stretching out his hand toward his disciples, he said, "Here are my mother and my brothers! ⁵⁰For whoever does the will of my Father in heaven is my brother, and sister, and mother."

This tiny section is the climax of the entire narrative begun at 11:1, the theme of which has been response to the deeds and the claims of Jesus. After the doubts expressed by the disciples of John the Baptist (11:2–6), the indifference of "this generation" (11:16–19) and the unrepentant towns (11:20–24), Jesus had hailed his acceptance by the disciples as a special gift of God (11:25–27) available to those who would come to him (11:28–30). This pattern was repeated in chapter 12, as Jesus' conflict with the Pharisees worsened, climaxing in the dispute about the spirit behind Jesus' miracles and the spirit behind the accusations of his enemies. Now this second sub-section ends on a similar positive note spotlighting again the disciples.

In the parallel passage of Mk 3:34, Jesus looks around at those about him, but Matthew dramatizes the action even more: Jesus "stretches out his hand toward his disciples." Jesus rejects natural family ties as having any value for the kingdom. Some disciples during Jesus' ministry must have felt the tension between family loyalties and the itinerant discipleship, but in the church for which Matthew is writing the tension was grave, since the split of the Christian community from the synagogue was complete and many families were torn in their al-

legiance. Jesus is categoric. Those who make the decision to
follow Jesus and his way of life ("the will of my Father in
heaven") become his mother and brothers.

The natural family of Jesus is not classified with "this evil
generation." Matthew eliminates Mk 3:21, where Jesus' family
go out to seize him because "they [or: "people"] said, 'He is
beside himself.' " This omission fits not only Matthew's concern
to avoid any statement of disrespect about Jesus but also probably his concern to avoid implying that she who conceived Jesus
by the Holy Spirit would have so drastically misunderstood
him. According to Luke's tradition, many of them were among
the believers in Jerusalem awaiting the coming of the Spirit
(Acts 1:14; see also "James, the brother of the Lord," Gal 1:19).
Here the natural family simply stands for all those who would
make the claims of the flesh alone a basis for closeness to Jesus.
Such persons will forever stand "outside." The new family of
Jesus enjoys intimacy with him, and because it is based on
those "who do the will of my Father," it can also embrace the
outcast, publicans, sinners, gentiles as well as Jews.

## DISCOURSE: THE SWITCH TO PARABLES (13:1–53)

If we were to accept the symmetrical organization of Matthew's gospel, this would be the central chapter, the keystone
of the entire gospel. However attractive such an alternative,
and however remarkable symmetry may be in certain portions
of the gospel, we do not think that the parables of the kingdom
are more important teaching than, say, the Sermon on the
Mount. What is new and significant here is not so much the
content of Jesus' teaching as his method.

In the Sermon on the Mount there is a distinction between
the circle of the disciples and the circle of the crowds, but the
instruction is given to the disciples in the *sight* of the crowds
and in language understandable by all. There is thus an implied
continuity between the disciples and the crowds, a continuity
prolonged in chapter 10 when Jesus sends the disciples to the
lost sheep of the house of Israel. But now the distinction between the crowds and the disciples becomes sharper. Jesus has

been rejected not only by the scribes and Pharisees but by the villages of Corozain, Bethsaida, and even Capernaum (11:20–24). The non-committal passivity of the crowds, which was tolerable in the early days of Jesus' ministry, has now become dead weight equivalent to opposition: "Whoever is not with me is against me" (12:30). Not to decide for Jesus is to decide against him. While the crowds are present Jesus speaks in mysterious language, reserving the explanation of his teaching for the private instruction of the disciples.

We are speaking here, of course, of Matthew's *use* of the parables of Jesus at this point in the composition of his gospel. Mark places Jesus' parabolic teaching early in his ministry, and this may well be closer to the original historical situation. But Matthew introduces the parables here as a change in Jesus' teaching method and as a further step in the mounting plot that will end on Calvary.

## The Sower Parable, Its Explanation, and the Reason for Parables (13:1–23)

13 THAT SAME day Jesus went out of the house and sat beside the sea. ²And great crowds gathered about him, so that he got into a boat and sat there; and the whole crowd stood on the beach. ³And he told them many things in parables, saying: "A sower went out to sow. ⁴And as he sowed, some seeds fell along the path, and the birds came and devoured them. ⁵Other seeds fell on rocky ground, where they had not much soil, and immediately they sprang up, since they had no depth of soil, ⁶but when the sun rose they were scorched; and since they had no root they withered away. ⁷Other seeds fell upon thorns, and the thorns grew up and choked them. ⁸Other seeds fell on good soil and brought forth grain, some a hundredfold, some sixty, some thirty. ⁹He who has ears, let him hear."

10 Then the disciples came and said to him, "Why do you speak to them in parables?" ¹¹And he answered them, "To you it has been given to know the secrets of the kingdom of heaven, but to them it has not been given. ¹²For to him who has will more be given, and he will have abundance; but

from him who has not, even what he has will be taken away.
[13]This is why I speak to them in parables, because seeing
they do not see, and hearing they do not hear, nor do they
understand. [14]With them indeed is fulfilled the prophecy of
Isaiah which says:
'You shall indeed hear but never understand,
and you shall indeed see but never perceive.
[15]For this people's heart has grown dull,
and their ears are heavy of hearing,
and their eyes they have closed,
lest they should perceive with their eyes,
and hear with their ears,
and understand with their heart,
and turn for me to heal them.'
[16]But blessed are your eyes, for they see, and your ears, for
they hear. [17]Truly, I say to you, many prophets and righteous men longed to see what you see, and did not see it,
and to hear what you hear, and did not hear it.

18 "Hear then the parable of the sower. [19]When any one
hears the word of the kingdom and does not understand it,
the evil one comes and snatches away what is sown in his
heart; this is what was sown along the path. [20]As for what
was sown on rocky ground, this is he who hears the word
and immediately receives it with joy; [21]yet he has no root in
himself, but endures for a while, and when tribulation or
persecution arises on account of the word, immediately he
falls away. [22]As for what was sown among thorns, this is he
who hears the word, but the cares of the world and the
delight in riches choke the word, and it proves unfruitful.
[23]As for what was sown on good soil, this is he who hears
the word and understands it; he indeed bears fruit, and
yields, in one case a hundredfold, in another sixty, and in
another thirty."

Jesus has been "in the house," i.e., in the company of his
disciples. Now he leaves the house and addresses the crowds
directly by using the *mashal*, a word that can mean story or
proverb or allegory, or almost any indirect teaching device.
The reason for this change is given in 13:13. Matthew edits

Mark slightly by using "because" instead of "in order that" to make it clear that the cause of the change is in the listeners, not in the speaker. Jesus continues to teach, but now he uses enigmatic language, which will be more difficult to understand and meaningless to those whose hearts are blinded. In Matthew Jesus himself quotes Is 6:9–10 as fulfilled in the lack of response to his message. Matthew inserts v. 12 from another place in Mark to reinforce the idea of grace needed to understand and accept the word. Just as in the secular world the rich get richer and the poor poorer, so in the realm of the spirit those who say an early "yes" to God find it easy and natural to say "yes" to subsequent invitations of his grace. And those who refuse an initial grace will find it all the more difficult to accept the subsequent invitations.

The disciples who have accepted Jesus stand in contrast not only to those who do not really see nor hear nor understand, but even to the prophets and saints of the OT who longed to see and hear the one who now stands in the midst of the disciples (vv. 16–18).

Now let us look at the parable itself and its possible meanings. Nowhere better than in the parables do we learn the difference between Jesus' original use of the story, the church's later use of it, and finally the evangelist's use of it. In the original life situation of Jesus, the parable of the sower was Jesus' figurative way of expressing his confidence in the harvest that would eventually spring from his ministry. Though some of his efforts are apparently wasted, just as some of the sower's seed is lost, there will be a harvest in Messianic abundance (thirty to a hundredfold is an intentional exaggeration). The meaning, then, is confidence in the power of the word, and a reminder that the minister of the good news need not be concerned about immediate, tangible results. God's word will bear abundant fruit in due time.

The explanation of the parable given in 18–23 shifts the interpretation from the sower and the seed to the various kinds of response to the word, reflecting the sorting-out process the struggling community experienced in the years after Jesus' resurrection. It also sets a pattern for understanding the church history of subsequent generations. There are four categories:

(1) The first are those who do not accept the word in the first place. Matthew uses the word "understand" here because it echoes the Isaian text. But the kind of comprehension at issue here is more than an intellectual grasp. It involves a conversion, a surrender of one's whole being to the God who speaks, a standing-under the word rather than over it. One does not *grasp* the word of God. One is grasped by it.

The path is the temporary short-cut across the field that will be plowed under after the sower scatters the seed by hand. It is of easiest access to birds because it is hard, flattened ground. Sometimes the birds even snatch the grain in flight before it touches the ground. A fine symbol of those whom the word never penetrates. No further theorizing is made here of the degree of responsibility for this refusal, though surely there must be some subjective disposition which renders the person so vulnerable to being robbed of the life-giving word.

(2) In the early church there were those enthusiasts who rejoiced in the message but under stress or persecution apostatized from their new-found faith. These must have been a burden for those disciples who remained faithful at all costs. In countries of at least nominal Christian culture today one may wonder how many Christians would consider their faith worth clinging to in the event of persecution. (3) Matthew's second-generation church, like Luke's, experienced enemies more subtle than persecution: worry and riches (Luke adds "pleasures"). The NABR translates the first "worldly anxiety." In the Sermon on the Mount Jesus had warned of this enemy of trust in the Father (6:25–34), and here we see it actually threatening the Christian life of the early church. It is basically a search for ultimate security in the world first, and only then, if there is time, in the kingdom—a reversal of priorities which ends by "choking the word." Similarly the *delight* in riches threatens the life of the community because it rapidly erodes trust in the Father and the sharing within and outside the community that builds brotherhood.

(4) Finally, there are those who hear and *understand*. Matthew again inserts the word *understand*, missing from Mark and Luke, because it prepares the faithful of Matthew's day to accept the teaching authority of those early disciples (and their

successors) who have the authentic interpretation of Jesus' teaching because they *understand* all that Jesus taught (see 13:51). Only they, and those who have the same understanding, bear fruit in Messianic abundance.

## Weeds among the Wheat (13:24-30; 36-43)

24 Another parable he put before them, saying, "The kingdom of heaven may be compared to a man who sowed good seed in his field; <sup>25</sup>but while men were sleeping, his enemy came and sowed weeds among the wheat, and went away. <sup>26</sup>So when the plants came up and bore grain, then the weeds appeared also. <sup>27</sup>And the servants of the householder came and said to him, 'Sir, did you not sow good seed in your field? How then has it weeds?' <sup>28</sup>He said to them, 'An enemy has done this.' The servants said to him, 'Then do you want us to go and gather them?' <sup>29</sup>But he said, 'No; lest in gathering the weeds you root up the wheat along with them. <sup>30</sup>Let both grow together until the harvest; and at harvest time I will tell the reapers, Gather the weeds first and bind them in bundles to be burned, but gather the wheat into my barn.'"

36 Then he left the crowds and went into the house. And his disciples came to him, saying, "Explain to us the parable of the weeds of the field." <sup>37</sup>He answered, "He who sows the good seed is the Son of man; <sup>38</sup>the field is the world, and the good seed means the sons of the kingdom; the weeds are the sons of the evil one, <sup>39</sup>and the enemy who sowed them is the devil; the harvest is the close of the age, and the reapers are angels. <sup>40</sup>Just as the weeds are gathered and burned with fire, so will it be at the close of the age. <sup>41</sup>The Son of man will send his angels, and they will gather out of his kingdom all causes of sin and all evildoers, <sup>42</sup>and throw them into the furnace of fire; there men will weep and gnash their teeth. <sup>43</sup>Then the righteous will shine like the sun in the kingdom of their Father. He who has ears, let him hear.

Only Matthew has this parable. Jesus in his public ministry attacked the exclusiveness he found in Jewish society, promoted especially by the Pharisees but practiced by other groups as well. He formed his community of tax collectors and sinners as well as respectable people. This practice applies in turn to the post-resurrectional church, which is now a mixture not only of social classes but of saints and sinners, of those who are trying to live up to Jesus' high expectations and those who care little about them. The tendency of the latter is to drift along, while the former grow impatient and want a quick house-cleaning. The parable is a two-edged sword. To the lax it promises inexorable judgment. To those who cry "Shape up or ship out," it counsels patience, for time itself is grace, and what may be judged a weed at the moment may in the end be wheat, and vice-versa. Had Augustine and Charles de Foucauld been judged on the conduct of their youth, they would never have become saints. That is not to say the community has no right to certain standards of membership—as will be clarified in chapter 18. But there is an impatient zeal for perfection which is not faithful to the mercy and patience of the Father (see Luke 15:11–32).

The explanation of the parable given later in the discourse (13:36–43) allegorizes its elements and extends the teaching. The field is not the church but the *world*. The division between the saved and the lost is not between the church and those outside it, for conceivably some who are not in the church will be saved and some presently within the church will be lost. It is not those who cry, "Lord, Lord!" (externally Christians) who will be saved, but only those who do the will of the Father in heaven (7:21–23).

## Small Beginnings, Great Results (13:31–33)

31 Another parable he put before them, saying, "The kingdom of heaven is like a grain of mustard seed which a man took and sowed in his field; ³²it is the smallest of all seeds, but when it has grown it is the greatest of shrubs and becomes a tree, so that the birds of the air come and make nests in its branches."

33 He told them another parable. "The kingdom of

heaven is like leaven which a woman took and hid in three measures of flour, till it was all leavened."

The parables of the mustard seed and the leaven are parables of confidence. At the very moment Jesus is preparing to withdraw from the crowds he throws at them images that promise the ultimate success of his mission. The mustard seed is tiny, yet it produces a large bush; Matthew, using the Q source, even calls it a tree big enough to provide nests for birds. This is doubtless an allusion to the tree symbolic of the kingdom in Dan 4:10–12: "I saw . . . a tree in the midst of the earth; and its height was great . . . It was visible to the end of the whole earth. Its leaves were fair and its fruit abundant, and in it was food for all. The beasts of the field found shade under it, and *the birds of the air dwelt in its branches*, and all flesh was fed from it." A similar image appears in Ezek 31:6: "All the birds of the air made their nests in its boughs." Both passages refer to an earthly kingdom that covers the entire earth. Matthew no doubt found this Bunyanesque contrast congenial to his theme that the church would one day house all the nations (20:19).

The same contrast appears in the image of the leaven, though with a slightly different nuance. Leaven is active within the flour, yet it does not attract attention to itself. Rather it enables flour to become fully what it is meant to be, palatable food. Thus the gospel and the church that preaches it promote all that is good and noble in the world, bringing it to perfection, a role also taught by the image of salt (5:13). For the Jews leaven was also a symbol of corruption and ritual impurity. For this reason during Passover all leaven was to be cast out of the house. Jesus' community is made of sinners and outcasts (9:13), yet it is precisely this community that will bring about the kingdom in this world.

## Another Reason for Parables (13:34–35)

34 All this Jesus said to the crowds in parables; indeed he said nothing to them without a parable. 35This was to fulfil what was spoken by the prophet:

"I will open my mouth in parables,
I will utter what has been hidden since the
foundation of the world."

  Up to this point the reason for parables was apparently
polemical, Jesus' withdrawal into allusive language because of
the bad dispositions of his listeners. Here, however, we have
a more positive reason given: Jesus is divine wisdom, a role
we have already seen him fulfill in the sayings of 11:25–27. And
to buttress this role Matthew again resorts to his favorite technique of a Scriptural citation, this time from Psalm 78:2, which
Matthew attributes to "the prophet" since he considers everything in the OT prophetic. Jesus' use of parables shows he is
a wisdom teacher revealing profound mysteries in figurative
language. These mysteries are not merely "from of old," as the
Psalm text originally says, but "from the foundation of the
world." Jesus' reveals what was hidden in God's heart from the
very beginning of creation (see Eph 1:4).

## The Treasure and the Pearl (13:44–46)

  44 "The kingdom of heaven is like treasure hidden in a
field, which a man found and covered up; then in his joy he
goes and sells all that he has and buys that field.
  45 "Again, the kingdom of heaven is like a merchant in
search of fine pearls, ⁴⁶who, on finding one pearl of great
value, went and sold all that he had and bought it.

  These two briefest of parables are proper to Matthew. The
traditional interpretation is as follows. In the ancient world, as
still in many tribal regions today, banks were not trusted, especially in times of political or economic upheaval. Even the
wealthy might bury their treasure in the ground. The assumption here is that the owner took the secret of his buried treasure to the tomb with him. A poor farmer, perhaps even a hired
worker, plowing the field, discovers the treasure. He quickly
covers it again, gathers all his possessions and buys the field.
Thus the person who discovers the kingdom preached by Jesus
joyfully forgoes everything else in order to have the kingdom.

It is another way of seeking first the kingdom of God (6:33), of carrying it away "by violence" (11:12); of losing one's life in order to find it (10:39). This is the kind of total commitment which makes saints.

The parable of the pearl teaches the same thing, except that the seeker is a merchant. So too the person who discovers Jesus' secret, the kingdom, is willing to sacrifice everything to have it.

The incomparable treasure is captured in the well-known hymn by Lynn DeShazo:

> Lord, you are more precious than silver
> Lord, you are more costly than gold
> Lord, you are more beautiful than diamonds
> And nothing I desire compares with you.

This traditional interpretation sees the farmer and the merchant as disciples or would-be disciples. But it is possible that both are images of God himself, who has given what is most precious to him, his own Son (see 21:37), to purchase (=redeem) his people. Perhaps it is only when the human person realizes the extent of God's extravagance that he can respond with similar totality.

## The Net and the Final Haul of Fish (13:47–50)

47 "Again, the kingdom of heaven is like a net which was thrown into the sea and gathered fish of every kind; 48when it was full, men drew it ashore and sat down and sorted the good into vessels but threw away the bad. 49So it will be at the close of the age. The angels will come out and separate the evil from the righteous, 50and throw them into the furnace of fire; there men will weep and gnash their teeth.

Another parable proper to Matthew. Like the other parables, this too is taken from daily life in Galilee. An individual fisherman might cast into the sea a net with weights. Then he waits for schools of fish to pass above it. When they do, he

draws in the net, full of various kinds of fish. Or the net may
be the much larger kind, hauled between two boats. The number and variety of fish are even greater. Then comes the selection. The teaching is basically the same as that of the parable
of the weeds among the wheat: good and evil will exist side by
side in this life, to be separated at the final judgment. However,
the emphasis here is on the judgment of the wicked, since the
lot of the good is only implied. Like the image of the field, the
net may stand for the church with its presently mixed composition, or the whole world, where the good and the wicked
now exist side by side. But we cannot ignore the repeated
warning of Jesus in Matthew that there will be a final judgment
from which no one can escape. Not a popular preaching theme
these days!

## The New and the Old (13:51–53)

51 "Have you understood all this?" They said to him,
"Yes." ⁵²And he said to them, "Therefore every scribe who
has been trained for the kingdom of heaven is like a
householder who brings out of his treasure what is new and
what is old."
53 And when Jesus had finished these parables, he
went away from there.

Again the theme of understanding (see above, 13:14–15,
19). In Matthew the disciples may at times be weak in faith
(8:26; 14:31), but they do understand the teaching of Jesus. This
is a different emphasis from that of Mark, for whom the disciples remain obtusely blind to the meaning of Jesus during the
whole of his public ministry. But Matthew's community, buf-
feted by the winds of false prophecy and teaching, must cling
to the tradition going back to these first disciples who, in the
evangelist's view, are the only authentic teachers because their
understanding of Jesus is the correct one.
Some scholars have spoken of "the school of St. Matthew,"
referring to a group of Jewish-Christian scribes who sought to
interpret Jesus in the light of their knowledge of the OT. The
evangelist himself, in any case, given his intimate knowledge

of the Scriptures, may well have been a converted scribe. If so, v. 52 describes the advantageous position such a person enjoys. Formed by the Scriptures, he is also "trained for the kingdom of heaven"—that is, he has undergone formation as a disciple of Jesus. He has the best of both worlds. He can show how Jesus brings all the meaning of the old law to its perfection (5:17) and yet affirm his master's distinctive newness, thus preserving both the old and the new (9:17).

At the conclusion of the discourse Jesus leaves Capernaum to continue his itinerant ministry. ■

# Book Four:

## Preparing for the Passion and the Church (13:54–18:35)

### STORY: CONTINUING HIS MINISTRY, JESUS PREDICTS HIS PASSION (13:54–17:27)

From here on Matthew picks up the narrative order of Mark with few major changes. The additions he makes focus on Peter (14:28–31; 16:16–19; 17:24–27) and the community of the church (chapter 18). Thus, as the gap widens between the non-believing Jews and Jesus with his disciples, the outlines of the future church begin to take shape. Jesus predicts that the opposition will lead to his passion, death and resurrection, through which the new age and the church will be born.

### Jesus Is Rejected at Nazareth (13:54–58)

54 and coming to his own country he taught them in their synagogue, so that they were astonished, and said, "Where did this man get this wisdom and these mighty works? ⁵⁵Is not this the carpenter's son? Is not his mother called Mary? And are not his brothers James and Joseph and Simon and Judas? ⁵⁶And are not all his sisters with us? Where then did this man get all this?" ⁵⁷And they took offense at him. But Jesus said to them, "A prophet is not without honor except in his own country and in his own house." ⁵⁸And he did not do many mighty works there, because of their unbelief.

From Matthew's narrative perspective, the synagogue is *their* synagogue (as in 4:23; 9:35), since the church is now a separate entity. The astonishment of the townspeople is not one of admiration but of indignation. And it comes from a distorted egalitarianism. There is a spirit of equality that is supportive solidarity. All are brothers and sisters, without hierarchical status for the privileged few. Jesus will demand that kind of equality among his disciples (23:8–12). But there is an egalitarianism that would reduce everyone in the community to the lowest common denominator and meet any creative initiative with the riposte, "Who do you think you are?" Among tribal peoples I have seen both the angelic and the demonic face of this spirit. And it is the demonic face that meets Jesus here. In v. 57 Matthew omits Mark's "among his own kin," probably to avoid implying that Mary, who conceived Jesus by the power of the Holy Spirit, could possibly *not* have honored him.

## Herod and John the Baptist (14:1–12)

14 AT THAT time Herod the tetrarch heard about the fame of Jesus; ²and he said to his servants, "This is John the Baptist, he has been raised from the dead; that is why these powers are at work in him." ³For Herod had seized John and bound him and put him in prison, for the sake of Herodi-as, his brother Philip's wife; ⁴because John said to him, "It is not lawful for you to have her." ⁵And though he wanted to put him to death, he feared the people, because they held him to be a prophet. ⁶But when Herod's birthday came, the daughter of Herodi-as danced before the company, and pleased Herod, ⁷so that he promised with an oath to give her whatever she might ask. ⁸Prompted by her mother, she said, "Give me the head of John the Baptist here on a platter." ⁹And the king was sorry; but because of his oaths and his guests he commanded it to be given; ¹⁰he sent and had John beheaded in the prison, ¹¹and his head was brought on a platter and given to the girl, and she brought it to her mother. ¹²And his disciples came and took the body and buried it; and they went and told Jesus.

In Mark the departure of the disciples on mission provides the occasion for the interlude about the Baptist's beheading. Since Matthew does not report the disciples' return as does

Mark (Mk 6:30), the account is not an interlude. It is rather another shadow in the escalating opposition to Jesus. Rejected by his own people, Jesus may well see in the execution of the Baptist a prefiguring of his own destiny. Matthew edits Mark to suggest this. He trims many of the colorful details, such as others' opinions about Jesus (Mk 6:15) in order to focus on Herod himself. Herodias' hatred is not mentioned, and whereas in Mk 6:19 Herodias wants to kill John, in Mt 14:5 it is Herod himself who wants to. His only reason for not killing him sooner is not his fear of John's holiness (Mk 6:20) but his fear of the crowds—a theme that will appear in Jesus' passion (21:46; 26:5). Matthew will not relate Jesus' appearance before Herod during the passion. But we are prepared to see what fate a prophet may expect at the hands of the authorities.

### Feeding the Five Thousand (14:13-21)

13 Now when Jesus heard this, he withdrew from there in a boat to a lonely place apart. But when the crowds heard it, they followed him on foot from the towns. [14]As he went ashore he saw a great throng; and he had compassion on them, and healed their sick. [15]When it was evening, the disciples came to him and said, "This is a lonely place, and the day is now over; send the crowds away to go into the villages and buy food for themselves." [16]Jesus said, "They need not go away; you give them something to eat." [17]They said to him, "We have only five loaves here and two fish." [18]And he said, "Bring them here to me." [19]Then he ordered the crowds to sit down on the grass; and taking the five loaves and the two fish he looked up to heaven, and blessed, and broke and gave the loaves to the disciples, and the disciples gave them to the crowds. [20]And they all ate and were satisfied. And they took up twelve baskets full of the broken pieces left over. [21]And those who ate were about five thousand men, besides women and children.

In Mark Jesus' leaving for a quiet place is prompted by the return of the disciples from their mission and the implicit need for debriefing. But in Matthew, it is the report of John's disciples about the death of their master that prompts Jesus to *withdraw*—a technical Matthean term we have noted elsewhere to indicate Jesus' reaction to an irresponsive environment (4:12; 9:24; 12:15; 15:21). But Jesus cannot escape the crowds. His compassion moves him to heal the sick, but he does not, as in Mark, teach them because, in Matthew's presentation of the developing plot, Jesus has ceased to teach the crowds in 13:36. The question is: what kind of language is appropriate for presenting the word of God? Jesus used the clear language of direct teaching in the Sermon on the Mount. When this was not accepted, he turned to the veiled language of parables in chapter 13. He will now try the language which is hardest to refuse because it brings immediate physical benefits—healing. And when the day of healing draws to a close he will use still another language of physical benefit—feeding the crowds.

Christians who live today in countries closed to the direct preaching of the gospel can find encouragement here to proclaim the good news as Jesus did in similar circumstances through the ministry of healing and feeding the hungry. Jesus himself here sets the example for those who will be welcomed into the kingdom because they have tended the sick and fed the hungry (25:35–36), even when the beneficiaries were not ready to hear the source of the healing and feeding love.

Here the challenge turns on the disciples, for there is not even enough food to feed themselves, as they are quick to point out. Jesus, however, tells them to bring the loaves and fish to him. He thanks God (that is the meaning of "blessed") for the meager resources, then returns them to the disciples to distribute. We can well imagine the consternation of the disciples. For Jesus did not magically create a stockpile of food whereby it would be obvious there was enough for all. The loaves will be multiplied only in the distributing. A lesson in discipleship: give to Jesus what little you have, with him thank the Father for it, then share it, and it will be multiplied.

Another effect: through the sharing of the bread the crowd becomes a community. This suggests the possibility of a Eucharistic motif, which is indeed grounded in the text. The rhythmic "blessed . . . broke . . . gave . . ." will recur at the last supper when Jesus institutes the Eucharist (26:26). And the fish disappear from the account here with v. 19, Matthew omitting them from Mark's account of the cleanup (Mk 6:43), so that the focus is entirely on the bread.

The story then looks backward to the OT events of the manna in the desert (Ex 16) and Elisha's feeding of a hundred men (2 Kgs 4:42–44) and forward to the Eucharistic banquet, though its basic meaning here is to manifest Jesus as the compassionate feeder of his people "until they are satisfied" (14:20).

## *Walking on the Sea—a Lesson in Faith (14:22–33)*

22 Then he made the disciples get into the boat and go before him to the other side, while he dismissed the crowds. [23]And after he had dismissed the crowds, he went up on the mountain by himself to pray. When evening came, he was there alone, [24]but the boat by this time was many furlongs distant from the land, beaten by the waves; for the wind was against them. [25]And in the fourth watch of the night he came to them, walking on the sea. [26]But when the disciples saw him walking on the sea, they were terrified, saying, "It is a ghost!" And they cried out for fear. [27]But immediately he spoke to them, saying, "Take heart, it is I; have no fear."

28 And Peter answered him, "Lord, if it is you, bid me come to you on the water." [29]He said, "Come." So Peter got out of the boat and walked on the water and came to Jesus; [30]but when he saw the wind, he was afraid, and beginning to sink he cried out, "Lord, save me." [31]Jesus immediately reached out his hand and caught him, saying to him, "O man of little faith, why did you doubt?" [32]And when they got into the boat, the wind ceased. [33]And those in the boat worshiped him, saying, "Truly you are the Son of God."

We do not know why Jesus separates himself from the disciples before dismissing the crowd, but we do know that this story, and particularly Matthew's addition to it about Peter, was preserved for its catechetical value. For it beautifully symbolizes the situation of the church after the resurrection. Jesus sends the disciples out on their own, while he is with the Father interceding for them. They are tossed on the waters of chaos and darkness, a motif that appears repeatedly in the OT (Gen 1:2; Ps 18:5; 42:8; 69:2; 88:8). This has happened before, with the same ecclesial symbolism (8:23–27), except that there Jesus was with them in the boat. Here they feel alone and exhausted, as the persecuted church of the first century must often have felt. Jesus appears to them, like the Lord standing over the chaotic waters in the OT (Ps 77:19). But the first effect is only to add fear to their discouragement, for they think they see a ghost. Jesus reassures them not only with the "fear not" typical of theophanies (Jgs 6:23; Dan 10:12; Lk 1:13,30) but with the words the Lord spoke to Moses at the burning bush (Ex 3:14): "It is I" is literally "I am." Here, as there, the meaning is: "I am here *for you*," that is, your covenant savior to rescue you from your misery. For Matthew this is another instance of Jesus as Emmanuel, God-with-us in every circumstance (1:23; 18:20; 28:20).

Up to this point Matthew has followed Mark closely, but now he inserts the story about Peter drawn from his own sources. From here on Peter emerges as a major figure in the increasingly ecclesiastical thrust of the next chapters. Addressing Jesus as "Lord," Peter vents his desire. Whether it is a desire to share Jesus' miraculous power (stressing *on the water*) or just a desire to be with Jesus (*bid me come to you*), Jesus invites him to come. He is temporarily successful. *But seeing the wind* is a strange expression, for normally the wind is heard or felt, not seen, save perhaps in its effects of mounting waves. But the wind is the threefold link tying the story together. It is the cause of the disciples' struggle (v. 24), the cause of Peter's fear (v. 30), and its ceasing the sign of Jesus' conquest (v. 32). In reporting that Peter *sees* the wind, Matthew is implying that Peter no longer sees Jesus, for he has taken his eyes off him. And this is the beginning of his failure. Fear strikes him, and he begins to sink. Mustering what faith he has, Peter cries out in the same words the disciples used in the storm (8:25) and Christians would use in succeeding centuries, "Lord, save me!"

Peter illustrates what Matthew understands by "little faith." It is not a lack of understanding, nor is it a basic disbe-

lief. It is the trust that falters out of fear. That too is the
meaning of *doubt* here—apparently something that will accompany the church even after the resurrection (28:17). It is the
state of mind which constantly needs the reassurance of Jesus'
presence, dramatized here by the calm which returns when
Jesus gets into the boat with Peter. It is a reassurance which
is the final, monumental word of the gospel: "I am with you
always, until the end of the world" (28:20). The story concludes
with the disciples worshipping Jesus, as they do in 28:17 in the
midst of doubt, and with a profession of faith that anticipates
Peter's (16:16) and the centurion's at the cross (27:54).

### Healings at Gennesaret (14:34–36)

34 And when they had crossed over, they came to land
at Gennesaret. [35]And when the men of that place recognized
him, they sent round to all that region and brought to him
all that were sick, [36]and besought him that they might only
touch the fringe of his garment; and as many as touched it
were made well.

Despite the crowd's increased resistance to Jesus' teaching, they are no less enthusiastic about his healing, the only
language Jesus has used since 13:36 for the multitudes and will
continue to use to the very end of his ministry in Jerusalem
(15:29–31; 21:14). His power to heal is not diminished, for those
who touch even the hem of his clothing are healed (compare
9:20–21).

### The Conflict on Defilement (15:1–20)

15 THEN PHARISEES and scribes came to Jesus from
Jerusalem and said, [2]"Why do your disciples transgress the tradition of the elders? For they do not wash their
hands when they eat." [3]He answered them, "And why do
you transgress the commandment of God for the sake of
your tradition? [4]For God commanded, 'Honor your father
and your mother,' and, 'He who speaks evil of father or

mother, let him surely die.' ⁵But you say, 'If any one tells
his father or his mother, What you would have gained from
me is given to God, he need not honor his father.' ⁶So, for
the sake of your tradition, you have made void the word of
God. ⁷You hypocrites! Well did Isaiah prophesy of you,
when he said:
　⁸"This people honors me with their lips,
　　but their heart is far from me;
　⁹in vain do they worship me,
　　teaching as doctrines the precepts of men.'"
　10 And he called the people to him and said to them,
"Hear and understand: ¹¹not what goes into the mouth defiles a man, but what comes out of the mouth, this defiles
a man." ¹²Then the disciples came and said to him, "Do you
know that the Pharisees were offended when they heard
this saying?" ¹³He answered, "Every plant which my heavenly Father has not planted will be rooted up. ¹⁴Let them
alone; they are blind guides. And if a blind man leads a blind
man, both will fall into a pit." ¹⁵But Peter said to him,
"Explain the parable to us." ¹⁶And he said, "Are you also
still without understanding? ¹⁷Do you not see that whatever
goes into the mouth passes into the stomach, and so passes
on? ¹⁸But what comes out of the mouth proceeds from the
heart, and this defiles a man. ¹⁹For out of the heart come evil
thoughts, murder, adultery, fornication, theft, false witness, slander. ²⁰These are what defile a man; but to eat with
unwashed hands does not defile a man."

　To the modern reader this dispute may seem of only archival interest. But for Jesus and the early church, it was a
life-or-death matter; in practice probably more critical in the
turning of the tide of Judaism against Jesus than any doctrinal
dispute. Where Christians today live among Hindus and Mus-
lims, differences are daily experienced more in what people eat
or don't eat than in what they believe. The exclusion of certain
foods is the exclusion of certain people. So the real dispute here
is not about food. It is about community.
　Matthew rearranges the Markan material to put the law
before the prophets and otherwise edits the story to stress

teaching needed by his community. Jesus' popularity is such that an official delegation of Pharisees and scribes comes from Jerusalem to question his life-style. Jesus and his disciples are transgressing sacred traditions, for in fact they are eating like gentiles. To this Jesus retorts by an *ad hominem* argument: your tradition of Corban is worse, for it transgresses the commandment of God himself concerning the honor due to parents. After quoting the Exodus commandment, Jesus cites the prophet Isaiah 29:13. To pretend to honor God while dishonoring one's parents is to give God lip-service, replacing true worship with man-made laws.

Following Mark, Matthew permits one exception to his general rule about Jesus no longer teaching the crowds. Jesus calls the people together and lays down a principle more far-reaching than excluding the washing ritual. Matthew does not repeat Mark's "thus he declared all foods clean" (Mk 7:19), because it is not necessary. For in v. 11 Jesus basically declares all foods clean—and the implication is sociologically profound: Jesus' community must never exclude anyone on basis of food. The only defilement is moral, not dietary. This was also a revision of the levitical law, and it must have surprised the disciples as much as it enraged the Pharisees. To this Jesus replies in terms similar to those found in John's gospel: "Every plant which my heavenly Father has not planted will be rooted up." The plant is a figure known in both the OT and Qumran as an image of the community. The Pharisees are not planted by the Father. They will be rooted up. "Let them alone" means, "Do not accept their leadership, do not follow them"—an important directive for Matthew's second generation community to hear when, after the fall of the temple, the Pharisees, sole surviving party, sought to exert their leadership over the scattered elements of the people, including the Jewish Christians.

The prominence Matthew gives Peter reappears here as he becomes the spokesperson for the disciples. In Acts 10–15 and Gal 2:11–14 Peter is predominantly involved in the issue of the admission of the gentiles, food being the critical issue. Here Peter calls the saying of v. 11 a parable, meaning that it is a mysterious saying to him. Raised as a good Jew, Peter is probably resisting the newness of Jesus' teaching rather than misunderstanding his words. Jesus' response is clear: defilement for him is not ritual but ethical. Echoing the Sermon on the Mount, Jesus begins with the sins of the heart, then in Matthew's revision of Mark, lists the sins according to the decalogue, adding "false witness," a sin by which the persecuted community of the eighties has no doubt been wounded. The concluding verse is not a limitation of Jesus' teaching to the issue of washing of hands but merely an inclusion with the opening v. 2, the meaning being, "If defilement is not a matter of what you eat but of what you speak and do, then even less it is a matter of eating with unwashed hands."

Once again we meet Jesus' concern to translate his understanding of his heavenly Father (v. 13) in terms of an inclusive human community. While Jesus is clear about the ethic he expects of his disciples, he is equally clear that no humanly made barrier should keep the Father's children from sharing the same table. It is a constant challenge to every Christian community to ask itself what walls, conscious or unconscious, it has erected.

In a church in Trichy, India, the long standing caste system had led to the building of a wall in the cemetery separating the graves of the high-caste Christians from those of the low-caste. An enlightened pastor one night tore down the wall. The high-caste parishioners were furious, took the case to court, and succeeded in getting the wall rebuilt!

## A Contrast: The Canaanite Woman (15:21–28)

21 And Jesus went away from there and withdrew to the district of Tyre and Sidon. [22]And behold, a Canaanite woman from that region came out and cried, "Have mercy on me, O Lord, Son of David; my daughter is severely possessed by a demon." [23]But he did not answer her a word. And his disciples came and begged him, saying, "Send her away, for she is crying after us." [24]He answered, "I was sent only to the lost sheep of the house of Israel." [25]But she came and knelt before him, saying, "Lord, help me." [26]And he answered, "It is not fair to take the children's bread and throw it to the dogs." [27]She said, "Yes, Lord, yet even the

dogs eat the crumbs that fall from their masters' table."
²⁸Then Jesus answered her, "O woman, great is your faith!
Be it done for you as you desire." And her daughter was
healed instantly.

In contrast to the exclusive nature of the Pharisees' dietary laws, we now have a story illustrating, among other
things, inclusiveness, again with a clear reference to table-fellowship.

Jesus is met by a gentile woman, whom Matthew calls a
"Canaanite," changing Mark's more precise "Syro-Phoenician"
to evoke perhaps the history of Israel's cohabitation with the
pagan inhabitants of the land. Textual criticism also indicates
Matthew added "and Sidon" to Mark's simple "Tyre" to suggest
perhaps a parallel with the gentile widow of Sidon who fed
Elijah. As in the genealogy of chapter 1, Matthew is interested
in evoking OT justifications for the role of the gentiles in the
church. Matthew has further edited Mark to dramatize the dialogue between the woman and Jesus. She addresses him with
the titles "Lord" and "Son of David." "Lord" already reveals
her faith, for from Matthew's viewpoint, it is the title Christians give to Jesus. "Son of David" is amazing, for thereby she
confesses Jesus to be the Jewish Messiah, a title the Jewish
crowds, hesitant to give Jesus at 12:23, do give him at his entry
to Jerusalem (21:9, 15), to be opposed of course by the Pharisees (12:24), the chief priests and the scribes (21:15-16). While
the Jewish leaders reject Jesus as Son of David, a gentile
woman acclaims him.

Her cry both echoes the Psalms and foreshadows the liturgical prayer of the church. Jesus' silence is broken by the
disciples' request, "Send her away," which, judging from Jesus'
response in v. 24, means, "Grant her request." Jesus reaffirms
his mission, and that of his disciples presently, only to Israel
(see 10:5-6). The second of her three requests is a brief, "Lord,
help me." Jesus intensifies his refusal by echoing the Jewish
epithet for the gentiles as "dogs." The woman, unrebuffed by
the remark, latches on to it in agreement, even accepts the
title and asks only for the scraps that fall from the *master's*
table. In Mark, it is the children's crumbs; in Matthew the

crumbs are those left by the Master, Jesus. The third request, clever and persistent, wins Jesus' admiration of the woman's *faith*. Working the healing she requested, Jesus himself illustrates the power of persistent prayer (see Lk 11:5–8; Mt 7:7–11).

Worth noting is the fact that it is Jesus who in his initial refusal introduces the image of table fellowship—and the Jewish practice of exclusiveness. But the faith of a gentile woman breaks down the barrier, thus foreshadowing the entrance of the gentiles into full communion with the believing Jews—something the Pharisees and scribes in the preceding story would have greeted with horror.

## Jesus Heals and Feeds the Crowd Again (15:29–39)

29 And Jesus went on from there and passed along the Sea of Galilee. And he went up on the mountain, and sat down there. ³⁰And great crowds came to him, bringing with them the lame, the maimed, the blind, the dumb, and many others, and they put them at his feet, and he healed them, ³¹so that the throng wondered, when they saw the dumb speaking, the maimed whole, the lame walking, and the blind seeing; and they glorified the God of Israel.

32 Then Jesus called his disciples to him and said, "I have compassion on the crowd, because they have been with me now three days, and have nothing to eat; and I am unwilling to send them away hungry, lest they faint on the way." ³³And the disciples said to him, "Where are we to get bread enough in the desert to feed so great a crowd?" ³⁴And Jesus said to them, "How many loaves have you?" They said, "Seven, and a few small fish." ³⁵And commanding the crowd to sit down on the ground, ³⁶he took the seven loaves and the fish, and having given thanks he broke them and gave them to the disciples, and the disciples gave them to the crowds. ³⁷And they all ate and were satisfied; and they took up seven baskets full of the broken pieces left over. ³⁸Those who ate were four thousand men, besides women and children. ³⁹And sending away the crowds, he got into the boat and went to the region of Magadan.

This story opens with a scene inviting the reader to recall the setting of the Sermon on the Mount (5:1). But, as we already noticed in 14:14, Jesus does not teach. He only heals, for this is the language the crowd understands. Instead of following Mark's story of the healing of the deaf-mute, however, Matthew, who has already related two such stories in 9:32-53 and 12:22, provides us with a summary of all Jesus' healings similar to the ones given in 4:23-34; 8:16; 9:35; 11:4-5 and recalling the healings prophesied by Isaiah: "Then the eyes of the blind shall be opened, and the ears of the deaf unstopped; then shall the lame man leap like a hart, and the tongue of the dumb sing for joy" (Is 35:5-6). "The deaf shall hear the words of a book, and out of their gloom and darkness the blind shall see" (Is 29:18).

The crowd is so caught up in praise that it seems to have forgotten its need for food. But Jesus hasn't, and in his compassion (noted before at 9:36 and 14:14) he takes the initiative. Only at this point do we learn the crowd has been with Jesus three days. Feeling that Jesus' initiative lays the responsibility on their shoulders, the disciples complain of their predicament. Again the sequence of events is the same as in the preceding story of the multiplication, with the exception of the number of loaves and the word for giving thanks, already used in Mark, *eucharistesas*, which strengthens the already eucharistic overtones of the story.

The similarities of this story with the one in 14:13-21 lead many scholars to say that this is simply another version of the story told there. Mark, after all, has two stories of the multiplication, and Matthew is fond of doublets. On the other hand, even in Mark, there are important differences in the two stories—the absence of many graphic details of the first story, different numbers for the crowds, the loaves, the baskets of scraps, one day of teaching in the first story, three in the second. And most importantly, as Augustine already noted, the first crowd was Jewish, the second gentile (in Mark Jesus is in the Decapolis). Most likely Mark himself was heir to a double tradition before him, whether two different stories or two versions of the same story, and Matthew simply chooses to relay that tradition here. In any case, Matthew does not exploit the detail about it being a gentile crowd. He seems satisfied to use this story, like the previous one, as an illustration of Jesus' compassion, expressing in the physical language of healing and feeding the divine mercy he can no longer effectively communicate in words.

## Jesus Rejects the Teaching Authorities (16:1–12)

**16** AND THE Pharisees and Sadducees came, and to test him they asked him to show them a sign from heaven. ²He answered them, "When it is evening, you say, 'It will be fair weather; for the sky is red.' ³And in the morning, 'It will be stormy today, for the sky is red and threatening.' You know how to interpret the appearance of the sky, but you cannot interpret the signs of the times. ⁴An evil and adulterous generation seeks for a sign, but no sign shall be given to it except the sign of Jonah." So he left them and departed.

5 When the disciples reached the other side, they had forgotten to bring any bread. ⁶Jesus said to them, "Take heed and beware of the leaven of the Pharisees and Sadducees." ⁷And they discussed it among themselves, saying, "We brought no bread." ⁸But Jesus, aware of this, said, "O men of little faith, why do you discuss among yourselves the fact that you have no bread? ⁹Do you not yet perceive? Do you not remember the five loaves of the five thousand, and how many baskets you gathered? ¹⁰Or the seven loaves of the four thousand, and how many baskets you gathered? ¹¹How is it that you fail to perceive that I did not speak about bread? Beware of the leaven of the Pharisees and Sadducees." ¹²Then they understood that he did not tell them to beware of the leaven of bread, but of the teaching of the Pharisees and Sadducees.

The Sadducees surprisingly now join the Pharisees, their ideological rivals, in asking Jesus for a sign "from heaven." Very well, Jesus replies ironically, look at the heavens. (*Heaven* and *sky* are the same word in Greek, *ouranos*.) There is a similar proverb in English: "Red sky at night, sailor's de-

light; red sky in the morning, sailor's warning." It is Jesus' way
of saying that his critics have enough signs in what Jesus has
done already.

Because verses 2 and 3 are missing from important manuscripts, some scholars doubt whether they belong originally to
Matthew. However, there are reasons to believe they are authentic: 1) They are not copied from the parallel saying in Luke
12:54–56 but represent an independent tradition of the same
teaching, which Luke may have already adapted to a more universal meterological situation: cloud means rain. 2) Their omission in certain manuscripts may be explained by the fact that
in certain climates like Egypt a red morning sky does not indicate rain. 3) There is a close ironical connection between the
request for a sign from heaven and Jesus' response about a
sign from the sky.

With verse 4 Matthew again follows Mark. To Mark's "evil
generation" Matthew adds, as he does also in 12:39, "adulterous," for Israel's wickedness is worse than the gentiles'. It is
an infidelity to its covenant with the Lord. Likewise, whereas
in Mark no sign will be given, in Matthew there is one exception: the sign of Jonah, which we know from 12:40 is the sign
of Jesus' death and resurrection.

Jesus' departure signifies for Matthew his rejection of the
authority of the Pharisees and Sadducees and is meant to lead
directly into the following teaching for the disciples. They are
upset because they have no bread, not adverting to the fact
that in their midst is the twice-shown multiplier of bread. They
are like the Pharisees and Sadducees because they have not
read the signs of Jesus' power available to them. This is their
*little faith*, the kind of discouragement that plagues the disciples of all ages—being overwhelmed by the circumstances and
difficulties and not relying on the Lord present in their midst.
Jesus means "leaven" in its spiritual sense. Leaven is a per-
vasive and corrupting influence. The disciples have become in-
fected by the teaching of the Pharisees and Sadducees. In the
Aramaic which Jesus spoke, the word leaven (*hamir'a*) sounds
almost the same as teaching (*'amir'a*). At the end of the story
the disciples "catch" his meaning. Matthew adds this to Mark's
account because, though the disciples are at times weak in

faith, they do understand Jesus' teaching and thus are qualified
to replace the Jewish magisterium as teachers of the new Israel. This point is now dramatized in the section that follows.

## *Jesus, Peter and the Church (16:13-20)*

13 Now when Jesus came into the district of Caesarea
Philippi, he asked his disciples, "Who do men say that the
Son of man is?" [14]And they said, "Some say John the Baptist,
others say Elijah, and others Jeremiah or one of the prophets." [15]He said to them, "But who do you say that I am?"
[16]Simon Peter replied, "You are the Christ, the Son of the
living God." [17]And Jesus answered him, "Blessed are you,
Simon Bar-Jona! For flesh and blood has not revealed this
to you, but my Father who is in heaven. [18]And I tell you,
you are Peter, and on this rock I will build my church, and
the powers of death shall not prevail against it. [19]I will give
you the keys of the kingdom of heaven, and whatever you
bind on earth shall be bound in heaven, and whatever you
loose on earth shall be loosed in heaven." [20]Then he strictly
charged the disciples to tell no one that he was the Christ.

Here we encounter a major turning point of the gospel, a
passage that reveals not only who Jesus is but what the church
is and the role of Peter within it. The passage will be followed
by Jesus' first prediction of his passion. Because of its critical
importance, we shall examine the passage in the detail it merits.

Jesus has gone to the northernmost reaches of his mission,
to the city built by Herod Philip to honor Caesar (whence the
name "Philip's Caesarea"). Jesus asks his disciples who people
say the *Son of Man* is. Matthew replaces Mark's simple "I"
with this solemn title, which is used in the gospels to describe
Jesus in his earthly ministry and passion as well as in his glorious coming on the clouds of heaven. Herod had spoken of
Jesus as John the Baptist come-to-life, others had thought of
Elijah come back, others—and it is Matthew alone who records
this—Jeremiah. At one level Jesus' preaching may have reminded the people of Jeremiah, but at the level of Matthew's

editing, Jeremiah is the suffering prophet who predicted the fall of Jerusalem and was rejected by his people, a clear figure of Jesus himself. But the hearsay identity is not enough for the disciples. Matthew has progressively distanced the disciples from the crowds, and now the key difference is called for and called forth—their personal confession of who Jesus is.

Peter does not wait for the others to respond. He gives two titles to Jesus. "You are the Messiah." Such a confession has not been made by any disciple until now. And Peter's original understanding of the title was clearly charged with Jewish political, temporal understandings, which Jesus will shortly correct. Even so, it is the true Christian confession. To it, how-ever, Peter adds the solemn, "Son of the living God." "The living God" was a title used for the Lord in the OT to distinguish Israel's living and life-giving God from the lifeless idols of the nations. Many scholars think "Son of the living God," like "Son of God" in 14:33, is a post-resurrectional title retrojected by Matthew to complete Mark's simple "You are the Messiah" (Mk 8:29). But adding *the living God* here could simply be a fulfilment application of Hosea 2:1, where the new covenant people will be called "sons of the living God." Changing the plural to the singular could be still another way that Matthew shows how Jesus is corporate Israel realized in his person, as we have seen repeatedly in this gospel. Peter alone makes this confession, and Jesus responds by reciprocally entitling Peter.

The entitling is prefaced by a beatitude, indicating a special personal blessing to Peter. No other disciple receives such a blessing. "Flesh and blood" is one of the many Aramaisms in this section, strongly suggesting Matthew is using a pre-existing source. It means "mere human beings." Not from these but from the Father alone has the grace of such a revelation come. In turn Jesus entitles Peter as "Rock." "Peter" in English comes from the Greek *Petros*, which in turn comes from *petra*, "rock." In Aramaic, which Jesus spoke, *Kepha* (used of Peter 9 times in the NT) meant "rock" but also was a personal name. The distinction between the masculine name and the female noun occurs only in Greek, so Jesus' original Aramaic would have been, "You are Rock." Like the Lord changing Abram's name to Abraham, Jesus' changing Simon's name to "Rock" focuses on his mission. Abraham was the stone from which God quarried his people (Is 51:1–2), Peter will be the foundation stone on which Jesus will build his church. Matthew's is the only gospel where the word *ekklesia* is used (twice, the other being 18:17). In the Greek OT it means the assembly of the people called out of Egypt by the Lord. Among the Christians the word quickly replaced the more restrictive *synagogue* used by the Jews for their local assembly. "My" church here goes beyond any local assembly, however, and indicates the unity of all believers committed to Christ and built on Peter. The rock is not the faith of Peter but the person of Peter, whose faith is, of course, implied.

To his promise of building his church on Peter Jesus now adds another, astounding promise: "The powers of death shall not prevail against it." The Greek literally reads "the gates of Hades." Hades is not appropriately translated "hell." It means the abode of the dead. "Gates" is metonymy for "powers," since the ancients thought of a city's gates as symbols of its might, and sometimes "gates" stood for "keepers of the gates." The "powers of death" are, on the one hand, death itself. Jesus promises his church *will not die*. That would be good news enough. But the powers of death are also all demonic forces which will battle against the church, including the forces of deceit and error.

To Peter personally are given the "keys to the kingdom of heaven." The OT text most frequently cited here is Is 22:15–25. Shebna, Hezekiah's prime minister, is deposed and replaced by Eliakim, on whose shoulders God places "the key of David; he shall open . . . and he shall shut"—referring to the power of the "Master of the Palace" to allow or refuse entrance and hence access to the king. If this is the background, then Jesus is giving to Peter the power to admit to the kingdom or to reject from it whomever he decides.

A second suggestion evokes Rev 1:18, "I have the keys of death and of Hades," and understands the power of the keys to be the *preaching* by which Peter will open the kingdom of heaven to allow believers to enter, unlike the Pharisees who close the kingdom of heaven (23:13).

The correct interpretation of the power of the keys is sharpened, however, by the binding and loosing image which follows. Among the rabbis the image occasionally means to impose or lift a ban of excommunication. This is the likely meaning of 18:18. But here the meaning is by far the more common rabbinic one: to impose or remove an obligation by handing down an authoritative decision, and this will ordinarily involve an authoritative interpretation of Scripture. That would mean to Peter is granted the power of binding decisions for the church and of authoritative interpretation of the teaching of Jesus.

One more refinement: The Greek text literally says, "Whatever you bind on earth *will have been bound* in heaven, and whatever you loose on earth *will have been loosed* in heaven." The peripharastic future perfect, rare in the NT, indicates something that happens in heaven *before* it happens on earth. The text thus looks forward to a future event, only *after* which Peter's teaching will become authoritative magisterium.

This would be a different order from what we may be accustomed to understand by the simple future used in most translations: "Whatever you bind/loose on earth will be bound/loosed in heaven"—as if God would be promising to ratify Peter's decisions. The reverse is rather true: God establishes his order first, and Peter's decisions ratify it for the church.

How can this be? We have noted how, for Matthew, the disciples are not given the mission to teach until after the resurrection (contrast 10:6; 28:20 with Mk 6:30). We have also pointed out how Matthew understands the law to be fulfilled in the death and resurrection of Jesus (see Excursus, pp. 72–73). Thus Jesus' new understanding of the law, his authoritative interpretation of it, his binding more stringently certain aspects of the law and loosing others such as the dietary laws, becomes effective and is promulgated with his death and resurrection, after which he proclaims: "All authority is given to me *in heaven* and on earth" (28:18). This is the future event, the definitive binding and loosing "in heaven," and when Peter will exercise his office of authoritative interpreter, it will be a manifestation on earth of the divine authority of the risen Jesus and the application of his new law to the church.

This is the astounding role given to Peter. Like the other disciples he is often weak and accused of being "of little faith."

But he is endowed with authority to teach and legislate in Jesus' name, and we can even say Jesus continues to teach and rule through him. It is Jesus' authority "on earth" (28:18) which Peter is exercising. The other disciples share in this ministry no doubt (18:18; 28:20), but Peter has it in a special way. He receives a special divine revelation and blessing given to no other disciple.

If the disciples in Matthew's gospel stand for the successors to those first disciples, who are to be followed against the false prophets of the day, who, in the church Matthew knows, is the successor of Peter, who was dead at the time Matthew wrote? Was Matthew's interest in Peter merely archival, or was there a *present* situation and a *present* authority which Matthew was envisioning? The Roman Catholic Church has found in this text a confirmation of its belief in the indefectibility of the church to the end of time and the particularly nuanced doctrine of the infallibility of the bishop of Rome in ultimately deciding matters of faith and morals.

In v. 20 Matthew returns to Mark's text commanding silence concerning the title "Messiah," which would so easily be popularly misunderstood. For the disciples it also needs much clarification, which Jesus now proceeds to give.

## The Passion of Jesus and His Disciples (16:21–28)

21 From that time Jesus began to show his disciples that he must go to Jerusalem and suffer many things from the elders and chief priests and scribes, and be killed, and on the third day be raised. 22And Peter took him and began to rebuke him, saying, "God forbid, Lord! This shall never happen to you." 23But he turned and said to Peter, "Get behind me, Satan! You are a hindrance to me; for you are not on the side of God, but of men."

24 Then Jesus told his disciples, "If any man would come after me, let him deny himself and take up his cross and follow me. 25For whoever would save his life will lose it, and whoever loses his life for my sake will find it. 26For what will it profit a man, if he gains the whole world and forfeits his life? Or what shall a man give in return for his life? 27For

the Son of man is to come with his angels in the glory of his Father, and then he will repay every man for what he has done. [28]Truly, I say to you, there are some standing here who will not taste death before they see the Son of man coming in his kingdom."

"From that time . . . ," like the same expression in 4:17, marks an important turning point of the gospel, as Jesus predicts his passion for the first time. Yet it is intimately connected with the preceding revelation and confession as a corrective. Jesus will go to Jerusalem (Matthew inserts the name of the city into Mark's account) but not to be acclaimed as the political Messiah but to suffer at the hands of the three groups from which the Sanhedrin drew its membership—the lay elders, the priests and the scribes. He will be killed and on the third day he will be raised (Matthew replaces Mark's "he will rise" with the passive, indicating the Father's role in raising Jesus, as in 1 Cor 15:4).

Peter's "God forbid!" may also be translated, "God is kind to you"—i.e., he would not let such a thing happen to you. In either case Peter cannot conceive of the Messiah, the Son of God, suffering. Not only does Peter speak for the other disciples, but he voices the universal belief of contemporary Judaism that the Messiah would come to remove all suffering and certainly would not himself suffer. Even as late as the third century A.D. the crucifixion of the Messiah was a major difference in the discussion of Trypho the Jew with Justin the Martyr (*Dialog*, 89, 1, 2).

In his retort to Peter Jesus uses the same language as he did in the temptation (4:10). Peter at this moment is Satan reappearing at the crossroad and offering Jesus an easier way out, blocking his way to the cross. Peter, just hailed by Jesus as the rock, is now the rock of stumbling (RSV: hindrance, Greek *skandalon*). It is the third of the "You are" statements in this section:

| 16:16: | Peter: | "You are the Christ, the Son of the living God." |
| 16:18: | Jesus: | "You are Rock . . ." |

16:23:     Jesus:     "You are a stumbling stone for me . . ."

The RSV translation of the last part of v.23 misses the exact meaning of the Greek, which is: "You are not thinking the way God thinks, but the way human beings think." Implicit here is that Peter—and every reader of the gospel—will need a conversion in his way of thinking in order to grasp the cross as God's way for Jesus. At this point the issue is really whether Jesus will be a stumbling block for Peter, who is confronted by the "scandal of the cross," of which Paul writes: "Jews demand signs and Greeks seek wisdom, but we preach Christ crucified, a stumbling block to Jews and folly to Gentiles, but to those who are called, both Jews and Greeks, Christ the power of God and the wisdom of God" (1 Cor 1:22–24).

Not only will the Messiah suffer, but his disciples will too. We had heard this language before in 10:38, but now it comes back in the light of Jesus' own cross-bearing. "To deny oneself" here does not primarily mean doing penance through deprivation. To "deny" is language used in the courts when a witness denies he knows or recognizes a given person. Here the verb, used in the reflexive, means the disciple no longer knows himself as the center of his world, he has forgotten himself. He now knows and recognizes only Jesus and wishes to be with him in everything, including his cross: "to know him and the power of his resurrection and the fellowship of his sufferings" (Phil 3:10).

Each disciple will have his own particular cross to carry. It may be the kind of long-term burden of caring for a disabled relation, or living with one's own physical or intellectual limitations. Or it may be a short-term cross like making a painful decision or confronting someone. The Christian is not immune to the kinds of sufferings which befall everyone in the human race. In addition, he will have the cross that comes from just being a Christian and witnessing to the values of Jesus in a world that does not accept them. But it is one thing to be *burdened* by the cross—its actual weight or the fear of its coming. It is quite another to *take it up*, that is, to make a conscious decision to embrace it as one's call to follow Jesus. The burden of the cross usually comes from *not taking it up*, not appropriating it, refusing to surrender to the call. It is the kind of clutching to one's own definition of life, which ends in losing it. Jesus calls to the kind of abandonment that brings life in abundance. He does not want disciples who are calculating, unwilling to risk, fearful of losing their security if they leap into his arms.

The life we experience upon embracing the cross is often immediate or at least forthcoming. But in the text here Jesus looks to the final life-giving judgment which will be directly related to our cross-choosing decisions here and now (v. 27).

A modern reader of v. 28 might reflect: "It has been a long time since Jesus said these words, and neither I nor previous generations have seen the second coming of Jesus. So what does this promise mean here?" Interestingly, Matthew's readers could easily have asked the same question, for they were a generation or two removed from that first generation who would have heard Jesus pronounce these words. Matthew himself was surely aware of this. That is why he deals with the delay of Jesus' second coming by focusing repeatedly on the final judgment, not on the imminence of Jesus' return. How then does he understand the promise here to have been fulfilled? Mark gives us a clue by having the statement lead directly to the transfiguration, in which the disciples see the kingdom coming in power. Matthew accepts this connection and by heightening the coming as the royal enthronement of the Son of Man, prepares us to see the transfiguration as the disciples' experience of that enthronement. It is only an anticipation, of course, of that other coming and that other enthronement which takes place through the death and resurrection of Jesus. In that event God gave signs that the old world was ending and a new age beginning. The climactic appearance of Jesus to his disciples on the mountain in 28:16–20 has the character of a parousia, a coming of Jesus as king of heaven and earth. The disciples who witness it then, and proleptically in the transfiguration, are those who were with Jesus ("standing here") in his public ministry (16:28).

*Jesus Is Transfigured (17:1–9)*

**17** AND AFTER six days Jesus took with him Peter and James and John his brother, and led them up a high mountain apart. [2]And he was transfigured before them, and his face shone like the sun, and his garments became white as light. [3]And behold, there appeared to them Moses and Elijah, talking with him. [4]And Peter said to Jesus, "Lord, it is well that we are here; if you wish, I will make three booths here, one for you and one for Moses and one for Elijah." [5]He was still speaking, when lo, a bright cloud overshadowed them, and a voice from the cloud said, "This is my beloved Son, with whom I am well pleased; listen to him." [6]When the disciples heard this, they fell on their faces, and were filled with awe. [7]But Jesus came and touched them, saying, "Rise, and have no fear." [8]And when they lifted up their eyes, they saw no one but Jesus only.

9 And as they were coming down the mountain, Jesus commanded them, "Tell no one the vision, until the Son of man is raised from the dead."

The reader who has, with the disciples, just heard the hard words of Jesus about the cross, is now given a glimpse of the glory to which it leads. "After six days" is an unusual precision. Following Mark, Matthew uses this detail to connect this story to the confession of Peter, as a confirmation of Jesus' divine sonship and also as a balancing consolation to the prediction of the passion. A Jewish Christian, listening to this story, would hear echoes of Ex 24 and 34, describing Moses' vision of God on Mount Sinai (the mountain, "after six days," the cloud, the voice, the companions, the radiant face) or of 1 Kgs 19:9–13, Elijah's ascent to the same mountain, along with Deut 18:15 foretelling the prophet-like-Moses about whom Moses commands, "To him you shall listen." But the differences between these OT scenes and our story are too great to suppose, as some scholars do, that the transfiguration was created from these OT passages. It is rather an attempt to describe, in terms meaningful to a Jew, a deep mystical experience in which the three disciples perceive the reality and the divine glory of the

Son of God acknowledged in Peter's confession and confirmed here as the fulfillment of the law (Moses) and the prophets (Elijah).

Matthew gives special emphasis to the element of light by three editorial touches: (1) Jesus' face shines like the sun (v. 2); (2) his garments are white as *light* (Mark simply has them bleached—v. 2); (3) the cloud is a *bright* cloud (v. 5). These changes and the placing of Moses' name before Elijah's mean that for Matthew Jesus has a brightness like but greater than that of Moses (Ex 34:29–35). Thus he is once more presenting Jesus, as we have seen in the infancy accounts and in the Sermon on the Mount, as the new and more authoritative instrument of God's revelation.

Matthew cuts many of Mark's colorful details in order to reach the climactic point, the voice from heaven, which interrupts Peter's inane and somewhat self-centered offer to be helpful ("*I* will make . . ." instead of Mark's "Let *us* make . . ."). For "while he was still speaking" the cloud and the voice take over the stage and the Father, who earlier revealed to Peter that Jesus is God's Son, now proclaims it before the three disciples. The words are the same as those at Jesus' baptism, with the important addition of "Listen to him." These words not only echo Deut 18:18, the prophet-like-Moses who must be listened to. They not only confirm Peter's confession of Jesus as Son of God. They tell the disciples that they must also listen to Jesus' prediction of his passion, which Peter did not want to hear.

Matthew adds to the account of Mark that the disciples fell on their faces, as did other apocalyptic visionaries (Dan 8:17; 10:9–11; Rev 1:17; 1 Enoch 14:14–25), and that Jesus touched them, brought them back to their senses and reassured them. As they now see "only Jesus" they realize that the one in whose company they have been since the beginning is more than they ever dreamed.

There are two other mountain scenes that help us understand this one: the mount of the temptation (4:8–10) and the mount of the great commission (28:16–20). In the temptation story, Satan tests Jesus' title as Son of God. He invites him to take three false paths. The third of these, offered on a "very high mountain" (the same expression used here), presents to him all the kingdoms of the world and their glory. Jesus, the Son who rejects royal power and glory on Satan's terms, receives them in an anticipated way in the transfiguration because of his obedience to the Father. For the transfiguration is a glimpse of the Son coming in his kingdom (16:28).

There are many editorial details by which Matthew ties this story also to the great commission scene in 28:16–20. In both scenes Jesus *comes* to his disciples on a *mountain*. In both the disciples are on their knees with doubts or fears, in both Jesus speaks to them a word of reassurance, and in both there is an authoritative voice—in the first the command to listen, in the second the command to teach.

The three mountains, then, pinpoint the trajectory of the whole gospel. On the mount of temptation Jesus is declared Son of God but rejects Satan's proposed path to royal power. On the mount of transfiguration Jesus, having been declared Son of God by Peter and again rejecting the way of Satan proposed by Peter in favor of the way of obedient sonship (16:16, 21–23), reveals his royal power (16:28) and is vindicated by the Father (17:5). In the third, having followed the path of obedient sonship to its end, Jesus is enthroned by the Father with full royal power as Lord of heaven and earth. The transfiguration scene is then an anticipated vindication of the path that Jesus has taken.

The journey of every Christian is marked by moments of transfiguration which vindicate his earlier choices of Jesus over other voices and other values. Such Taboric experiences are rare graces giving a foretaste of the promised glory, as v. 9 indicates: the transfiguration is a forecast of the resurrection.

## Elijah and John the Baptist (17:10–13)

[10]And the disciples asked him, "Then why do the scribes say that first Elijah must come?" [11]He replied, "Elijah does come, and he is to restore all things; [12]but I tell you that Elijah has already come, and they did not know him, but did to him whatever they pleased. So also the Son of man will

suffer at their hands." [13]Then the disciples understood that
he was speaking to them of John the Baptist.

The question of the disciples is abrupt, and the reader does
not see its connection with the preceding. According to the
scribes' interpretation of Mal 4:5–6, Elijah was to return before
the Messiah would come. If Jesus is already the Messiah (as
Peter confessed in 16:16) and is confirmed proleptically as royal
Son of God by the vision, then what of the scribal opinion about
Elijah? This question doubtless reflects disputes of the scribes
with the early Jewish believers in Jesus. Jesus does not dispute
the belief but says Elijah has already come in the person of
John the Baptist. "They" did not recognize him as Elijah, just
as they will not recognize Jesus as the Messiah. Instead "they"
(a generalized statement embodied in King Herod) martyred
him, just as they will do with Jesus—another oblique prediction of his passion.

## *Faith and the Healing Ministry (17:14–21)*

14 And when they came to the crowd, a man came up
to him and kneeling before him said, [15]"Lord, have mercy on
my son, for he is an epileptic and he suffers terribly; for
often he falls into the fire, and often into the water. [16]And
I brought him to your disciples, and they could not heal
him." [17]And Jesus answered, "O faithless and perverse generation, how long am I to be with you? How long am I to
bear with you? Bring him here to me." [18]And Jesus rebuked
him, and the demon came out of him, and the boy was cured
instantly. [19]Then the disciples came to Jesus privately and
said, "Why could we not cast it out?" [20]He said to them,
"Because of your little faith. For truly, I say to you, if you
have faith as a grain of mustard seed, you will say to this
mountain, 'Move from here to there,' and it will move; and
nothing will be impossible to you."

In Mark this story has many colorful details which Matthew pares to the bone in order to focus on the single miracle
and the lesson on faith at the end. Matthew's zoom lens moves

in on the father who approaches as a believer, on his knees and addressing Jesus with "Lord, have mercy" (compare Mark where the man addresses Jesus as *teacher* and merely describes the illness). The illness is often translated "epileptic" (RSV, TEV, NIV), but "lunatic" (NABR, JB) is more exact. The inability of the disciples to heal wrings from Jesus a general exclamation addressed neither to the father nor to the disciples but to the "faithless and perverse generation," a general picture of the progressive resistance Jesus is meeting in his ministry. The healing, which is actually an exorcism, is described in the briefest detail, the boy being healed instantly by the word of Jesus. In Mark, Jesus attributes his disciples' inability to cure to their lack of prayer. But in Matthew it is their *little faith*, a description often used by Jesus to describe faith that is hesitant and doubtful. Elsewhere the little faith was manifested in the disciples' lack of awareness of Jesus' power in a life-threatening situation. Here it concerns their lack of reliance on his power in their ministry.

From this concrete situation Jesus now draws a more universal lesson. Though their faith be as small as a mustard seed, if they use it they can move a mountain—a parabolic saying explained by "nothing will be impossible for you."

The challenge to the disciple's faith touches every area of his life, including his ministry.

## Second Prediction of the Passion (17:22–23)

22 As they were gathering in Galilee, Jesus said to them, "The Son of man is to be delivered into the hands of men, 23and they will kill him, and he will be raised on the third day." And they were greatly distressed.

This second passion prediction is the most skeletal of the three. We miss "the elders, the chief priests and the scribes" mentioned in the first prediction (16:22). We even miss now the active decision of Jesus to *go* to Jerusalem (16:21). Everything is passive, including the play on words, "The Son of *Man* is to be delivered into the hands of *men*." It appears that Jesus will be the victim of "this faithless and perverse generation" (17:17).

The passives, however, reveal the Father's permissive will to which Jesus is totally committed. He will be raised on the third day, but this prophecy does not prevent the disciples from being disheartened. Again, Matthew avoids Mark's "they did not understand" because for Matthew the early disciples *do* understand. They just are depressed by what they understand.

## Freedom and Prudence (17:24–27)

24 When they came to Caperna-um, the collectors of the half-shekel tax went up to Peter and said, "Does not your teacher pay the tax?" [25]He said, "Yes." And when he came home, Jesus spoke to him first, saying, "What do you think, Simon? From whom do kings of the earth take toll or tribute? From their sons or from others?" [26]And when he said, "From others," Jesus said to him, "Then the sons are free. [27]However, not to give offense to them, go to the sea and cast a hook, and take the first fish that comes up, and when you open its mouth you will find a shekel; take that and give it to them for me and for yourself."

This story, which is more a parabolic teaching than the narrative of a miracle, is found only in Matthew. To uncover its meaning, it will be necessary to examine the various historical and literary strata on which it stands. At the time of Jesus, every male Jew 20 years of age or older was required to pay a yearly half-shekel tax for maintaining the sacrifices in the temple. Jews outside Palestine considered this a privileged way of expressing their solidarity with the faith of Palestinian Jews and of atoning for their sins, particularly when it was not possible for them to come to Jerusalem to offer sacrifice in person. When the Romans destroyed Jerusalem and the temple in 70 A.D., Vespasian converted the tax into a Roman one in support of the temple of Jupiter Capitolinus in Rome—a move that was offensive to Jews and Jewish Christians as well. Finally, in the religious vacuum following the loss of the temple, Johanan ben Zakkai received permission from Vespasian to found a school for the study of the Law in Jamnia, southwest of Jerusalem. The Pharisaic Jewish scholars who resided there gradually became the central teaching authority for all Jews of the post-temple era. The study of the law replaced the temple cult, and they taught that repentance and good works could now replace the sacrifices that had atoned for sin in the temple. Eventually, with the emperor's sanction a legal tax was established to support this Jewish Council, and this tax was the true successor of the half-shekel temple tax.

Now think of the historical trajectory of Matthew's gospel. Here he is relating an incident from the life of Jesus prior to the destruction of the temple. Yet the community for which he is writing is now required to pay the Roman tax and is being asked by its fellow Jews whether it will pay the tax for the Jewish leadership in Jamnia. With this setting and these questions, let us look at the text.

The collectors of the temple tax, knowing that Peter is the leader of the disciples, ask him rather than Jesus whether "your [plural] teacher" pays the tax. Without further reflection or even consulting Jesus, Peter as an observant Jew answers yes. But as he enters what is probably his own house in Capernaum, Peter is immediately confronted by Jesus who shows his supernatural knowledge of the situation. "The kings of the earth" is an expression taken from the psalms; here it is meant to contrast with the implied "king of heaven." The central teaching of the passage lies in the words, "The sons are free." That is, both Jesus and the disciples, who belong to the kingdom of the Father, are, strictly speaking, exempt from taxation. Jesus will pay the tax, but for a motive Peter has not thought of: not to give offense. Jesus here enunciates a principle that we will find again in Paul's treatment of table-fellowship in 1 Cor 8:1–13. A Christian may have rights, but peace and charity may at times lead him to refrain from exercising his rights, and such is the case here.

Peter's quaint foray to the sea to find the shekel is a lesson in the kind of trust in the Father's care which Jesus preached in the Sermon on the Mount (6:25–34).

A disputed question is what application Matthew sees in this story for his community, which lives at a time the original temple tax is defunct. Which of the other two taxes does he recommend paying by using this story from Jesus' ministry?

The tax to Rome or the tax to the rabbinate of Jamnia? Or both? The question is not settled, though, if choice must be made, it seems more likely that Matthew would be thinking of the tax paid to the Jamnia council, who were, after all, fellow Jews, than to pagan Rome. It was not a matter of doctrine but one of practice. Christians of all ages have had at times to face a similar question: when do you stand up for a matter of principle, and when do you go along with a situation you don't agree with but is not worth sacrificing civil peace to challenge?

Finally, the role of Peter in this story is surprising. He is, of course, the spokesperson for the other disciples. But more than that, he and Jesus seem to have a particularly close relationship. The dialogue takes place in Peter's house, and the one coin pays for both Jesus and Peter (one might ask who paid for the other disciples). This role of Peter fits with the prominence given him throughout Matthew's gospel, particularly in this ecclesiastical section. It also explains, perhaps, why the other disciples will now ask Jesus about ranks in the kingdom.

## *DISCOURSE:* THE SHEPHERDING COMMUNITY
## (18:1–35)

We now come to what is perhaps the most tightly and ingeniously organized section of this gospel, the Community Discourse. Matthew has gathered scattered sayings of Jesus from the tradition and woven them together in a symmetrical pattern of teaching on relationships of Christians with one another in community. Early in the Sermon on the Mount Jesus had held up to his disciples their vocation to be the salt of the earth and the light of the world. He then told them very concretely what they would have to do in order to fulfill that vocation of witnessing to the world, represented by the crowds. Now, as Jesus has withdrawn from the crowds and focused on forming his disciples more intensely, he instructs them privately on how they should behave toward one another. The Essenes at Qumran had a community rule. It is much more extensive and complex than this short chapter of Matthew, but there are some striking similarities as well as important differences. The point to be retained is that here we have the first Rule of Life of a Christian community, built upon Jesus' word. In its simplicity it should be the foundation of all other Christian rules or constitutions or groups that strive follow Jesus. There is rich teaching here for all Christian families, parishes and communities.

## Conversion Unlimited (18:1-4)

18 AT THAT time the disciples came to Jesus, saying, "Who is the greatest in the kingdom of heaven?" ²And calling to him a child, he put him in the midst of them, ³and said, "Truly, I say to you, unless you turn and become like children, you will never enter the kingdom of heaven. ⁴Whoever humbles himself like this child, he is the greatest in the kingdom of heaven.

This first and foundational article of Jesus' rule of life has to do with conversion. Asked by the disciples as a group this time (there being no designated spokesperson) who is the greatest in the kingdom of heaven, Jesus responds first by an action. He calls a child, contrasting the "little one" with the disciples' dream of being "the biggest." Then he tells them that unless they convert and become like children, not only will they not be greatest, but they will not even get into the kingdom.

The conversion of which Jesus speaks here is not the conversion preached by John the Baptist as an entry requirement for the kingdom. That was a moral conversion from sin, and Jesus presumes his disciples have gone through such a conversion. The conversion here is to spiritual childhood, and that is quite another thing. Children have many defects: they speak out of turn, they break things, they get into the cookie jar when they aren't supposed to, they are in constant need of correction. But there is one thing a child will ordinarily do that adults often will not. If you give the child a gift, he will take it. The Pharisees have been self-conscious adults, calculating defenders of the status quo. They were very righteous, and in terms of external conformity to the law were blameless. But they were unable to accept the new gift Jesus has offered. To accept that gift would have meant a new way of relating with God and a new way of relating with their fellow human beings. To know God as "Abba" one must be a child, and that would also mean entering into a barrier-free community with all God's other children. That takes a conversion more profound than turning away from sin. It means to accept a new way of imaging God, self and others. It is the foundational principle of the community Jesus established. It is not sufficient to be "good." One must be filial and fraternal. "Whoever does not receive the kingdom of God like a child shall not enter it" (Mk 10:15).

But this is also the process of a lifetime, and in the context here, it is clear that Christian community can be built only if there is a constant ongoing conversion, a willingness to change on the part of all ("Unless you change . . ."). Have you ever tried to hold a discussion in which one or both parties were not listening, that is, not open to be changed by the encounter? Spiritual childhood means a willingness to learn, a willingness to grow together. That makes true greatness in the kingdom.

## Concern for Others (18:5–7)

5 "Whoever receives one such child in my name receives me; [6]but whoever causes one of these little ones who believe in me to sin, it would be better for him to have a great millstone fastened round his neck and to be drowned in the depth of the sea.

7 "Woe to the world for temptations to sin! For it is necessary that temptations come, but woe to the man by whom the temptation comes!

If the disciple is to consider himself a child, he must consider the other to be the same. It may be threatening to welcome an adult, but who fears welcoming a child? Jesus welcomed each of his disciples in this way and in so doing gave each of them the freedom to shed their masks and pretenses. Judas abused that freedom, but Jesus did not make that possible refusal an excuse for not welcoming him. Similarly, the disciple makes himself vulnerable in welcoming the other, but the community of Jesus can be made in no other way, and the freedom experienced by those who do respond to the welcome is worth risking the pain from the few who do not.

"Child" here stands for any other disciple, whatever their chronological age. To welcome the other is to welcome Jesus himself. Thus within the community the disciples have a constant training ground for the kind of effective love Jesus will describe in the last judgment scene: "Whatever you did to one of these, my least brethren, you did to me" (25:40).

Like the word "child," "little one" now denotes any member of the Christian community. From the positive attitude of "welcoming," Jesus' instruction now turns to those who are a source of spiritual downfall to others in the community. The millstone to which Jesus refers is probably the type of enormous basalt stone animals were used to turn. "Temptations to sin" (RSV, v. 7) is literally "scandals." Today scandal merely suggests something that is shocking. The original meaning however was "stumbling block," something one would put in the path of another to make him fall. Hardly could Jesus have been more graphic in his condemnation of those who lead others into sin.

## Purification of the Community (18:8–9)

⁸And if your hand or your foot causes you to sin, cut it off and throw it away; it is better for you to enter life maimed or lame than with two hands or two feet to be thrown into the eternal fire. ⁹And if your eye causes you to sin, pluck it out and throw it away; it is better for you to enter life with one eye than with two eyes to be thrown into the hell of fire.

In Mark this dramatic saying of Jesus refers to the urgency of avoiding personal occasions of sin. Matthew, however, appropriates it for his discussion of community and understands "hand" or "foot" or "eye" to refer to a gangrenous member of the community that must be excised to save the life of the whole organism. It is clear that this saying of Jesus is being used to legitimate excommunication, as becomes clear from the corresponding passage in verses 15–18 examined below.

## Care for the Little Ones (18:10)

10 "See that you do not despise one of these little ones;
for I tell you that in heaven their angels always behold the
face of my Father who is in heaven.

This verse could be considered the conclusion of the preceding warning about scandal. But it merits standing alone because it urges upon all members of the community the importance of pastoral care for others and with v. 14 frames the
shepherd parable with an affirmation of how precious the "little
ones" are to the Father. Here that preciousness is shown in an
oblique way through the guardian angels. Since the rabbis held
that only the highest rank of angels beheld God's face, Jesus
is saying that if the disciples are cared for by the highest angels
in heaven, then they should be cared for with highest concern
by members of the community on earth. The community is the
earthly guardian of each of its members.

Verse 11 is missing from most translations, since it is missing from many of the better Greek manuscripts and was no
doubt imported by a scribe from Lk 19:10: "For the Son of Man
came to save the lost."

## The Shepherd (18:12–13)

¹²What do you think? If a man has a hundred sheep, and one
of them has gone astray, does he not leave the ninety-nine
on the mountains and go in search of the one that went
astray? ¹³And if he finds it, truly, I say to you, he rejoices
over it more than over the ninety-nine that never went
astray.

In Luke Jesus relates this parable to justify his going out
to the sinners and outcasts of his day. By inserting the parable
here in the community discourse Matthew is giving it a new
twist. The attitude of the shepherd must be that of the whole
community. The one sheep is not *lost* (as in Luke) but *straying*
because it is, hopefully, merely in a temporary limbo awaiting

reintegration. The community must not look on its weak and straying members with passive regret but must take an active initiative to reclaim them, like the shepherd who leaves the ninety-nine in search of the stray.

This beautiful parable occupies the keystone position in the symmetrical arch of this chapter. It sheds its interpretative light on those passages that are rigorous about standards of membership and on those that counsel prayer, intervention and reconciliation. Like the church of the catacombs which chose to have this scene dominate so many of its walls, the community of Jesus gathers under the good shepherd who constantly reminds them that they must now exercise his own shepherding of the little ones and the straying. They must be the shepherding community.

## Care for the Little Ones (18:14)

[14]So it is not the will of my Father who is in heaven that one of these little ones should perish.

Like verse 10, which it matches to frame the shepherd image, this verse comes neither from Mark nor Q but from Matthew's own source. The Father's will, for which the disciples have learned to pray (6:10), is that none of the little ones, some of whom are straying, should perish. Thus the shepherd, whether this be Jesus or the community which continues his mission, is a missionary of the Father's love.

## Purification of the Community (18:15–18)

15 "If your brother sins against you, go and tell him his fault, between you and him alone. If he listens to you, you have gained your brother. [16]But if he does not listen, take one or two others along with you, that every word may be confirmed by the evidence of two or three witnesses. [17]If he refuses to listen to them, tell it to the church; and if he refuses to listen even to the church, let him be to you as a

Gentile and a tax collector. [18]Truly, I say to you, whatever
you bind on earth shall be bound in heaven, and whatever
you loose on earth shall be loosed in heaven.

The term "brother" now replaces "child" and "little one."
It refers not to a blood brother and even less to relationships
with outsiders but envisages rather other disciples of the covenant community. The words "against you," which appear in
some translations of v. 15 (RSV, TEV, NABR in brackets) are
missing from important Greek manuscripts and may well have
been introduced by a scribe from v. 21. They are omitted by
JB, correctly we believe, because what appears to be at issue
here, unlike Peter's problem in v. 21, is a sin against the community as such. The brother who has sinned is not, or at least
is not yet, the kind of corruptive influence envisaged in the
excommunication passage above (vv. 8–9). He is at this point
a "backslider," one who because of weakness has failed to live
up to the new ethic demanded by Jesus. By the second generation of disciples such problems were not uncommon in the
community, and Christians sought guidance for how to deal
with them in the words of Jesus.

The procedure is amazing in its concreteness and simplicity. The first step is to approach the failing brother or sister
one-to-one. One of the most difficult things to do! How much
easier to find a sympathetic soul upon whom to unburden one's
grievance, or worse, to air it at once before the whole community; or even worse to take one's grievance to outsiders! It
takes courage to approach the brother or sister personally, and
it also takes wisdom to know how. But whether out of cow-
ardice or fear of rejection or passing the responsibility to someone else, how often this simple and direct method is avoided!
On the other hand, how rewarding can be the success of the
direct approach: reconciliation with the brother or sister: "If
he listens to you, you have won back your brother." The ambiguous support of others enlisted in our "righteous" cause cannot match the joy of fraternal reunion.

But it is possible that the other will not listen. In that case,
confrontation by a small group of fellow-disciples is called for.
Matthew, the scribe initiated into the kingdom, recalls the leg-

islation of Deut 19:15: "Only on the evidence of two witnesses, or of three witnesses, shall a charge be sustained."

Finally, realism must admit it is possible for the recalcitrant disciple not even to listen to the community ("the church"). In that case the verdict is exclusion: "Let him be to you as a Gentile or a tax collector." This may appear like a severity not at all in keeping with the mercy of Jesus, and indeed if it is a formulation arrived at in the early days when the community was exclusively Jewish, it may well have been. But if we recall how Jesus relates to gentiles and tax collectors throughout Matthew's gospel, it is obvious he relates to them as *persons to be evangelized.* The conclusion then is this: The one who refuses the authority of the community, an authority behind which Jesus stands (10:40; 16:19; 18:18; 28:18–20), can only be choosing to relate to the community as an outsider, and the community has no choice but to relate reciprocally, and the point comes, after due process, when this situation must be acknowledged openly. But that does not mean the community consigns the person as hopelessly lost. If the person is no longer open to the direct invitation to return, as presumably the straying member of v. 12–13 is, there is still hope, and that hope lies in the intercession of the community, as the next verses show.

## Prayer for Others (18:19–20)

[19]Again I say to you, if two of you agree on earth about anything they ask, it will be done for them by my Father in heaven. [20]For where two or three are gathered in my name, there am I in the midst of them."

These two verses are proper to Matthew. If Jesus has just assured the community that his full authority stands behind the decisions of the community regarding its membership (v. 18), that is not the only nor even the preferred way that Jesus shows his power, nor the community theirs. There is another way to deal with those who reject the community: intercession. If Jesus is with the community in its authoritative decisions, he is also with it when it prays in his name—and even more so, as the introduction, "Again I say to you," suggests. The intercession here is not private prayer; it is shared prayer, communal prayer. And it assumes an agreement of mind and heart in the persons who come together to pray. In Jewish tradition, the divine presence was represented by the *shekinah*, the cloud of glory that hovered over the meeting tent in the desert and later over the Ark in the temple. The rabbis so prized the study of the law that they held that where two persons gathered to study it, "the *shekinah* is between them" (*Aboth*, 3:2). For Matthew, when two or more disciples come together and agree in Jesus' name, *he* is the *shekinah*, the divine presence, between them. Here again is the theme that is the backbone of Matthew's gospel. Jesus is Emmanuel, our companion God.

## Forgiveness Unlimited (18:21–35)

21 Then Peter came up and said to him, "Lord, how often shall my brother sin against me, and I forgive him? As many as seven times?" ²²Jesus said to him, "I do not say to you seven times, but seventy times seven.

23 "Therefore the kingdom of heaven may be compared to a king who wished to settle accounts with his servants. ²⁴When he began the reckoning, one was brought to him who owed him ten thousand talents; ²⁵and as he could not pay, his lord ordered him to be sold, with his wife and children and all that he had, and payment to be made. ²⁶So the servant fell on his knees, imploring him, 'Lord, have patience with me, and I will pay you everything.' ²⁷And out of pity for him the lord of that servant released him and forgave him the debt. ²⁸But that same servant, as he went out, came upon one of his fellow servants who owed him a hundred denarii; and seizing him by the throat he said, 'Pay what you owe.' ²⁹So his fellow servant fell down and besought him, 'Have patience with me, and I will pay you.' ³⁰He refused and went and put him in prison till he should pay the debt. ³¹When his fellow servants saw what had taken place, they were greatly distressed, and they went and reported to their lord all that had taken place. ³²Then

his lord summoned him and said to him, 'You wicked servant! I forgave you all that debt because you besought me; [33]and should not you have had mercy on your fellow servant, as I had mercy on you?' [34]And in anger his lord delivered him to the jailers, till he should pay all his debt. [35]So also my heavenly Father will do to every one of you, if you do not forgive your brother from your heart."

We have seen repeatedly how forgiveness is radically central to the teaching of Jesus in Matthew. It is one of the three "we" petitions of the Lord's prayer (6:12), the only one meriting a commentary (6:14–15). And brother must be reconciled with brother before presenting a gift acceptable to the Lord (6:23–25). The love of enemies is presumed (5:43–48), but sometimes it is more difficult to forgive those closest to us, because unlike the outsiders who might be excused for their ignorance or insensitivity, the brother "should know better." Those who can hurt us the most and those it is easiest to hate are those to whom we have somehow been covenanted in love. Not without reason, then, does Matthew save this teaching on forgiveness as the climax of the chapter. What is at issue here is not forgiveness in general, but Jesus' demand that it be *unlimited*.

That it is a matter of a personal offense and not some general offense against the community appears now in Peter's question, "How often shall my brother sin *against me*?" Peter, aware that he must forgive, implies that there is a limit to forgiveness, but he is willing to be exceedingly generous and thus presents to Jesus the perfect biblical number, expecting no doubt a commendation like the "Blessed are you, Simon . . ." of 16:17. In fact, seven times is all that is expected in the parallel saying of Jesus in Lk 17:4. Peter is surprised—and so are we!—by Jesus' response: not seven but seventy times seven.

Jesus here echoes the story of Lamech in Gen 4:23–24. According to the portrait in Genesis, when man and woman in the garden turned against God, one of the effects of their sin was to turn in some way against each other, Adam casting blame on Eve, and Eve passing the responsibility on to the serpent. This situation of alienation deteriorates when Cain kills his brother Abel. Then the situation of sinful humankind deteriorates even more with Lamech:

> Lamech said to his wives [plurality of wives a further sign of deterioration from the original ideal of monogamy]: "Adah and Zillah, hear my voice; you wives of Lamech, hearken to what I say: I have slain a man for wounding me, a young man for striking me. If Cain is avenged sevenfold, truly Lamech seventy-sevenfold."

Escalation of revenge has been the program of sinful humankind ever since. Jesus reverses this principle: unlimited revenge is to give way to unlimited forgiveness. And community cannot be built on a limitation of forgiveness any more than it can be built on a limitation of love. Experience shows that one cannot live very long in community with another or others without misunderstandings and hurts, and if there is no commitment to resolve differences and forgive hurts, the community will self-destruct. And that commitment cannot be fenced with conditions and limitations if it is to reflect the mind and the heart of Jesus.

Jesus now proceeds with a parable which we find only in Matthew. Commentary on this magnificent story would almost be like ruining a joke by explaining it. Still, a few short comments may be helpful. "Ten thousand talents" in the economy of the times was an astronomical figure to which our only comparison would be the national debt. The solution to such a situation was to be sold with one's family into slavery, the proceeds going *towards* payment of the debt. The servant does what every pressed debtor does: he does not ask to be released from the debt but "just give me time." The absurdity of the parable is that the king, in a moment of compassion, does not give him time at all. He forgives the entire debt. There will be no burden of either time or slavery. The freed debtor then refuses to release a fellow servant of a small amount (a denarius was a day's wages). He even seizes his debtor by the throat and demands payment. When the debtor repeats the same plea for time, the creditor-servant has him thrown in jail—a magnificent figure for resentment which keeps the offender in bondage until he pays for what he has done. But in so doing the unforgiver finds himself in bondage, as his lord in anger hands *him* over to the jailers to be tortured (the Greek word translated "jailers" by the RSV really means "torturers"). And the story concludes with the one really strident description of the otherwise merciful Father of Jesus: That is exactly what my heavenly Father will do to each of you, if you do not forgive your brother from your heart.

The point is clear: the disciple has received from the Father the forgiveness of an unpayable debt. Forgiveness of others is simply the naturally expected behavior of one who has been forgiven all. If, on the other hand, the disciple refuses to forgive the other, he will lose the forgiveness he has already received and find himself in a worse state than before, for it adds to unforgiveness the sin of a blasphemous ingratitude to God.

And the forgiveness must not be in words only. It must come from the heart. If my own experience is a common one, I know that it may take time to *feel* the forgiveness I have given outwardly. I remember once being offended by a brother in my community. It was not a small matter; I felt quite hurt by what he did. Eventually he did ask my forgiveness, and I assured him I forgave him. But the words that came out of my mouth were formal. It was an act of the will at that moment, because I did not feel in my heart the forgiveness that was on my tongue. It was almost a year later when somehow I realized the sin of my own self-righteousness toward him and, confessing it, found myself one in heart with him in the common embrace of the Father's forgiveness.

The only way then, to be able to forgive without limits, as Jesus expects, is to live in the grateful awareness of the Father's infinite love and forgiveness already received.

## Conclusion: The Arch

We are now in a position to draw some conclusions about Matthew's theology of Christian community from the overall arrangement of this chapter. While the symmetrical pattern

*Companion God*

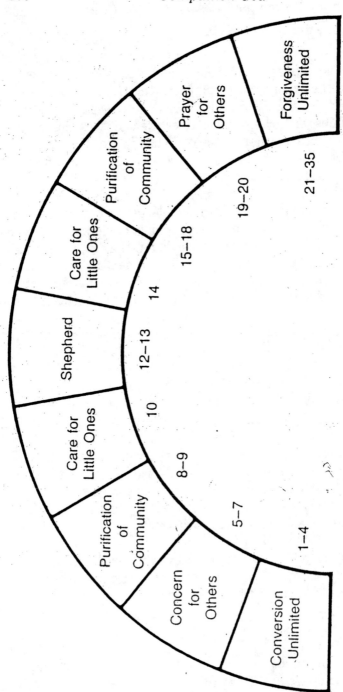

The Shepherding Community
Matthew 18

may not be the pattern Matthew had in mind for his entire gospel, a definite symmetrical pattern can be discerned in this chapter, and it is instructive beyond the teaching of its individual parts. It will help at this point to glance at the graphic on page 206.

There are two foundation stones for any Christian community. The first, represented on the left side of the arch, is *conversion*, that is, a willingness to be changed daily, to become more and more like a little child before the Father and before our brothers and sisters in community. This is not a childishness, but the mature stance of one who realizes that all is gift, that the Father loves and cares, and that one belongs to a family created by the Father's love and Jesus' gift of himself for all (1–4).

But one cannot live long in a community of committed relationships without hurting others and being hurt, even if one has the best intentions. And thus the second foundation stone (on the opposite side of the arch) is *forgiveness*, a forgiveness that does not keep a record of failures or previous pardons but is always willing to start over and create anew (21–35).

Then there must be openness to welcome the other as one would a child and a genuine care not to be a source of sin in the community (5–7), a love that, in the case of those alienated from the community, is translated into intercessory prayer (19–20). But this love is not what has been called "sloppy *agape*." It is tough love, for the community has been called into being by the word of Jesus, and that word is demanding. There are standards of membership, and excommunication is possible and may at times be necessary (8–9). But this should only be a last resort. Normally, if brothers and sisters follow the Lord's directive and process their grievances with each other, beginning with one-to-one, face-to-face encounters, they will overcome their difficulties and experience the joy that comes when brothers and sisters grow together in the Lord (15–18). The care such members should have for each other is illustrated by the fact that the guardian angel of each disciple faces both the Father and the disciple he is guarding, and on earth the community that knows the Father should show the same respect and care for each member, in particular for those who are straying and in danger of being lost (10,14).

But where do the disciples get the power to achieve this impossible dream, the shepherding community? Daily conversion, unlimited forgiveness, fraternal correction—who has the strength to persevere in this ideal, or even to undertake it? The only way this arch can hold together is by the keystone which is Jesus himself, the good shepherd, who has done for each member of the community what the shepherd of the parable has done for the lost sheep. Lost, separated, away from the community of God's love, the disciple knows the shepherd left the ninety-nine to bring him back. This rescue, this forgiveness, this love is what the disciples must now as a community share because they have received it and continue to receive it from the Source. The sheep must now become the shepherd.

An arch is held together by tension. There is tension in this arch between standards of membership on the one hand and compassion, outreach and forgiveness on the other. In his exquisite handling of the tensions in his community, Matthew models the pastoral balance needed in every age of the church. ■

*Book Five:*

======================

# Collision Course and the Final Times (19:1–25:46)

*STORY:* MINISTRY IN JUDEA AND JERUSALEM
## (19:1–22:46)

We begin here the last of the five books into which Matthew has gathered the public ministry of Jesus. Though we classify chapters 19–22 as narrative, much of it is teaching because Matthew is limited in his organization of the Judean material by his decision to follow Mark, who was less concerned about separating narrative and teaching. These chapters have two principal themes—the requirements of discipleship, with application to various states of life, and Jesus' victory in debates with his enemies.

*Departure to Judea; Divorce and Celibacy (19:1–12)*

19 NOW WHEN Jesus had finished these sayings, he went away from Galilee and entered the region of Judea beyond the Jordan; ²and large crowds followed him, and he healed them there.

3 And Pharisees came up to him and tested him by asking, "Is it lawful to divorce one's wife for any cause?" ⁴He answered, "Have you not read that he who made them from the beginning made them male and female, ⁵and said, 'For this reason a man shall leave his father and mother and be joined to his wife, and the two shall become one flesh'? ⁶So they are no longer two but one flesh. What therefore God has joined together, let not man put asunder." ⁷They said to him, "Why then did Moses command one to give a certificate of divorce, and to put her away?" ⁸He said to them, "For your hardness of heart Moses allowed you to divorce

your wives, but from the beginning it was not so. ⁹And I say
to you: whoever divorces his wife, except for unchastity,
and marries another, commits adultery."

10 The disciples said to him, "If such is the case of a
man with his wife, it is not expedient to marry." ¹¹But he
said to them, "Not all men can receive this saying, but only
those to whom it is given. ¹²For there are eunuchs who have
been so from birth, and there are eunuchs who have been
made eunuchs by men, and there are eunuchs who have
made themselves eunuchs for the sake of the kingdom of
heaven. He who is able to receive this, let him receive it."

The Galilean ministry is finished. Jesus leaves for Judea,
perhaps at the approach of Passover. The crowds continue to
follow him, and he heals them. Again Matthew has substituted
healing for Mark's "teaching." This is a legitimate transfer, for
in Mark Jesus teaches also through his healing power (Mk 1:21–
28). But Matthew is consistent with his previous picture of
Jesus after 13:36. The crowds are now open to hear only the
language of healing.

In Jesus' day there was a debate between the schools of
Shammai and Hillel on what grounds were sufficient for divorce, Shammai holding that only adultery permitted it, while
Hillel allowed it for any motive whatever. Jesus is not being
asked to take sides in this debate, because that would hardly
be the trap which Matthew assures us was hidden in this question. The Pharisees are trying to catch Jesus on the more fundamental issue of the authority of the law itself. Jesus sends
them back to the creator's plan in Genesis, affirming that monogamy is made by God, and if one chooses to divorce, he is
breaking up a divinely-established unity. (Note that Matthew
reflects the Jewish tradition of the times, according to which
only the man could initiate divorce. Mark 10:12 envisages the
Roman practice which recognizes a woman's right to do so.)
But the Pharisees have a retort from the law itself: Deut 24:1–
4, to protect the woman's rights, commanded the husband to
give a written bill of divorce, thus declaring her free to marry
any man who would take her.

Jesus' response implies that in the Old Law there were degrees of authority and that the law of Deuteronomy was a relaxation of the original divine mandate of monogamy "because of *your* hardness of heart." The retort is aimed at the Pharisees listening, whether they followed the liberal Hillel or the conservative Shammai. That *your* also separates the Pharisaic interpretation from that to be followed by Jesus' disciples. The meaning of the clause "except for unchastity" is the same as in 5:32, more correctly rendered by the NABR, "unless the marriage is unlawful." See our commentary on 5:32. Converts living with a partner within the forbidden degree of kinship could not appeal to this teaching of Jesus to perpetuate their irregular affair.

The Pharisees disappear from the scene, and the disciples express their amazement: "Then it is better not to marry." The next line (v. 11) could refer to the monogamy teaching just given or to the celibacy saying that follows. If it refers to the preceding prohition of divorce, it would mean that not everyone can accept that demand of Jesus. This is certainly less likely, for Jesus' statement about divorce is so categoric it would hardly allow for monogamy being a "special grace," whereas he expressly says celibacy for the kingdom is, in almost the same words, at the end of v. 12. Hence this saying (*logos*, which does not mean command but only "word") supports the call to celibacy "for the sake of the kingdom of heaven."

Celibacy for the kingdom is clearly a matter of initiative and free choice (they have "made themselves eunuchs"). For this reason most commentators think the passage does not refer to the state of the innocent party who remains celibate after being divorced by the other—although this interpretation is not clearly excluded. Nevertheless, the choice of this state is a special gift ("let him receive it who can"). The translation "for the sake of" suggests "with a view to"—i.e., marriage is given up in order to be more ready for the coming kingdom (with the idea that it is imminent, which we find in 1 Cor 7:26–35) or to be more available to work for it. But the Greek *dia* more ordinarily means "because of," and if that is to be preferred here, it suggests that the disciple has so experienced the kingdom already in his life that he wishes to remain single in order not to be distracted from it (a view also found in 1 Cor 7:35).

### Children in the Kingdom (19:13–15)

13 Then children were brought to him that he might lay his hands on them and pray. The disciples rebuked the people; ¹⁴but Jesus said, "Let the children come to me, and do not hinder them; for to such belongs the kingdom of heaven." ¹⁵And he laid his hands on them and went away.

This is the one scene in the gospels where petitioners come to Jesus for nothing more than a blessing. Children are dependent, and infant mortality was high in ancient times. A parent too thinks of the child's future and hopes it will be bright. Thus the elders bring children to Jesus that he might lay hands on them and *pray* (Matthew's addition to Mark). But the disciples think Jesus has more important things to do than to waste time with children. They have forgotten the teaching of 18:1–5. Jesus had invited all the burdened to come to him (11:28). Now he invites those who as yet have no adult burdens but typify those who can receive the kingdom as a gift and trust totally in the care of the Father.

Some scholars have proposed that this story was kept in the early church because it helped resolve the question of infant baptism. Some of the language, especially the word *hinder* was common in early baptismal liturgies and figures in Jesus' own baptism (3:14). The argument is plausible but not certain.

### The Rich and Salvation (19:16–26)

16 And behold, one came up to him, saying, "Teacher, what good deed must I do, to have eternal life?" ¹⁷And he said to him, "Why do you ask me about what is good? One there is who is good. If you would enter life, keep the commandments." ¹⁸He said to him, "Which?" And Jesus

said, "You shall not kill, You shall not commit adultery, You shall not steal, You shall not bear false witness, [19]Honor your father and mother, and, You shall love your neighbor as yourself." [20]The young man said to him, "All these I have observed; what do I still lack?" [21]Jesus said to him, "If you would be perfect, go, sell what you possess and give to the poor, and you will have treasure in heaven; and come, follow me." [22]When the young man heard this he went away sorrowful; for he had great possessions.

23 And Jesus said to his disciples, "Truly, I say to you, it will be hard for a rich man to enter the kingdom of heaven. [24]Again I tell you, it is easier for a camel to go through the eye of a needle than for a rich man to enter the kingdom of God." [25]When the disciples heard this they were greatly astonished, saying, "Who then can be saved?" [26]But Jesus looked at them and said to them, "With men this is impossible, but with God all things are possible."

In Mark and Luke the man who comes to Jesus addresses him as "Good Teacher." Matthew moves the word "good" to the deed to be done, so that the man addresses Jesus merely as "teacher," Matthew's signpost of inadequate dispositions. The petitioner is looking for some specific good deed he must do. Matthew will not allow Jesus to say, "Why do you call me good?" (Mk 10:18) but instead, "Why do you ask me about *what* is *good?*" Whether the "one who is good" is God himself or whether the "one good" is the law (a disputed point among scholars), Jesus, in this question-and-answer session, directs the young man away from any grandiose project and to the heart of the OT, the commandments. That the questioner should ask *which* commandments is likewise not in his favor, but, in listing the second part of the decalogue, Jesus has the opportunity to add what we don't find in Mark: "You shall love your neighbor as yourself," Jesus' summary of the entire law. The young man responds that he has kept all these, including the all-encompassing love of neighbor. But he is still not satisfied. "What do I still lack? Should I become a Pharisee? Should I join the monastery at Qumran? Is there a different life-style I should embrace?"

"If you would be perfect . . ." Jesus replies. This text has been used in the past, in the Catholic Church at least, to promote a two-tiered class of Christians—those who follow the commandments (the "laity") and those who in addition follow the counsels (religious). And it is easy to see how such an interpretation could come about. After all, the young man is invited to give up his possessions, perhaps even the hope of wife and family, to undertake the itinerant life-style of Jesus. But the original text suggests something else. First of all, the young man who keeps the commandments is a Jew who has not yet come to faith in Jesus. Then in the Bible and in the contemporary documents of Qumran, "good" and "perfect" are interchangeable terms, and that would suggest that to do the good (v. 16), to enter life (v. 17) and to be perfect (v. 20) might all have to do with the same reality. And v. 25 indicates that Jesus is talking about the surrendering of riches as a means of salvation.

In the light of Matthew's particular pastoral situation, the best understanding of the passage is this: Among Jesus' contemporaries and even among contemporaries of the second and third generation disciples, there were good Jews, particularly among the Pharisees, who kept the law integrally and who were even outstanding in their love of neighbor. They could say, with the young man, "All these I have observed." But they felt that was enough. They were satisfied with their own spiritual performance. Perhaps, impressed with Jesus as an outstanding *teacher* (v. 16), they were even attracted to him. But they could not bring themselves to make a commitment to him. The law was enough. Jesus was too much, because Jesus asked more than the law. He asked a personal commitment to himself. And in practice what distinguished Jesus' life style from that of even good Jews was his attitude toward wealth. Many good Jews considered wealth a sign of God's blessing and a confirmation of their righteousness in observing the law. Whatever else they liked about Jesus, the stone of stumbling for them was the demand he made on their pocketbook. The decisive question was not doctrinal but economic. Though Jesus did not ask all those who believed in him to follow him in the itinerant discipleship (Zacchaeus, for example, Lk 19:1–10), the itinerant

disciples who embodied Jesus' ideal life-style were surely an
irritant to the pious-wealthy Jews because they were a goad
constantly reminding them of what Jesus thought of mammon.

Thus when Jesus invited the wealthy young man he was
pushing to its logical conclusions the contrast already lurking
in the superficial attraction of this young man to Jesus. Will
you accept me—*and my life-style?*

It was too much to ask, and the young man went away
sad—quite a contrast to the man who joyfully sold all he had
to get the treasure of the kingdom (13:44).

In Matthew's day the scene was repeated, the only difference being that the Jew who wished to become a Christian
could not have the option of becoming a private, closet Christian while outwardly being a pious, wealthy, observant, re-
spected Jew. To be "perfect," that is, to have that completion
necessary to enter the life of the kingdom, he would have not
only to accept Jesus in his heart but to join that community of
disciples who, because they were ostracized and persecuted
even economically, probably looked little different from the
early disciples who tramped around Galilee and Judea with Jesus.

That is why salvation is not easy, particularly for those
attached to their wealth. Jesus' hyperbole about the camel and
the needle is serious. Isolating wealth may be the one thing
that blocks access to Jesus, and with him to eternal life.

Christians who read this passage today are challenged by
it to ask themselves: (1) Is my faith primarily an ethic or a
person? and (2) Do I allow my life-style to block me from entering into real community with my fellow Christians, or is my
independence, padded by my possessions, dearer to me than
*community* with Jesus?

### The Joy of the Disciples (19:27–30)

[27]Then Peter said in reply, "Lo, we have left everything and
followed you. What then shall we have?" [28]Jesus said to
them, "Truly, I say to you, in the new world, when the Son
of man shall sit on his glorious throne, you who have followed me will also sit on twelve thrones, judging the twelve

tribes of Israel. ²⁹And every one who has left houses or brothers or sisters or father or mother or children or lands, for my name's sake, will receive a hundredfold, and inherit eternal life. ³⁰But many that are first will be last, and the last first.

Through Peter's question, Matthew's eye now turns to that primitive group of disciples, representative of his own community, who are living the cost of discipleship. "What reward may we expect?" Before repeating the answer given in Mark, which concerns all the disciples, Matthew inserts a saying from the Q source which applies to the twelve. In the remaking of all things ("the new world" RSV, "the new age," NABR), they will share Jesus' glorious rule and "judge the twelve tribes of Israel." That can mean either that they will rule over the new Israel which is the church, or it may mean that they will, with Jesus, "judge" the old Israel for its unbelief.

Then Jesus' answer turns to all the disciples, "every one." The promise of the hundredfold in Mark is to be clearly realized "now in this time" (Mk 10:30), but by dropping this phrase, Matthew leaves the present reward ambiguous in favor of the certainty of its fulfillment in the eternal life.

The "first" in this life, i.e., the wealthy and powerful, will be last in the next, and the poor, persecuted followers of Jesus, the "world's rejects" (1 Cor 1:28), will be first in the kingdom, possessing what the rich young man wanted but could not sacrifice to attain. This concluding line about first and last provides the transition to the next parable.

## The Vineyard Workers (20:1–16)

20 "FOR THE kingdom of heaven is like a householder who went out early in the morning to hire laborers for his vineyard. ²After agreeing with the laborers for a denarius a day, he sent them into his vineyard. ³And going out about the third hour he saw others standing idle in the market place; ⁴and to them he said, 'You go into the vineyard too, and whatever is right I will give you.' So they went. ⁵Going out again about the sixth hour and the ninth

hour, he did the same. ⁶And about the eleventh hour he went out and found others standing; and he said to them, 'Why do you stand here idle all day?' ⁷They said to him, 'Because no one has hired us.' He said to them, 'You go into the vineyard too.' ⁸And when evening came, the owner of the vineyard said to his steward, 'Call the laborers and pay them their wages, beginning with the last, up to the first.' ⁹And when those hired about the eleventh hour came, each of them received a denarius. ¹⁰Now when the first came, they thought they would receive more; but each of them also received a denarius. ¹¹And on receiving it they grumbled at the householder, ¹²saying, 'These last worked only one hour, and you have made them equal to us who have borne the burden of the day and the scorching heat.' ¹³But he replied to one of them, 'Friend, I am doing you no wrong; did you not agree with me for a denarius? ¹⁴Take what belongs to you, and go; I choose to give to this last as I give to you. ¹⁵Am I not allowed to do what I choose with what belongs to me? Or do you begrudge my generosity?' ¹⁶So the last will be first, and the first last."

The problem with interpreting this challenging parable comes from our uncertainty as to which setting is primary here—that of Jesus' historical ministry, that of Matthew's developing community, or the final message of the evangelist. Except for the concluding line about "last" and "first," which occurs in all three synoptics (Mk 10:31; Lk 13:30), the parable appears only in Matthew. It is not an allegory, in which each element carries a symbolic meaning, nor is it a moral teaching on employment practices. The point lies in v. 15: "Do you begrudge my generosity?" or, in the NABR, "Are you envious because I am generous?"

During Jesus' public ministry, the righteous Pharisees were scandalized at Jesus' welcoming sinners and dining with them (9:11). Far from proving their righteousness by works and practices, as did the Pharisees, these common people ignored the law, violated it knowingly or unknowingly—and here is this so called "man of God" claiming that these people will get into the kingdom first (21:31)! This parable, like the three in Luke

15, could well have been addressed to the Pharisees and other observant Jews as a defense of Jesus' ministry, which is to reveal God's *saving* justice ("whatever is *just* I will give you," v. 4, and "I am doing you no *injustice*," v. 13) which is generous beyond human calculations. Instead of being envious of the attention Jesus was giving to sinners, the Pharisees should have rejoiced.

However, in Matthew this parable is not addressed to the Pharisees nor to the crowds but to the *disciples*, that is, to Christians, and in this setting it could have three possible meanings:

1) Addressed to the Jewish Christians who are uncomfortable or even opposed to the influx of gentiles into the community, it is a warning not to be envious of the late-comers, whom the Lord himself has called. Such envy could only betray that the labor done for the Lord in their earlier life under the law, or even their observance of the law now, was grudgingly done and looked to the reward as a strict payment in justice. Acts tells us that among the early Jewish converts were not only a large number of priests (Acts 6:7) but also Pharisees who continued to observe the Jewish law and even sought to impose it on gentile converts (Acts 15:5). Such converts would have been prime targets for Matthew's reuse of this parable.

2) The main characters, however, are *laborers* in the vineyard (a symbol of God's people), and as such they could represent Christian ministers, some of whom appear to receive more honor than others. In Mt 18:1 and shortly in 20:20–28 we see that this was indeed a problem among the early disciples. With Jesus, seniority has no claims on choice for ministry.

3) A more generalized interpretation would also fit the context. The parable concludes by the same saying used to conclude the preceding teaching on the rewards of discipleship, except that Matthew literally reverses the place of the first and last (compare v. 16 with v. 30)! Obviously both passages somehow illustrate the same point. In the earlier passage

Jesus promised that the twelve would sit on thrones judging Israel and that all the disciples would receive a hundredfold. It would be normal, then, for the disciples to congratulate themselves on their response to Jesus, which has assured them such honors and benefits. The parable of the vineyard laborers, however, would head off such a conclusion, reminding them that their call and their rewards were totally the grace and generosity of the Lord, and if they are to "judge" Israel, it is not because of work they have done but purely the goodness of the Lord. Thus the teaching here would be exactly the same as that we explained in Mt 11:25 above, where Jesus' judgment upon the unrepentant towns is followed by a praise of the *grace* given to the disciples.

In applying this parable to our lives and to the life of the church, any of these meanings can provide a legitimate inspiration for reflection and Christian living. The point of all of them is that we cannot apply human standards and limits to the generosity of God.

## *Third Prediction of the Passion (20:17–19)*

17 And as Jesus was going up to Jerusalem, he took the twelve disciples aside, and on the way he said to them, ¹⁸"Behold, we are going up to Jerusalem; and the Son of man will be delivered to the chief priests and scribes, and they will condemn him to death, ¹⁹and deliver him to the Gentiles to be mocked and scourged and crucified, and he will be raised on the third day."

We rejoin Mark here for the third prediction of the passion. Jerusalem is already ahead of Jesus now, and in this third prediction he addresses only the twelve—those to whom he has promised thrones judging the twelve tribes of Israel (19:28). No wonder Mark records the disciples' amazement as well as fear, for Jesus' ministry and predictions range from zenith to nadir. Matthew, however, omits this Markan detail, assuming the reader will experience the same amazement unaided. This is the most detailed of the three predictions. For the first time

Jesus mentions the role of the Romans ("gentiles") in his coming passion. The details of "mocked, spit upon and scourged" given already in Mark clearly identify Jesus as the fulfillment of the Servant prophecy in Is 50:6: "I gave my back to the smiters, and my cheeks to those who pulled out my beard; I hid not my face from shame and spitting" and Psalm 22:6-7, "scorned by men, and despised by the people, all who see me mock at me." But Matthew omits the spittle and inserts instead, for the first time, the word *crucify*. Even so, Jesus will be raised on the third day, himself the first to enjoy the hundredfold promised to those who do the Father's will.

## *Lordship and Servanthood (20:20-28)*

20 Then the mother of the sons of Zebedee came up to him, with her sons, and kneeling before him she asked him for something. [21]And he said to her, "What do you want?" She said to him, "Command that these two sons of mine may sit, one at your right hand and one at your left, in your kingdom." [22]But Jesus answered, "You do not know what you are asking. Are you able to drink the cup that I am to drink?" They said to him, "We are able." [23]He said to them, "You will drink my cup, but to sit at my right hand and at my left is not mine to grant, but it is for those for whom it has been prepared by my Father." [24]And when the ten heard it, they were indignant at the two brothers. [25]But Jesus called them to him and said, "You know that the rulers of the Gentiles lord it over them, and their great men exercise authority over them. [26]It shall not be so among you; but whoever would be great among you must be your servant, [27]and whoever would be first among you must be your slave; [28]even as the Son of man came not to be served but to serve, and to give his life as a ransom for many."

Hardly has Jesus finished his graphic description of the darkness that lies ahead for the Servant, when the mother of James and John, heedless of the prediction, comes forward and kneels with a request. Matthew enjoys describing this religious detail, though its significance should not be excessively pressed, since in eastern cultures such gestures of fervent petition are commonplace (I was so besought a number of times in India and Nepal). She asks a favor without specifying what, as if to get Jesus to commit himself before he knows what he's getting himself into. Is this a hint that even the woman has some doubts about the righteousness of her desire or whether Jesus might grant it? When asked to specify she says, "*Command* that my sons may sit . . . ," thus trusting in the power of Jesus' word to make anything happen. (Mark's version has simply "*Grant* . . .") As Jesus is approaching Jerusalem, the woman thinks that Jesus is about to be enthroned, and she asks that her two sons may be his chief ministers.

But neither she, nor her two sons (the only petitioners in Mark) know the true nature of Jesus' kingdom nor the price he is about to pay for it. The "cup" is a frequent biblical image for God's judgment which his people in some cases, their enemies in others, must drink for their sins (Ps 75:8; Jer 25:15–29; Is 51:17–23). Though not mentioned specifically in the Servant prophecy of Is 53:4–9, the vicarious suffering mentioned there is clearly what Jesus is referring to, for he has taken on the sins of his people, as he wished to show already in asking to be baptized by John. Matthew omits, however, the reference to baptism, which in Mark means simply immersion in suffering, either because by Matthew's time it has become a technical sacramental term in the church (cf. 28:19) or because he knows that only James, not John, suffered a martyr's death (Acts 12:2).

That they should even ask for the first places in the kingdom shows how little they have grasped the teaching of Jesus at 18:1–5, where Jesus told them that to be the greatest they must strive to become the least. The indignation of the other ten disciples shows that they too are victims of the same spirit of rivalry, so Jesus calls them all together for a formal teaching on the matter. Today we would say, "Ambition for positions of power and domineering exercise of leadership belong to the ways of the world. You are to be different." Whoever wishes to be first must become the servant, even the slave. There is a slight difference in the two terms. "Servant" refers primarily to one who waits on tables (Acts 6:2), while "slave" is one who is available for any kind of service.

One day I was interviewing a young Indian candidate for our community, and I wanted to know whether he had an acceptable understanding of the relationship of the brotherhood and the priesthood. Our religious community follows the spirit of St. Benedict who founded numerous monasteries but remained a layman all his life. Thus, what is primary for us is the religious life itself, and those called to the priesthood merely exercise a priestly ministry within the brotherhood. Most of our members are brothers. In places where we are not known and especially where there is a highly clericalized notion of church, we find it difficult to get prospective candidates to think first in terms of the religious life itself, and only later to ask the question about priestly ministry. Unfortunately, often such candidates (and their parents!) think of priesthood as a status rather than a service (the original meaning of "ministry"). Thus I was a bit anxious when I asked this bright young man, "Are you thinking about becoming a priest or a brother?" His answer astounded me, and I had no doubt it was coming straight from his heart, "Father, I just want to *serve*."

Jesus roots this teaching in his own example: "The Son of man came not to be served but to serve." The Lord comes as a table servant (see Luke 22:27) and as a slave (see the footwashing scene in John 13:1–20). But the addition of the phrase, "to give his life as a ransom for many" expands the servant image to theological and cosmic dimensions. More clearly than any other text, it evokes the entire song of the Suffering Servant in Is 52:13–53:12, who, though innocent, willingly endures the humiliation, suffering and death of a criminal and thus atones for the sins of the "many." "Many" here does not imply the exclusion of some. It is simply a way of referring to the whole people in contrast to the one servant (Is 53:11). "To give his life" means to submit voluntarily to martyrdom (1 Macc 2:50; 6:44). "Ransom," as we have come to know painfully in this age of terrorism, means the price for the deliverance or liberation of one held captive, but in the ancient world it was also the price for setting a slave free (Lev 25:51–52; Is 45:13). It is the role of theology to shed light on the mystery of how in God's eyes the suffering of the one innocent man sets sinners free, but some measure of understanding will be given in the parable of the wicked tenants (21:33–43), which we shall discuss further on. For the moment, this lapidary statement expresses the entire mystery of the redemption, being introduced by Jesus as a model for Christian life in community. It will be richly exploited by Saint Paul for the same purpose (Phil 2:6–11).

## The Blind Become Disciples (20:29–34)

29 And as they went out of Jericho, a great crowd followed him. [30]And behold, two blind men sitting by the roadside, when they heard that Jesus was passing by, cried out, "Have mercy on us, Son of David!" [31]The crowd rebuked them, telling them to be silent; but they cried out the more, "Lord, have mercy on us, Son of David!" [32]And Jesus stopped and called them, saying, "What do you want me to do for you?" [33]They said to him, "Lord, let our eyes be opened." [34]And Jesus in pity touched their eyes, and immediately they received their sight and followed him.

This is the last major event in Jesus' ministry in Judea before he reaches Bethphage, the ante-room of Jerusalem. Both in Mark and in Matthew the healing of the blind here is a climactic event because of its significance for discipleship. This is the only story in which we are told that the one healed becomes a disciple. We have just seen how those who were already Jesus' disciples have proved to be blind to his prophecy of the passion. *They* need healing as much as the two blind men of Jericho. And the reader of the gospel is challenged to have his own blindness healed.

We have discussed Matthew's penchant for doubling his characters above under 8:28–34 and again at 9:27–31. Whatever his intention, in the text here the two stand in contrast to the spiritually blind James and John. Twice they address Jesus as Son of David, and twice, perhaps even three times (since the text of v. 30 is uncertain) they use the Christian title, "Lord." And crying, "Have mercy on us," they are voicing what had doubtless since become the liturgical cry of the Matthaean community. Jesus insists that they name their need, thus evoking more commitment of their faith. Moved with pity (a favorite Matthaean trait of Jesus, 9:36; 14:14; 15:32; 18:27), Jesus *touches* their eyes. This detail is all the more remarkable because it is not found in Mark's account and Matthew generally prefers to describe Jesus healing by his word.

The last words, "and followed him," mean here that they become disciples and willingly join Jesus on his journey to the passion. Implicit perhaps in this story is the teaching that any disciple who cannot "see," that is, accept the cross in his life, can come to that sight and that acceptance by asking Jesus for healing.

## Jesus Enters Jerusalem (21:1–11)

21 AND WHEN they drew near to Jerusalem and came to Bethphage, to the Mount of Olives, then Jesus sent two disciples, ²saying to them, "Go into the village opposite you, and immediately you will find an ass tied, and a colt with her; untie them and bring them to me. ³If any one says anything to you, you shall say, 'The Lord has need of them,' and he will send them immediately." ⁴This took place to fulfil what was spoken by the prophet, saying,
     ⁵"Tell the daughter of Zion,
     Behold, your king is coming to you,
     humble, and mounted on an ass,
     and on a colt, the foal of an ass."
⁶The disciples went and did as Jesus had directed them; ⁷they brought the ass and the colt, and put their garments on them, and he sat thereon. ⁸Most of the crowd spread their garments on the road, and others cut branches from the trees and spread them on the road. ⁹And the crowds that went before him and that followed him shouted, "Hosanna to the Son of David! Blessed is he who comes in the name of the Lord! Hosanna in the highest!" ¹⁰And when he entered Jerusalem, all the city was stirred, saying, "Who is this?" ¹¹And the crowds said, "This is the prophet Jesus from Nazareth of Galilee."

With the disciples and the crowds we have followed Jesus through Galilee, southeastern Judea and the city of Jericho. He is approaching Jerusalem from the east, as pilgrims did for the feasts. Any pilgrimage to the Holy City speeds the pilgrim's heartbeat as the goal nears, but this is no ordinary pilgrimage, and Jesus no ordinary pilgrim. The arrival of the Messiah in the capital city was something every Jew aspired to behold.

What will Jesus do? Arrived at Bethphage, a village between Bethany and Jerusalem, he sends two of his disciples to fetch an ass and a colt. Both animals are mentioned by Matthew to prepare us for the fulfillment text in v. 5, which mentions both ass and colt. If challenged, the disciples are to say, "The Lord needs them." *Lord* here can mean "owner," or it may be Jesus' way of referring to God. If Jesus means "Lord" to refer to himself, this would be the only place in the gospel where he so applies this title. Probably Matthew intends a multivalent meaning here: God is the real owner of the ass and colt, and so is Jesus. Of course, Matthew's community is completely comfortable with the title *Lord* being applied to Jesus.

The scripture text is a fusion of Is 62:11 and Zech 9:9. The full text of the first reads: "Say to the daughter of Zion [Jerusalem], 'Behold, your salvation comes; behold his reward is with him, and his recompense before him.' " The second reads: "Rejoice greatly, O daughter of Zion! Shout aloud, O daughter of Jerusalem! Lo, your king comes to you; triumphant and victorious is he, humble and riding on an ass, on a colt the foal of an ass." Matthew has taken the first part of the first text and the second part of the second. This scripture testimony may well have been part of a list of OT texts drawn up by early Christians prior to the writing of our gospels and pointing to fulfillment in Jesus. They would be used in instruction with converts and in apologetic encounters with the Jews.

In the Zechariah text, the ass and the foal are really two descriptions of the same animal, the repetition being simply common Hebrew parallelism. But Matthew understands the text as two animals, and that is why, concerned to show fulfillment in detail, he says Jesus sat *on them*. The point of Matthew's interest, however, is the humility of Jesus' entry. He

does not choose a chariot but the poorest means of conveyance.
Imagine today Jesus entering a modern city not in a limousine
but on a bicycle.

The people do for Jesus what the Israelites did at the
anointing of Jehu as king (2 Kgs 9:13), as the Jews did on their
victorious entering of the temple (1 Macc 13:51) and the festival
of its purification (2 Macc 10:7). In Jesus' day "Hosanna" simply
meant "Hail" or "Long live . . ." Proclaiming Jesus as Son of
David was equivalent to hailing him as the Messiah. The people
chant a line of Psalm 118, one of the Hallel psalms sung at
Passover, from which Jesus will later quote in the parable of
the wicked tenants (21:42). The original meaning was a blessing
invoked on the pilgrim who comes into the temple, and it is
remarkable that the Psalm text continues with the invitation,
"Join in procession with leafy boughs" (Ps 118:26–27). Here,
however, "Blessed is he who comes in the name of the Lord"
refers to Jesus, the "coming one" announced by John the Baptist (3:11; 11:3) and anointed by the Lord as Messiah. "Hosanna
in the highest" is a festive shout for "Praise God!"

Though the crowd that accompanied Jesus may well have
been a modest one, his coming into Jerusalem "rocks" the city
(the NABR "shaken" reflects the earthquake language Matthew uses here better than the weak RSV "stirred"). Already
at the arrival of the Magi looking for the new-born king, Herod
had been "troubled, and all Jerusalem with him" (2:3), but the
language here is stronger. The crowds in v.11, however, identify Jesus only as the prophet. Though this title falls far short
of Jesus' full identity, it does enable the reader to see Jesus
as the fulfillment of the Scripture that a prophet like Moses
would come (Deut 18:15), and particularly it sets the stage for
Jesus' indictment that Jerusalem is the city that murders its
prophets (23:37).

### *Jesus Restores the Temple (21:12–17)*

12 And Jesus entered the temple of God and drove out
all who sold and bought in the temple, and he overturned
the tables of the money-changers and the seats of those who
sold pigeons. [13]He said to them, "It is written, 'My house

shall be called a house of prayer'; but you make it a den of robbers."

14 And the blind and the lame came to him in the temple, and he healed them. ¹⁵But when the chief priests and the scribes saw the wonderful things that he did, and the children crying out in the temple, "Hosanna to the Son of David!" they were indignant; ¹⁶and they said to him, "Do you hear what these are saying?" And Jesus said to them, "Yes; have you never read,
'Out of the mouth of babes and sucklings
thou hast brought perfect praise'?"
¹⁷And leaving them, he went out of the city to Bethany and lodged there.

Jesus now enters the very heart of Judaism, the temple. Recent archaeological excavations have revealed how magnificent a building this was in Jesus' day. Gentiles were forbidden, under pain of death, to enter the inner courts reserved to the Jews, but they were provided with an immense outer court where those attracted to Judaism could pray. The Jews, of course, needed to purchase animals for the sacrifices, or pigeons or doves if they were poor (Lev 12:6; Lk 2:22–24), and they needed money changers to convert their Roman coinage into the Tyrian shekel necessary to pay the annual temple tax. Originally there were four market-places approved by the Sanhedrin for the necessary business connected with temple worship, and all of these were at some distance, in the Mount of Olives area. But when Caiphas became High Priest he allowed this trading to move to the court of the gentiles in the temple area, an abuse which effectively prevented the gentiles from praying there.

In Mark's account, it is this exclusion of the gentiles which is the key motivation for Jesus' prophetic activism. "My house shall be called a house of prayer *for all the nations*" (Mk 11:17). We would expect Matthew to exploit this gentile-oriented thrust of Mark, but surprisingly he omits "for all the nations" and condemns the rampant commercialism that changes the very nature of this house of prayer. For once this Jesus who in the Sermon on the Mount had counseled turning the other cheek, resorts to physical violence. In purifying the temple he fulfills the promise of Malachi 3:1–4 that the Lord would send a mighty purifier of temple and priesthood. This is a prophetic action, not of forecast but of fulfillment. Jesus did not preach against the temple commercialism nor hold meetings with the establishment. He made a whip and went to work.

But then he does something else equally prophetic. Blind and lame people were not only forbidden to exercise the priesthood. They were, on the basis of 2 Samuel 5:6–8 (Greek version), even forbidden entry to the temple. The community at Qumran, like the Jerusalem temple, excluded the crippled, blind, deaf and dumb as unworthy "of the holiness of the congregation" (IQSa II.5–9). But now they come to Jesus. He admits them to the temple and in healing them enables them to be totally reintegrated into the worshipping community.

Now this helps us to understand why Matthew does not exploit the gentile theme at this point. Jesus has been sent only to the lost sheep of the house of Israel (15:24). The time will come when the gentiles will be fully incorporated but that will be the time of the church, after the resurrection. And by the time Matthew writes his gospel, the temple is no more, having been physically destroyed by the Romans and replaced by the one greater than the temple (12:6) and his community. Thus there is no need to claim the Jewish temple for the gentiles. In the church they will be welcomed not merely in the outer court, but as "fellow citizens with the saints and members of the household of God" (Eph 2:19).

But Jesus does model and foreshadow the future gentile mission domestically, as it were, by embracing and healing the outcast in his own society. Mark and Luke record no miracles of Jesus in the capital city, apparently considering Jerusalem as a whole unworthy of signs because of its lack of faith. But in Matthew Jesus continues to heal unto the very end of his ministry, just as John reserves Jesus' greatest miracle, the raising of Lazarus, for the climactic moment of his Judean ministry.

And surprisingly, at this point at least, it is not the cleansing of the temple that angers the chief priests and the scribes but the "wonderful things" Jesus is doing and the unbridled enthusiasm of the children chanting "Hosanna to the Son of David," hailing him, in effect, as the Messiah. Miracles and "Messiah" was more than they could handle. There is tremendous irony in the fact that it is Jesus' healing that will lead to his death and that the ruling establishment is threatened by the sing-song chant of children. To their defense Jesus quotes Psalm 8, leaving the listeners who know this psalm to infer that God's only defense against his enemies are children who can be amazed at his works and spontaneously praise him. The reader of Matthew hears an echo of 11:25: "I thank thee, Father, Lord of heaven and earth, that thou hast hidden these things from the wise and understanding and revealed them to babes."

## The Fig Tree Withers (21:18–22)

18 In the morning, as he was returning to the city, he was hungry. ¹⁹And seeing a fig tree by the wayside he went to it, and found nothing on it but leaves only. And he said to it, "May no fruit ever come from you again!" And the fig tree withered at once. ²⁰When the disciples saw it they marveled, saying, "How did the fig tree wither at once?" ²¹And Jesus answered them, "Truly, I say to you, if you have faith and never doubt, you will not only do what has been done to the fig tree, but even if you say to this mountain, 'Be taken up and cast into the sea,' it will be done. ²²And whatever you ask in prayer, you will receive, if you have faith."

My mother once went through a depression and a crisis of faith. In tears she asked me a question I was not expecting: "Why did Jesus curse the fig tree?" At that point I wished I could have climbed into a time machine and persuaded the evangelists to give us a little more help in properly interpreting this scene, which causes such an obvious difficulty to the modern reader. On the surface, it seems that Jesus acts irrationally and spitefully. Can this be the same Jesus who said, "Look at the lilies, see how they grow"?

The first key to a proper interpretation is to note that this scene is a parable in action, a prophetic action like that of Jeremiah when he took a clay pot and dashed it to the ground to dramatize what was going to happen to the city of Jerusalem because of its repeated rejection of God's word (Jer 19:1–13). The second key is to note the role that the image of the fig tree, like that of the vineyard, had in the religious culture of Jesus' people. The prophets often used the destruction of the fig tree as a symbol of judgment (Is 34:4; Hos 2:2; 9:10, 16; Joel 1:7). The tree that has leaves but no fruit symbolizes a nation that has not lived up to its calling.

"Woe is me!" cries Micah. "For I have become as when the summer fruit has been gathered, as when the vintage has been gleaned: there is no cluster to eat, no first-ripe *fig which my soul desires*. The godly man has perished from the earth, and there is none upright among men; they all lie in wait for blood . . . The day of their watchmen, of their punishment, has come . . . Put no trust in a neighbor, have no confidence in a friend. . . . A man's enemies are those of his own house. But as for me, I will look to the Lord, I will wait for the God of my salvation; my God will hear me" (Mi 7:1–7). Notice how this passage, beginning with the prophet's hunger for a fig, contains elements that would fit both the coming judgment upon Jerusalem and Jesus' own passion, including his betrayal by a friend. Jeremiah 8:8–13 begins with a condemnation of "the false pen of the *scribes*" who will be judged for having rejected the word of the Lord, and the *priests* who will be punished and overthrown for promoting a false peace. Jeremiah then concludes: "When I would gather them, says the Lord, there are no grapes on the vine, nor figs on the fig tree; even the leaves are withered, and what I gave them has passed away from them."

It is quite clear, then, that Jesus is performing a symbolic action. Lord of the harvest, he has come to Jerusalem and the temple looking for the fruits he has the right to expect. (Shortly he will relate the parable of the son who comes to collect the fruit of the vineyard, 21:36–46.) But the city and its authorities are sterile. If the fruit of a tree is not good, the tree is not good (7:16–20), and it will wither under the judgment of God.

In the early tradition, however, even before Matthew, another lesson was drawn from this action: the power of faith, not only to wither a fig tree but to move mountains (see the similar saying in 17:20). Matthew adds to Mark's text the words "and never doubt," because doubting is an important mark for Matthew of that "little faith" which dogs the disciples even after the resurrection (28:17).

## By Whose Authority? (21:23–27)

23 And when he entered the temple, the chief priests and the elders of the people came up to him as he was teaching, and said, "By what authority are you doing these things, and who gave you this authority?" 24Jesus answered them, "I also will ask you a question; and if you tell me the answer, then I also will tell you by what authority I do these things. 25The baptism of John, whence was it? From heaven or from men?" And they argued with one another, "If we say, 'From heaven,' he will say to us, 'Why then did you not believe him?' 26But if we say, 'From men,' we are afraid of the multitude; for all hold that John was a prophet." 27So they answered Jesus, "We do not know." And he said to them, "Neither will I tell you by what authority I do these things.

In the midst of the temple Jesus appears once more as teacher of the crowds, a function that was eclipsed toward the end of his Galilean ministry, in favor of healing alone. The crowds in Jerusalem are new and, while their adherence to Jesus is ambiguous, as events will show, they are at least open to listen to Jesus, as the authorities are not. The latter, probably members of the Sanhedrin that will eventually condemn Jesus, are disturbed by "these things"—Jesus' cleansing of the temple, his welcoming and healing the blind and the lame there, and now his teaching. *They*, after all, are, along with their scribes, the teaching authority, and they certainly have not authorized Jesus. Who then has?

In rabbinic debate, as among campaigning politicians, it was often more important to "stump" the opponent than to move the discussion forward to a conclusion acceptable to both. One of the ways of responding was to ask an alternative question. Jesus considers the attitude of his opponents such that only such a sparring question could meet them. His opponents, as well as the crowd, are aware that both John and Jesus preached conversion in view of the coming kingdom of God. John thus provides a camouflaged alter-ego for Jesus himself. Was John's baptism from God ("heaven") or from men?

They are caught on the horns of a dilemma. To admit John was authorized by God would be to condemn themselves for not believing and repenting at his preaching (some did go for the external ritual only to receive John's condemnation, 3:7–10). But to deny John's authority would be to alienate the common people who revered John as a prophet even more so now that he had been martyred. In side-stepping the issue, the authorities ironically say more than they intended. "We do not know" at one level is an escape from the dilemma. At another level, it is an unintended admission that they are incapable of teaching Israel and thus have no real authority at all. Jesus therefore refuses to submit to their questioning.

The reader, of course, knows full well by whose authority Jesus is acting.

## The Parable of the Two Sons (21:28–32)

28 "What do you think? A man had two sons; and he went to the first and said, 'Son, go and work in the vineyard today.' ²⁹And he answered, 'I will not'; but afterward he repented and went. ³⁰And he went to the second and said the same; and he answered, 'I go, sir,' but did not go. ³¹Which of the two did the will of his father?" They said, "The first." Jesus said to them, "Truly, I say to you, the tax collectors and the harlots go into the kingdom of God before you. ³²For John came to you in the way of righteousness, and you did not believe him, but the tax collectors and the harlots believed him; and even when you saw it, you did not afterward repent and believe him.

This is the first of three parables, all of which have as basic theme Israel's rejection of Jesus which results in tragedy for Israel and the admission to the kingdom of those hitherto excluded.

In this first parable, which is proper to Matthew, Jesus now takes the initiative in posing a question to his opponents. Whatever the circumstances in which this parable originated or its use during an earlier oral stage, the meaning of it here in Matthew appears to be as follows. The first son, who at first refused to obey his father, represents the tax collectors and sinners who were not living according to the law of God but who converted at the preaching of John the Baptist. Though Jesus speaks of John, the same reversal also took place at his own preaching. The second son, who addressed his father more respectfully ("sir," which can also be translated "Lord") but did not *do* his father's will, represents those teachers in Israel who professed to do the will of God in law or cult but who, when confronted by the new invitation of the Father presented by John/Jesus, refused to obey. Those who converted enter the kingdom; those who refused to convert do not. (In light of its probable Aramaic background, the saying "go into the kingdom before you" implies exclusion of the others and not merely delay.) The judgment is more severe in that the authorities witnessed the conversion of the tax collectors and sinners (the repentant "doing" of the other son) but not even that moved them to a change of heart.

But for Matthew, the tax collectors and sinners of Jesus' ministry are also prophetic symbols of the gentiles embraced by Jesus' community after the resurrection, and so there is a lesson here for those Jewish members who may be finding it difficult to accept their gentile brothers and sisters. Beyond that, the Christian reader even today is challenged not to rely on the *yes* he pronounced yesterday to assure he will respond to God's will today.

## The Parable of the Tenants (21:33–46)

33 "Hear another parable. There was a householder who planted a vineyard, and set a hedge around it, and dug

a wine press in it, and built a tower, and let it out to tenants, and went into another country. ³⁴When the season of fruit drew near, he sent his servants to the tenants, to get his fruit; ³⁵and the tenants took his servants and beat one, killed another, and stoned another. ³⁶Again he sent other servants, more than the first; and they did the same to them. ³⁷Afterward he sent his son to them, saying, 'They will respect my son.' ³⁸But when the tenants saw the son, they said to themselves, 'This is the heir; come, let us kill him and have his inheritance.' ³⁹And they took him and cast him out of the vineyard, and killed him. ⁴⁰When therefore the owner of the vineyard comes, what will he do to those tenants?" ⁴¹They said to him, "He will put those wretches to a miserable death, and let out the vineyard to other tenants who will give him the fruits in their seasons."

42 Jesus said to them, "Have you never read in the scriptures:

'The very stone which the builders rejected
  has become the head of the corner;
  this was the Lord's doing,
  and it is marvelous in our eyes'?

⁴³Therefore I tell you, the kingdom of God will be taken away from you and given to a nation producing the fruits of it." ⁴⁴And he who falls on this stone will be dashed to pieces; but when it falls on anyone, it will crush him.45 When the chief priests and the Pharisees heard his parables, they perceived that he was speaking about them. ⁴⁶But when they tried to arrest him, they feared the multitudes, because they held him to be a prophet.

This extremely rich parable, with its following commentary, is undoubtedly the most comprehensive teaching in the synoptics on the meaning of Jesus and his saving death in the whole sweep of salvation history. The opening lines describing the householder who planted and developed a vineyard would recall to any Jew the scene of Isaiah 5:1–2: "My beloved had a vineyard on a very fertile hill. He digged it and cleared it of stones, and planted it with choice vines; he built a watchtower in the midst of it, and hewed out a wine vat in it . . ." Verse 7 identifies the vineyard as "the house of Israel." The vineyard here therefore symbolizes Israel, but whereas in Isaiah God's judgment falls on the vineyard for not producing the desired fruit, in Jesus' parable the focus is on the tenants who prevent the owner from receiving the fruits of the vineyard. In v. 45 these are identified as the chief priests and the Pharisees, who understand that the parable was directed against them. This is an important point, for elsewhere in Matthew it appears that Jesus is rejected by the people as a whole, whereas in reality it is their corrupt leadership that is at fault, although as so often happens in world history, the leadership brings tragedy on the nation.

Absentee landlords were common in the Israel of Jesus' day, and there is evidence of considerable unrest among tenants at the time. The landlord would periodically send inspectors and at harvest time send an agent to claim his share of the produce. In our parable, the servants who go to collect the lord's share are beaten, stoned, or killed. Matthew abbreviates Mark's graphic description of the various fates of the collectors, reducing them to two groups, the second more numerous than the first. At this point the parabolic nature of the story becomes evident, for no human landlord would put up with this repeated barbarity. But if the servants are prophets (the title "servant" was repeatedly used for the prophet in the OT, Am 3:7; Jer 7:25; 25:4; Zec 1:6), then the landlord is one whose patience and long-suffering are really divine. The owner is the Lord.

Instead of avenging himself, the lord will make one final, incredible attempt. "At last" or "finally" (NABR) is a better translation than the RSV's "afterward." This is the last move on the part of the householder. There will be no other. So much does the lord desire the fruit of the vineyard that he is willing to risk sending his own son. Surely the tenants will respect the son, who is as good as the landlord himself. Clearly, Jesus is more than another prophet!

On seeing the son, the tenants apparently assume that the landlord is dead and that the son has already inherited the vineyard (they call him "the heir"). This assumption at least lends a measure of malicious cleverness to what otherwise would be an ultimately suicidal plot. In Mark, the tenants kill the son inside the vineyard and then cast him outside. Matthew, conscious of the sequence of events in Jesus' passion, has the tenants take him outside the vineyard (=Jerusalem) where they kill him. The death of the son is the climactic point of the story. Jesus foretells his own death at the hands of those to whom he is telling the story, though this understanding by his listeners is withheld until v. 45. At this point they rightly conclude, in answer to Jesus' question, that the owner (*kyrios* also means "Lord") will come in judgment against the tenants. In Matthew the authorities quote a classical Greek pun, *kakous kakos apolesei autous*, found in Sophocles and Josephus, which the NABR tries to catch by rendering, "He will put those wretched men to a wretched death." Then the owner will lend out the vineyard to others who, Matthew adds, "will give him the fruits in their seasons." "Fruits" is a frequent Matthaean term for "good works," sign of that greater righteousness which Jesus proclaims and expects of his disciples (5:20).

Who are these "other tenants" who will render the desired fruits? Verse 43, which is Matthew's addition to the Markan story, says they are a "nation," *ethnos* the same word used in the plural for "gentiles." However, used in the singular here, it means a unified people and therefore surely the *church* Jesus has promised to build (16:18), a people composed of both Jews and gentiles.

But first Jesus quotes Psalm 118:22–23, lines of the Hallel song already used at Jesus' entry into Jerusalem (21:9). In the OT the verse was originally a parable for the just person who, despite rejection by the powerful, is defended and vindicated by God. It was understood to apply to David, the least of Jesse's sons, who was chosen as king. In succeeding generations it was applied to the incumbent king and then to the coming king, Son of David, the Messiah. In quoting this passage, Jesus is coming very close to claiming his Messianic identity. Jesus is the rejected stone whom the Lord will make the cornerstone of the new people of God.

If we wonder why Matthew did not put v. 43 immediately after v. 41, an order that would appear more logical, since both have to do with the new people of God, the reason may well be that he wishes first to portray Jesus as the foundation of this new "nation." By combining the building image with that of the vineyard, and identifying "tenants" and "builders," Jesus is using language that will become commonplace in the New Testament, where the church is God's field, his building (1 Cor 3:9), the temple of which Jesus is the central stone (Eph 2:20–21). The effect of placing verses 41–44 in the order in which we find them (instead of the more "logical" 41, 43, 42, 44), is that the stone of stumbling and crushing in v. 44 is not only Jesus but the church with him: to reject the church, as well as to reject Jesus, is to stumble on this stone and to imperil oneself to being crushed by it—a lesson Matthew wishes his community and the Jews of his age to hear.

Once again, then, we encounter Matthew's understanding of the church as one with Jesus, the Emmanuel who dwells in its midst.

## The King's Wedding Feast (22:1–14)

**22** AND AGAIN Jesus spoke to them in parables, saying, [2]"The kingdom of heaven may be compared to a king who gave a marriage feast for his son, [3]and sent his servants to call those who were invited to the marriage feast; but they would not come. [4]Again he sent other servants, saying, 'Tell those who are invited, Behold, I have made ready my dinner, my oxen and my fat calves are killed, and everything is ready; come to the marriage feast.' [5]But they made light of it and went off, one to his farm, another to his business, [6]while the rest seized his servants, treated them shamefully, and killed them. [7]The king was angry, and he sent his troops and destroyed those murderers and burned their city. [8]Then he said to his servants, 'The wedding is ready, but those invited were not worthy. [9]Go therefore to the thoroughfares, and invite to the marriage feast as many as you find.' [10]And those servants went out into the streets and gathered all whom they found, both bad and good; so the wedding hall was filled with guests.

11 "But when the king came in to look at the guests, he saw there a man who had no wedding garment; [12]and he said to him, 'Friend, how did you get in here without a wedding

garment?' And he was speechless. ¹³Then the king said to
the attendants, 'Bind him hand and foot, and cast him into
the outer darkness; there men will weep and gnash their
teeth.' ¹⁴For many are called, but few are chosen."

In many ways this parable resembles the previous one:
son, servants, rejection and violent treatment of the servants,
punitive judgment by the king, others replacing those who
proved unworthy. But the basic image is different. The OT
image of the coming kingdom as a feast (Is 25:6; Lk 14:15;
22:18) becomes in the NT a wedding feast. If the celebration
begins with the public ministry of Jesus, who is the bridegroom
(9:15), its consummation is in heaven (25:10; Rev 19:7–9). Here
it is a royal wedding, God obviously being the king and Jesus
his son, the bridegroom.

The first set of servants, we can guess already from the
previous parable, are the OT prophets. Even the OT inveighs
against the people for refusing to listen to its prophets, but in
this case the prophets are inviting to the royal wedding, the
messianic banquet, and in the east even today it is considered
a serious breach of courtesy to reject an invitation to a wedding! More precisely, however, the servants are *calling* those
who had earlier received an announcement of the coming wedding. In other words, they are saying, "The time has come; the
time is fulfilled." Thus the prophets are those whose messianic
predictions are now fulfilled, and those who refuse the invitation are not so much the past generations but the present who
will not believe the prophecies to be fulfilled in Jesus.

Who are the second set of servants? On the pattern of the
previous parable we would think automatically of another set
of OT prophets. But note: the son is not sent at all in this
parable; he is with his father. And the burning of the city by
troops, which follows the violent treatment of the servants, is
an obvious allusion to the destruction of Jerusalem. Consequently, it is much more probable that the second set of servants are the early Christian missionaries to the Jews. Their
message is one of urgency: "everything is ready" (v. 4). But
the response ranges from indifference to murder. Verse 7 is
such an intrusion on the parable (the banquet is held up while

a war is waged) that most scholars think it was added by Matthew himself as a commentary on the destruction of Jerusalem by the Romans in 70 A.D., Matthew having written after the event. In the OT, the armies of Israel's enemies are sometimes depicted as the scourge of the Lord (Is 10:5–11; Jer 4:5–12), and that would seem to be Matthew's meaning here. Personal vindictiveness is not, however, the way of the Father, whom Jesus describes in 5:43–48 as loving even his enemies. Consequently, the destruction of Jerusalem must be seen at most as resulting from the tragic inner logic of Israel's not recognizing the hour of her opportunity and the things that would make for her peace (Lk 19:41–44).

The unworthiness of those repeatedly invited comes only from their refusal of the invitation. By the same token, those who accept the invitation are worthy, not because of some prior virtue, but simply because they have said "yes" to God's gift.

The third group of servants are Christian missionaries to the gentiles. "Go therefore" (v. 9) is the same command given in 28:19, "Go therefore and make disciples of all nations . . ." They are to go wherever they can find people willing to come. They welcome both "good and bad." This can mean either of two things: 1) The new community of Jesus is made of those who were virtuous, outwardly at least, prior to their conversion, as well as sinners who on entering the community changed their ways; or 2) The church even now is a mixture of good and bad, there are weeds among the wheat (13:24–30, 36–43), bad fish among the good (13:47–50). In either case the expression prepares us for the epilogue scene, which is now directed squarely at the church.

The king comes in to "look at" the guests, a cue that this is a "final judgment" scene. Among the guests is a man who has come in shabby, dirty clothes. This is not a poor man who has stumbled in off the streets, for welcoming such a person would be fulfilling Jesus' concern for the poor (5:3; 11:5; 19:21; 25:35–36). It is rather a man whose life was in no way changed by the invitation or by entering the wedding hall; he flaunts his old way of living in the face of the king and the other guests. This is clearly a symbol for those second or third generation Christians who have fallen into laxity, who pay no heed to Jesus' high ethical demands (5:20), who expect the benefits of the banquet without paying the price of discipleship. Presumption indeed! When challenged by the king, the boor has no excuse. He is bound and thrown into the outer darkness to "weep and gnash his teeth." This is a particularly Matthean refrain of damnation reserved for Christians who have been unfaithful to their calling. It appears again in 24:51 and 25:30. Its two previous occurrences were at the judgment scene of the weeds among the wheat (13:42) and the bad fish among the good (13:50), a situation identical to our present parable.

Matthew is dealing with a very specific pastoral problem— those who presume that being a Christian will automatically gain them entrance into the kingdom. The frequency and the severity with which Matthew deals with this problem indicates how seriously he views it. Those who pretend to be Christians while in reality living a sinful life will fare no better than those who refused to accept Jesus in the first place. Such laxity is tantamount to refusing the invitation, and the tragic ending is the same. "Many are invited, but few are chosen" (NABR). Matthew drives a distinction between the "called" (or invited) and the "chosen" unknown to Paul, who uses the terms interchangeably. For him, to be called by God is to be chosen. He can barely conceive how anyone so graced by God could be lost. But Matthew's longer pastoral experience with the libertines in his community has convinced him otherwise, and he uses a saying of Jesus to drive his point home. The "called" here means all those invited, those who came as well as those who refused. The "chosen" means those who accepted the invitation and in addition persevered by a worthy life until the end. There is, of course, no numerical percentage given, but the sobering message is the same given in the Sermon on the Mount: "Enter by the narrow gate; for the gate is wide and the way is easy, that leads to destruction, and those who enter by it are many. For the gate is narrow and the way is hard, that leads to life, and those who find it are few" (7:13–14).

## What Is Caesar's and What Is God's (22:15–22)

15 Then the Pharisees went and took counsel how to entangle him in his talk. [16]And they sent their disciples to

him, along with the Herodi-ans, saying, "Teacher, we know that you are true, and teach the way of God truthfully, and care for no man; for you do not regard the position of men. <sup>17</sup>Tell us, then, what you think. Is it lawful to pay taxes to Caesar, or not?" <sup>18</sup>But Jesus, aware of their malice, said, "Why put me to the test, you hypocrites? <sup>19</sup>Show me the money for the tax." And they brought him a coin. <sup>20</sup>And Jesus said to them, "Whose likeness and inscription is this?" <sup>21</sup>They said, "Caesar's." Then he said to them, "Render therefore to Caesar the things that are Caesar's, and to God the things that are God's." <sup>22</sup>When they heard it, they marveled; and they left him and went away.

We now begin a series of four debates of Jesus with his enemies: the first with the Pharisees, the second with the Sadducees, the third with the scribes, and the fourth again with the Pharisees but with Jesus taking the initiative.

The Pharisees send their disciples to "entangle" Jesus in his talk. They team up with the supporters of Herod, whose politics of collaboration they despise but whose help they will gladly accept in this case. The Pharisees would have detested the Roman tax, the Herodians supported it. Addressing Jesus as "Teacher," they betray from the start their insincerity, for such a title is Matthew's flag for those of little or no faith in Jesus. They compliment Jesus on his forthrightness. The presence of the crowd is not mentioned, but we can assume the debate is public, and thus they use a tactic that will surely ingratiate them with the crowd and give them leverage for embarrassing Jesus.

The dilemma they propose is clever and simple. If Jesus supports the tax, he will lose the favor of the Jews who detest it. If he assails the tax, he can be accused of fomenting discontent against Caesar and even of being a Zealot. An insincere question does not demand a sincere answer, so Jesus calls them hypocrites and in brilliant rabbinic style throws the ball into their court. They supply the coin they have obviously been using, "lawful" or not. In saying "Give to Caesar the things that are Caesar's, and to God the things that are God's," Jesus does not state which things belong to whom, but he recognizes the legitimate rights of each and, more importantly for the

Pharisees present, he challenges them to give to God what they
have not given.

## The Sadducees and the Resurrection (22:23–33)

23 The same day Sadducees came to him, who say that
there is no resurrection; and they asked him a question,
²⁴saying, "Teacher, Moses said, 'If a man dies, having no
children, his brother must marry the widow, and raise up
children for his brother.' ²⁵Now there were seven brothers
among us; the first married, and died, and having no children left his wife to his brother. ²⁶So too the second and
third, down to the seventh. ²⁷After them all, the woman
died. ²⁸In the resurrection, therefore, to which of the seven
will she be wife? For they all had her."

29 But Jesus answered them, "You are wrong, because
you know neither the scriptures nor the power of God. ³⁰For
in the resurrection they neither marry nor are given in
marriage, but are like angels in heaven. ³¹And as for the
resurrection of the dead, have you not read what was said
to you by God, ³²'I am the God of Abraham, and the God of
Isaac, and the God of Jacob'? He is not God of the dead, but
of the living." ³³And when the crowd heard it, they were
astonished at his teaching.

The Sadducees attack Jesus from another front. They belonged to a party distinguished from the Pharisees in two important points: (1) They accepted as authoritative only the first
five books of the Bible, the Pentateuch or Torah (meaning
"Law") but not the prophets and the other books. They also
rejected the oral law by which the Pharisees sought to apply
the written law to everyday practice. (2) They rejected a belief
in the resurrection of the just. All human life ends with this
life, and the only immortality a man gains is through his descendants. These two points, converging in their claim that nowhere in the Pentateuch is the doctrine of the resurrection
taught, form the background for the dispute with Jesus.

Addressing Jesus as "Teacher," the title indicating little or
no faith in Jesus' identity now well known to the disciples and

to the reader, they evoke the levirate law from an acceptable Torah book, Deuteronomy 25:5. In a situation where a married man dies childless, the law provided that the next youngest brother would marry his brother's widow in order to raise up heirs for his brother. The Sadducees then present a case of a lamentable woman who went through seven husbands this way before dying herself. If indeed there is to be a resurrection, whose wife will she be? The question was not so ill-placed as might seem, because many of the Pharisees thought of the resurrection more as a resuscitation to earthly life on a grander scale than in spiritual terms.

Jesus responds that the Sadducees err on two counts: their interpretation of Scripture, and their limitation of the power of God. Taking up these points in reverse order, Jesus first situates the resurrection within God's power. That power guarantees immortality: "To know your power is the root of immortality" (Wis 15:3). But the condition of the resurrected just is not a return to bodily life as we know it here. It is a passage into a more perfect life in which the physical functions associated with marriage no longer hold. "Like angels" does not mean an immaterial existence, but the spiritualization of the body itself, in which the human person is transformed into a divine life such as Paul describes in 1 Cor 15:42–49.

As for the scriptural argument, Jesus knows it is useless to quote the prophets, whose teachings would be clearer on the subject. He chooses instead a text acceptable to the Sadducees and in fact addressed *to them* (Matthew's addition to Mark), from Ex 3:16. God there revealed himself to Moses as the God of Abraham, of Isaac, and of Jacob. It may be difficult for us to understand how Jesus' conclusion follows from this: He is not the God of the dead but of the living. Biblically speaking, however, the basis of immortality is not a philosophical doctrine of the immortality of the soul. Even less is it founded in some arcane constitution of the physical body. It is founded in *covenant*. In the Exodus passage the covenant relationship of the patriarchs is evoked by God's defining himself as the God *of* Abraham, the God *of* Isaac, the God *of* Jacob. Those who are bound in covenant with the Lord participate in his immortality, for they are part of his self-definition as "I *am*. . . ." A covenant established by God cannot be broken by the death of the human party. The book of Wisdom expresses it thus: "Righteousness [i.e., God's covenant union] is immortal" (Wis 1:15).

The error of the Sadducees is that in practice, they denied the power and the fidelity of Israel's covenant God. Jesus could very well have quoted to the Sadducees what he had just said "that same day" (v. 23) to the Pharisees: Give to God what belongs to God. God owns all those who live in his covenant love. When he raises them from death he is simply claiming what is his own.

The reaction of the Sadducees is not recorded. But the crowds are amazed at Jesus' teaching.

## The Greatest Commandment (22:34-40)

34 But when the Pharisees heard that he had silenced the Sadducees, they came together. [35]And one of them, a lawyer, asked him a question, to test him. [36]"Teacher, which is the great commandment in the law?" [37]And he said to him, "You shall love the Lord your God with all your heart, and with all your soul, and with all your mind. [38]This is the great and first commandment. [39]And a second is like it, You shall love your neighbor as yourself. [40]On these two commandments depend all the law and the prophets."

In Mark, a well-intentioned scribe, impressed with Jesus' handling of the Sadducees' dilemma, asks Jesus which commandment is the first of all. Pleased with Jesus' answer, he says so, and Jesus compliments him in return: "You are not far from the kingdom of God" (Mk 12:34).

Matthew's revision of Mark reflects the tense situation a generation later between the community and the Pharisees. The scribe (literally, "lawyer") is sent by the Pharisees, who "gather" as if in a conspiracy (see Ps 2:2) to trap Jesus in his speech. Either way, Jesus' teaching is the same. The lawyer, addressing Jesus as "teacher" only, asks which *one* commandment is the greatest. Jesus quotes from the *Shema* (Deut 6:5), the Jewish daily morning prayer, which is formulated in a way to impress upon the Jew a love for God that is total. The sur-

prise comes when Jesus adds that this commandment is insep-
arable from the second. Though taken from another part of
Scripture (Lev 19:18), it is *like* the first. In Leviticus "neighbor" means fellow-countryman, but Jesus both by act and word
shows that it extends to everyone, even enemies (5:41–48), and
the reason is the same as that given here, that human love is
to be modeled on God's way of loving. We touch here the core
of Jesus' teaching—which is neither love of God alone nor love
of neighbor alone, but the inextricable intertwining of the two,
an answer both to humanists and "religionists." Thus Jesus'
answer to the lawyer's question about the one commandment
is that there are *two* on which the whole law depends—and the
prophets as well, Jesus adding this to the scribe's scope of
inquiry. The word "depend" means "hang" as on a peg.
Remove the peg and everything hanging on it collapses. Thus
the double commandment is also the principle in the light of
which all other commands and practices are to be interpreted
and judged.

Matthew does not add, as Mark does, that "after that no
one dared to ask him any questions," reserving this for the
final silencing at the end of the next encounter.

## *David's Son and Lord (22:41–46)*

41 Now while the Pharisees were gathered together,
Jesus asked them a question, [42]saying, "What do you think
of the Christ? Whose son is he?" They said to him, "The son
of David." [43]He said to them, "How is it then that David,
inspired by the Spirit, calls him Lord, saying,

[44]"The Lord said to my Lord,
  Sit at my right hand,
    till I put thy enemies under thy feet'?
[45]If David thus calls him Lord, how is he his son?" [46]And no
one was able to answer him a word, nor from that day did
any one dare to ask him any more questions.

Again the Pharisees are in collusion, and it is as if Jesus,
in this final encounter, is taking them all on as a group. Up to
this point Jesus has been parrying his enemies' attacks. Now

he takes the ball into their court by asking them whose son
the Messiah is. Obviously he means not the Messiah's immediate father, but of what line he is descended. The Pharisees
hold to the mainstream of the Messianic hope which looked for
the Messiah to be descended from David. To understand Jesus'
counter-question, the following background is necessary. Psalm
110 was originally written to celebrate the enthronement of a
Judean king. The psalmist begins by saying, "The Lord [God]
says to my lord [the king], 'Sit at my right hand . . .' " The
palace of the king, Son of David, was in fact to the right of the
temple as one faced east. In NT times, David was held to be
author of all the psalms, hence also of this one. When the Judean kings were suppressed by the Babylonians, a situation
maintained by the Persians and the Greeks after them, psalms
referring to the king were applied by the Jews to the king-to-
come, the Messiah. And so it was with Psalm 110. But if David,
the assumed psalmist, calls the Messiah "Lord," how can he be
his son? A son, biblically speaking, is never greater than his
father.

In terms of debate, Jesus has vanquished his enemies.
They are reduced to silence, and certainly, since they cannot
explain the Scriptures, they are bankrupt as teachers in Israel
and must give way to Jesus, the authoritative interpreter of
the will of God.

But Matthew surely sees more in this text than victory in
a debate. By the time he wrote his gospel, Psalm 110 had been
used and reused in the Christian community to explain Jesus'
enthronement as Messiah, Lord and Son of God, which occurred dramatically at his resurrection (Acts 2:36; Rom 1:4).
The phrase "until I make your enemies your footstool" was used
to explain the interim between the resurrection and Jesus' glorious return (1 Cor 15:25).

Here, at Matthew's level, at once more primitive and more
developed, Jesus is certainly not denying his Messiahship. The
title of the gospel, the genealogy and the cries of the needy to
the "Son of David" throughout the gospel, and of the children
in the temple, assures that he is the Messiah. Though the Pharisees may not have caught his inference, he is claiming to be
*more* than David's son. The reader by now knows what that

*more* is. He is Son of God (14:33; 16:16), already revealed as such at his baptism (3:17). And the title "Lord" is indeed fittingly given to him. The approaching passion, death and resurrection will confirm his divine status, but the revelation of it already subtly underlies Jesus' question, "Whose son is he?"

## DISCOURSE: CONFLICT WITH THE PHARISEES AND THE FINAL TIMES (23:1–25:46)

Scholars dispute whether chapter 23 should be counted with the previous narrative section or with the discourse material of chapters 24 and 25. There is certainly a great difference between this discourse addressed to the Pharisees and that addressed to the disciples following. Yet, since both are discourse material, we will follow those scholars who group all the material together.

Jesus' strong attack upon the Pharisees presents some problems for the modern reader, inviting the following introductory remarks.

1) Jesus is a prophet, and a prophet's role is twofold: a positive one of building and planting, and a negative one of clearing the ground of the old stones and plants so that the new life can take place: "See, I place my words in your mouth! This day I set you over nations and over kingdoms, to root up and to tear down, to destroy and to demolish, to build and to plant" (Jer 1:9–10). In this assemblage of sayings against the Pharisees Jesus is fulfilling the mission of tearing down what stands in the way of the new kingdom he has come to proclaim and inaugurate.

2) In reading this section it is important to keep in mind that the present text has a history beginning with Jesus' original conflict with the Pharisees, but reused and adapted to the ongoing situation of Matthew's community, and finally edited by the evangelist around the year 90. Despite the condemnations of the Pharisees which we find everywhere in the gospels, there was among the first Jewish Christians a

strong and influential group who belonged to the Pharisee party and continued their life-style (Acts 15:1–5). It is likely that these went through a period in which even as Christians they still recognized the Pharisaic scribal leadership as authoritative and hesitated to accept fully the revisionist interpretations of the apostles, especially Paul. They must have defended their position by appealing to some early saying(s) of Jesus which admitted the competence of the scribes or at least commended obedience to their authority. Only such a situation, which surely changed with time, enables us to make any sense of 23:2–3, especially the clause, "practice and observe whatever they tell you," which clashes so discordantly with Matthew's increasing discreditation of the Pharisees.

Why did Matthew include this saying, then? Pastor that he is and a genius at using community tensions creatively (see chapter 18), Matthew incorporates an early saying of Jesus that legitimates those Jewish converts who wish to continue whatever in the Pharisaic tradition does not conflict with their new faith, but he immediately provides a corrective about saying and doing and the lengthy seven woes against the scribes and the Pharisees, reflecting the confrontational stage of Jesus' ministry and the struggle over leadership in the Jewish community at the time Matthew wrote his gospel. Now not only is Jesus the full and only authoritative voice of God, but he has authorized his disciples to be the new and only teachers of all nations (28:19–20).

3) While the spotlight is on the scribes and Pharisees outside the community, Matthew is using this whole section to address those members within who "say" but do not "do," the hypocrites among the Christians who utter false prophecies and say "Lord, Lord" but do not *do* the will of the Father (7:21–23). It is this "boomerang" intention of the discourse which enables the Christian reader today to be profoundly challenged by the text.

4) In the Sermon on the Mount, at the beginning of his ministry, Jesus pronounced the beatitudes, blessings on a series of persons whose dispositions made them ready for the com-

ing kingdom. In Luke's version of the Sermon, the beatitudes are followed by an equal number of woes upon those whose attitudes will exclude them from the kingdom (Lk 6:24–26). Matthew reserves the "woes" for the concluding hours of Jesus' ministry, where they not only fulfill an important function in warning the community against certain attitudes but also provide an inclusion with the blessings with which Jesus began his ministry.

## *Avoid the Style of the Scribes (23:1–12)*

23 THEN SAID Jesus to the crowds and to his disciples, 2"The scribes and the Pharisees sit on Moses' seat; 3so practice and observe whatever they tell you, but not what they do; for they preach, but do not practice. 4They bind heavy burdens, hard to bear, and lay them on men's shoulders; but they themselves will not move them with their finger. 5They do all their deeds to be seen by men; for they make their phylacteries broad and their fringes long, 6and they love the place of honor at feasts and the best seats in the synagogues, 7and salutations in the market places, and being called rabbi by men. 8But you are not to be called rabbi, for you have one teacher, and you are all brethren. 9And call no man your father on earth, for you have one Father, who is in heaven. 10Neither be called masters, for you have one master, the Christ. 11He who is greatest among you shall be your servant; 12whoever exalts himself will be humbled, and whoever humbles himself will be exalted.

Unlike any of the other discourses, this one is addressed both to the crowds and the disciples, Jesus thus resuming in Jerusalem the teaching role he had abandoned toward the end of his Galilean ministry. It is clear, therefore, that the indictment of the scribes and the Pharisees is something to be published openly, but it is also an instruction to the disciples to avoid the same attitudes in their new life within the Christian community. This becomes particularly clear in this first passage, which is addressed more to the disciples than to the crowds.

"Moses' seat" refers to Moses' teaching authority. For the teacher to sit was common rabbinic practice, followed by Jesus as well (5:1). The one who succeeds to the teacher's seat exercises the teacher's authority. Although the RSV translates, "the scribes and the Pharisees *sit* on Moses' seat," the aorist tense in the Greek really means "*took* the seat," possibly suggesting that they did it by their own authority rather than by God's. In any case, however, verse 3 accepts their teaching authority. For an explanation of this unusual text which is in tension with the rest of Matthew's gospel, see our discussion in the introduction above, #2.

The NABR catches the meaning of the "but" clause better: "Do not follow their example." When legitimate authority does not practice what it preaches, that is no excuse for those under it to do the same. The fact that an alcoholic bishop preaches sobriety does not justify his subjects' overindulgence. Such behavior is an adolescent projection of one's own responsibility onto the authority figure in order to be released from the demands of one's own conscience.

From the OT Torah the scribes had devised a list of 613 precepts, 365 negative and 248 positive, which had to be observed if one was to be truly pious and holy. The common people, represented here by the crowds, did not have the time nor the ability to study the law in such detail and thus transgressed it frequently, leading to the famous statement of rabbi Hillel, "The man who is not learned has no fear of sin; the common people cannot be pious" (*Aboth* II, 6). The picture we get from the gospels generally confirms that exceptions to the rules were allowed only in extreme cases. Thus, for example, one was allowed to heal on the Sabbath only if there were danger of death. Jesus considers burdens of this kind tantamount to killing people (Mk 3:4; Lk 6:9), and the scribes will do nothing to lift those burdens even when there is real human need. It was precisely here that Jesus came to lift the people's burdens, in a twofold sense: by lifting their infirmities through healing (8:17) and by substituting for the impossible burden of the law (admitted by Peter, Acts 15:10) his own freeing yoke of love and compassion (11:28–30). By healing on the Sabbath he attacked both burdens at once.

Jesus' second attack concerns the scribes' externalism and show of piety. Already in the Sermon on the Mount Jesus had warned his disciples against doing things "in order to be seen by people" (6:1). In literal fulfillment of the OT commands to keep the great deeds of the Lord and his statutes before one's eyes and on one's hands and heart (Ex 13:9, 16; Deut 6:8; 11:18), the practice developed of appending, by strips of cloth or leather, to the forehead and the arm at the level of the heart a small box or capsule containing parchments on which were written the full texts cited above. Every male Jew was required to wear the phylactery during his morning prayer. Here Jesus attacks the scribes' tendency to showy expansion of this practice.

The law prescribed the wearing of four tassels, one for each corner of the cloak (Deut 22:12) to remind the Jew of the Lord and his laws and the obligation to be holy (Num 15:38–39). The scribes apparently expanded on this practice as well. Since they were the learned teachers of the law, the scribes were shown marks of respect by the people, who would rise to greet them and at dinners give them the places of highest honor. In the synagogues they had special seats facing the congregation. They wore a long white stole called a *tallith* which easily distinguished them from others who generally wore colored clothing.

The element which draws most of Jesus' attention is the use of titles. "Rabbi" was the common Jewish word for "teacher," a title of high respect, though it may already have lost its original semantic meaning of "my great one." The disciples are to avoid using that title, lest it distract from the one teacher who is Jesus. Actually, we have noticed how only disbelievers or those coolly related to Jesus address him as *didaskalos* (teacher), and we shall notice further on that only Judas uses the Hebrew word *rabbi*. Christians know Jesus is more than a teacher. He is Messiah and Son of God. But precisely for that reason he is the supreme and only teacher who deserves the title. This does not negate the fact that Jesus will send his disciples with authority to teach in his name (28:19–20). Thus it is not the authority of the disciples that is at issue

here but status and rank which militates against the equality
which the disciples are to preserve as brothers and sisters.

Likewise the disciples are to call no one "Father." This
means, on the one hand, that even physical or adoptive parents,
though due the respect demanded by the fourth commandment,
become equals with their children before God. Thus a priest
celebrating Mass for his deceased father or mother will say,
"Remember our brother/sister, who has passed from this
life . . ." On the other hand it also rules out giving this title in
a spiritual sense to anyone else in the community—a practice
found more in the breach than in the observance in the Catholic
and Orthodox churches, though Paul himself sets the example:
"Even if you should have countless guides to Christ, yet you
do not have many fathers, for I became your father in Christ
Jesus through the Gospel" (1 Cor 4:15). The point of Jesus'
teaching is that the cult of the title *father* obscures the uniqueness of God as *Abba* and the consequent equality of brothers
and sisters in the community. Today, when some claim that the
word "father" for God reinforces an oppressive patriarchal system, it is enlightening to recall that Jesus subverted the oppressive claims of patriarchy precisely by appealing to the divine Father image. For our Indian novices, who had grown up
with a high degree of respect for their fathers and were used
to calling all priests "father," it was a difficult adjustment to
learn to call me, their novicemaster, just "George." Visitors
were sometimes shocked to hear what they thought was disrespect, but I wish they could have seen the tears in the eyes
of the novice who, at our parting, gave me a hug and said,
"You have been a real father to me." Titles do not assure, they
sometimes obscure, the reality.

The third title to be avoided is "Master," a comprehensive
term for a philosopher or spiritual guide, a bit more specific
than "teacher" but otherwise of the same scope. There is one
Master for the community, *the Christ*. This absolute use of the
title "Messiah" probably derives from the Christian community, since Jesus habitually avoids applying it to himself. Jesus
had already taught that the greatest should become the servant
in 26:20, but here the teaching is applied to the lust for titles,

In interpreting this whole chapter 23, one should be clear about the difference between externals and externalism. As human beings we need externals: uniforms for police and nurses, for example, indicate their availability for service to those in need. They also facilitate quick identification, as the celibate's religious habit immediately communicates the person's non-availability as a partner to the opposite sex. Externals can also be an expression of values the individual thinks important. So it was with the Pharisees. In itself the wearing of the phylacteries and tassels was not wrong. But in fact such externals were part of a much larger problem. They accentuated the Pharisees' separation from the "unclean," even when the "unclean" were people.

The same can be said of titles. If they serve for quick identification or availability for service or values the person holds, well and good. But if they are used to block genuine human and fraternal relationships they would fall under Jesus' condemnation.

which apparently had become a problem in Matthew's community.

## The Seven Woes (23:13–36)

13 "But woe to you, scribes and Pharisees, hypocrites! because you shut the kingdom of heaven against men; for you neither enter yourselves, nor allow those who would enter to go in. [15]Woe to you, scribes and Pharisees, hypocrites! for you traverse sea and land to make a single proselyte, and when he becomes a proselyte, you make him twice as much a child of hell as yourselves.

16 "Woe to you, blind guides, who say, 'If any one swears by the temple, it is nothing; but if any one swears by the gold of the temple, he is bound by his oath.' [17]You blind fools! For which is greater, the gold or the temple that has made the gold sacred? [18]And you say, 'If any one swears by the altar, it is nothing; but if any one swears by the gift that is on the altar, he is bound by his oath.' [19]You blind men! For which is greater, the gift or the altar that makes the gift sacred? [20]So he who swears by the altar, swears by it and by everything on it; [21]and he who swears by the temple, swears by it and by him who dwells in it; [22]and he who swears by heaven, swears by the throne of God and by him who sits upon it.

23 "Woe to you, scribes and Pharisees, hypocrites! for you tithe mint and dill and cumin, and have neglected the weightier matters of the law, justice and mercy and faith; these you ought to have done, without neglecting the others. [24]You blind guides, straining out a gnat and swallowing a camel!

25 "Woe to you, scribes and Pharisees, hypocrites! for you cleanse the outside of the cup and of the plate, but inside they are full of extortion and rapacity. [26]You blind Pharisee! first cleanse the inside of the cup and of the plate, that the outside also may be clean.

27 "Woe to you, scribes and Pharisees, hypocrites! for you are like whitewashed tombs, which outwardly appear

beautiful, but within they are full of dead men's bones and all uncleanness. ²⁸So you also outwardly appear righteous to men, but within you are full of hypocrisy and iniquity.

29 "Woe to you, scribes and Pharisees, hypocrites! for you build the tombs of the prophets and adorn the monuments of the righteous, ³⁰saying, 'If we had lived in the days of our fathers, we would not have taken part with them in shedding the blood of the prophets.' ³¹Thus you witness against yourselves, that you are sons of those who murdered the prophets. ³²Fill up, then, the measure of your fathers. ³³You serpents, you brood of vipers, how are you to escape being sentenced to hell? ³⁴Therefore I send you prophets and wise men and scribes, some of whom you will kill and crucify, and some you will scourge in your synagogues and persecute from town to town, ³⁵that upon you may come all the righteous blood shed on earth, from the blood of innocent Abel to the blood of Zechariah the son of Barachiah, whom you murdered between the sanctuary and the altar. ³⁶Truly, I say to you, all this will come upon this generation.

The eight beatitudes of the Sermon on the Mount are now balanced by seven woes, arranged by Matthew from sayings of Jesus from the Q source (which Matthew shares with Luke) and from his own source. Again it is helpful to recall that Matthew is using Jesus' critique of the religious leaders of his day to reinforce the church's rejection of the Pharisaic leadership after the fall of the temple. It is also helpful to remember that not all the Pharisees would merit the condemnation given here. An important number of them did, indeed, accept the faith (Acts 15:5). "Woe" was a common exclamation of the prophets proclaiming doom upon the wicked. Generally each woe was followed by a "therefore" clause detailing the punishment that is coming. Here the threat of punishment is reserved for the end of the series, in v. 34–36.

*Woe #1: Shutting out of the kingdom.* A most severe indictment of the religious leaders who are supposed to lead into the kingdom. In the context of Jesus' ministry, this could mean the rigorist "binding and loosing" which made holiness such a feat of ritual mountaineering that only the elite could achieve it. In the context of Matthew's later community, it could refer to the Pharisees and scribes hindering their fellow Jews from accepting Jesus and entering the church.

*Woe #2: Brainwashing of proselytes.* In many Jewish synagogues there were three circles of members: Jews by birth, converts to Judaism who accepted circumcision and the full observances of the law ("proselytes"), and the "God-fearers," as Luke calls them, who were attracted to Judaism and attended the synagogue services but did not embrace all its practices. Even prior to the Christian mission, then, Judaism was not only open to gentile converts but actively pursued them. The scribes and Pharisees made heroic efforts to secure these converts. In what sense did they make them "twice as much a child of hell" as themselves? Experience shows that converts are often twice as zealous for their new-found faith as those who convert them. This saying then probably aims at those gentile converts to Judaism who were most violent in their opposition to the Christian missionaries. Not only does Luke in *Acts* show Paul dogged by "Judaizers," some of whom may have been proselytes, but he had a particular difficulty with his gentile converts in Galatia who were being persuaded by other Judaizing missionaries to adopt the practices of Judaism. Paul's reaction to them is similar to the word of Jesus here (Gal 5:12).

*Woe #3: The Practice of Swearing.* Jesus has told his disciples earlier to avoid swearing altogether (5:33-37). Here he attacks the Pharisees' casuistry in oath-taking by two ridiculous examples. Though we do not know of this practice from any independent Jewish source, casuistry is always an attempt to find pockets of security against naked surrender to God's demands—like the interminable questions teenagers can ask in the classroom in discussing "How far can I go without committing a serious sin?" God is involved in every oath, no matter what kind of hair-splitting one resorts to to keep him out. Such casuistry makes one blind, incapable of leading others. With this Jesus again rejects the scribal magisterium.

*Woe #4: Tithing.* The law of committing one tenth of one's agricultural produce to the Lord (Num 18:12 and Deut 14:22-23) was extended by the Pharisees to even the smallest garden plants. Mint, which grew on the banks of streams and in moist places, was used in seasoning and for medicine. The aromatic dill seeds were used to flavor other vegetables. Cumin seeds were used for spice or relish. Jesus does not condemn this practice, but he tells the Pharisees they cannot see the woods for the trees. The "weightier matters of the law" are those foundations for all other practices. Jesus could have recalled his earlier teaching to the Pharisees about the love commandment on which law and prophets depend (22:34–40). This time, however, instead of quoting from the law, Jesus echoes, without directly citing, a text from the prophets. To the people anxious to know what sacrifice is most pleasing to God Micah says: "You have been shown, O man, what is good and what the Lord requires of you: to do justice, to love mercy, and to walk humbly with your God" (Micah 6:8). "Justice" here in Matthew is not *dikaiosune* but *krisis*, which means to give right judgments in matters of law. "Mercy" translates the Hebrew *hesed*, which means right and compassionate relationships with all other members of the covenant community. Implicitly, by their restrictions which have separated them from the unlearned "sinners" of the Israelite community, they have failed against the most fundamental requirement of the faithful Israelite: to love *hesed.* "Faith" can mean either fidelity or trust in God. To give minute matters such importance, while neglecting the graver is to strain out the gnat and swallow the camel.

*Woe #5: Purity.* From the meticulous and elaborate washing ritual of the Pharisees Jesus quickly jumps to the person who is outwardly vs. inwardly clean. Cleaning the outside of the dish reflects the Pharisees' concern for outward purity, disguising filth in the heart. The two words translated by the RSV "extortion and rapacity" are better rendered by the NABR, "plunder and self-indulgence." The Pharisees' concern for the appearances of purity veneer not only greed but intemperance. Again by stating "*First* cleanse the inside," Jesus does not condemn the ritual cleansing but only the inversion of values he finds in the Pharisees.

*Woe #6: External Righteousness.* The point begun in the fifth woe is now driven home with dramatic irony. Touching a corpse or a tomb rendered the Jew ritually unclean. For that reason, especially before Passover, tombs were whitewashed as a visible warning to the passersby. The Pharisees would have been particularly careful to avoid such contamination. But *they are the whitewashed tombs!* Outwardly they look clean and pure white. But inside they are full of death and "uncleanness"—the state most abhorred by the purity-conscious Pharisee. More than that, their state is not just a ritual one; it is moral. While outwardly looking righteous, they are full of hypocrisy and *lawlessness (anomia)*, they who are experts in fulfilling the externals of the law! As remarked above, here is another boomerang statement that strikes at the hypocrisy of certain members of Matthew's community, who, though saying "Lord, Lord," will be condemned for their practice of lawlessness (*anomia*, 7:23).

*Woe #7: Killing the Prophets.* The climactic woe is the most severe. In Jesus' day there was a widespread cult of murdered prophets of the past, whether these were the classical prophets or those popularized in apocalyptic literature. In some cases, prophets whose death is not recorded in the OT were held to have been martyred (e.g. Isaiah was said to have been sawed in half). Monuments were erected in and around Jerusalem to these heroes. Many of the Pharisees surely promoted this cult, since, unlike the Sadducees and the Samaritans, they accepted, in addition to the first five books of the Bible, the words of the prophets as God's revelation. The logic of vv. 30–31 may escape the modern reader. It is, in fact, as John Meier points out in his commentary on Matthew, a play on words. By referring to their "fathers" who killed the prophets, they admit they are "sons of" those murderers. And "sons of" in Hebrew means not only physical descendants but "party members" or "collaborators." Their collaboration in murdering the prophets has not happened yet, but it is about to take place in murdering Jesus and those he sends as his representatives to Israel, beginning with Stephen (Acts 7).

"Fill up the measure of your fathers" is equally enigmatic to the modern reader. In the apocalyptic imagery of the times, God has established a certain amount of suffering to be endured by the persecuted just. That measure has not yet been completed; with deep irony Jesus tells his enemies to go ahead and finish off the work begun by their fathers: killing him and the missionaries he sends. Jesus here is in the tradition of the OT prophets who lashed out at the wicked leaders of their own people and threatened them with dire punishment. Here Jesus does not promise hell fire, but simply asks the rhetorical question, "How can you avoid it?"

*The Punishment.* Above we noted that when the OT prophets pronounced a woe, after the specific accusation the threatened punishment would be announced by a statement beginning with *therefore.* After the seven woes pronounced by Jesus we now reach the "therefore" clause. But there is a surprise here. Instead of describing hell fire or the destruction of the city or some other great calamity, he describes the punishment as *another mission of grace!* The "prophets and wise men and scribes" are the Christian missionaries to the Jews (some think the titles describe offices in Matthew's community), to be sent by the risen Jesus, who here speaks as the personification of the Wisdom of God (compare Luke 11:49: "Therefore also the Wisdom of God said, 'I will send them prophets and apostles . . .' "). On the one hand, this is the post-resurrection parallel to the sending of the prophets and finally the Son to the wicked tenants (21:33–41), the manifestation of God's infinite grace and patience. But just as the sending of the Son, though the supreme grace on God's part, occasioned the consummate sin on the part of the tenants, so the sending of the Christian missionaries, in itself a supreme grace, will be the occasion of even greater sin on the part of those who persecute them. And thus those already blinded to the light bring upon themselves an even worse punishment. This is how, paradoxically, additional grace is the worst punishment to the spiritually blind.

The successors to those listening to Jesus will kill and crucify the Christian missionaries. Actually, crucifixion could not be accomplished without the involvement of the Romans, as in the case of Jesus. Short of that, Jesus predicts scourging and hounding of his disciples from town to town. Some of this we see detailed in the Acts of the Apostles.

Whenever one goes against the light to the extent of resorting to violence, one becomes part of the community of violence stretching across history, from the first shedding of innocent blood, Abel's murder by his brother Cain (Gen 4:1–16), down to the murder of the last OT prophet, Zechariah. It is irrelevant to the teaching of this text that Matthew here confuses the prophet Zechariah, son of Barachiah, with Zechariah, son of Jehoida, who after a prophetic condemnation of Israel's idolatry, was stoned in the temple (2 Chron 24:17–22). Biblical names were often confused in popular tradition. Jesus and his followers are merely the latest in a long line of martyred prophets, and when innocent blood is shed, it cries to heaven (Gen 4:10; see Heb 12:24). One cannot escape the fate that will befall the city of violence if one chooses to share its shedding of innocent blood. As we now see in the next section.

## Final Separation: Jesus and Jerusalem (23:37–39)

37 "O Jerusalem, Jerusalem, killing the prophets and stoning those who are sent to you! How often would I have gathered your children together as a hen gathers her brood under her wings, and you would not! ³⁸Behold, your house is forsaken and desolate. ³⁹For I tell you, you will not see me again, until you say, 'Blessed is he who comes in the name of the Lord.' "

From his attack on the scribes and Pharisees, Jesus now turns to the city of Jerusalem itself, addressing it as he would a person. People, buildings, social habits, whatever makes up the life of a commonwealth, are swept into the destiny chosen by the religious leadership. So it is with every nation in the earth's history. So it is with Jerusalem. Individuals may bear more or less responsibility for the fate of the commonwealth— or perhaps none at all. But the state or the city rises or falls as a collectivity, and that is what is envisaged here. Like the Lord of the OT, depicted as gathering under his wings people (Is 31:5) or individuals (Ps 17:8; 91:4), Jesus earnestly desired to gather and shelter his own people from the storm that is coming. "How often" may indicate the kind of repeated visits to Jerusalem we see in John's gospel, though the synoptics, perhaps for catechetical purposes, show Jesus coming only once to the capital city as the climax of his ministry. In any case Jerusalem has rejected not only the prophets sent to it, but the last and final envoy, the Son (21:37–39). The result is that "your house" (which could mean "your nation" but more probably the temple itself), is abandoned and desolate. The prophetic present is used to describe a future event, the destruction of Jerusalem and its temple. But the more immediate dereliction is that of Jesus himself who is leaving the temple to its own fate. The passive "is forsaken" is a typically biblical way for saying, "God has forsaken." The words "forsaken and desolate" evoke Isaiah's threat to sinful Jerusalem hundreds of years earlier: "Ah! sinful nation, people laden with wickedness, vile race, corrupt children! They have forsaken the Lord, spurned the Holy One of Israel. . . . Your country is waste, your cities burnt with fire; your land before your eyes strangers devour—and daughter Zion is left like a hut in a vineyard, like a shed in a melon patch, like a city blockaded" (Is 1:4–8 NAB).

Luke places the saying about not seeing Jesus until they say "Blessed is he who comes in the name of the Lord" before Jesus' triumphal entry into Jerusalem, thus allowing at least a partial fulfillment of the prophecy at that moment. But Matthew has already recorded the entry with the triumphal chant at 21:9, so that the only possible meaning here is the final coming of Jesus as judge. At that time the saying will be a dread acknowledgement of Jesus' Lordship which the city as a whole was not willing to acknowledge "at the time of her visitation." Jerusalem will obviously see Jesus again in the passion, but the emphasis here is on the closure of the time of grace, the last invitation and the last opportunity. As Jesus leaves the temple (24:1), the curtain has been rung down on Israel as a collectivity. The age of the church will soon begin.

## THE FUTURE: KNOWN AND UNKNOWN (24:1–36)

With the beginning of chapter 24 we leave the crowds, the scribes and the Pharisees, and enter into Jesus' final major instruction to the disciples. As the religious and political powers begin to close in on Jesus, he gives them a farewell discourse of sorts, but one quite unlike that at the last supper in John. As the end of Jesus' life draws near, Matthew and the reader of the gospel ask what meaning this coming event will have in the history of the world, and particularly in relation to the strong apocalyptic hopes of first century Jews. Mark's version of Jesus' eschatological discourse (Mk 13:1–32) already provided rich, if at times enigmatic, answers which Matthew incorporates with few changes in this first section, moving with mounting intensity from the destruction of the temple through future events to the glorious coming of the Son of Man (24:29–36). But Matthew also knows that the delay of Jesus' second coming has led to a cooling of fervor and even to abuses in his community. To deal with these concerns, Matthew, beginning with 24:37, will incorporate some parables from the Q tradition and add elements of his own, climaxing the discourse with the magnificent panorama of the final judgment.

## The Destruction of the Temple (24:1–2)

**24** JESUS LEFT the temple and was going away, when his disciples came to point out to him the buildings of the temple. ²But he answered them, "You see all these, do you not? Truly, I say to you, there will not be left here one stone upon another, that will not be thrown down."

Jesus' leaving of the temple is symbolic of his rejection, for himself and his disciples, of official Judaism. From now on Jesus gives his attention solely to instructing his disciples. At the level of Matthew's composition, the church has become a separate entity from Judaism. But the original disciples, unaware of the later symbolism of Jesus' departure, are impressed with the magnificence of the Herodian temple begun over 40 years earlier. Though not yet completed in Jesus' day, it was already sufficiently grandiose to command the awe of any visitor. Recent excavations of the temple site have confirmed beyond expectations what a huge and awesome complex it was. Jesus shocks his disciples by predicting the temple's total destruction.

*The End Is Not Yet (24:3–8)*

3 As he sat on the Mount of Olives, the disciples came
to him privately, saying, "Tell us, when will this be, and
what will be the sign of your coming and of the close of the
age?" ⁴And Jesus answered them, "Take heed that no one
leads you astray. ⁵For many will come in my name, saying,
'I am the Christ,' and they will lead many astray. ⁶And you
will hear of wars and rumors of wars; see that you are not
alarmed; for this must take place, but the end is not yet.
⁷For nation will rise against nation, and kingdom against
kingdom, and there will be famines and earthquakes in
various places: ⁸all this is but the beginning of the birthpangs.

As Jesus sits on the Mount of Olives facing the temple
area, the disciples ask him a double question. In Mark's version
both questions apparently refer to the destruction of the temple. They want to know when it will happen, and if Jesus cannot
give a date at least he could tell them of signs that it is about
to happen. From Jesus' answer we might infer that their question also concerned the end-time, but the question itself does
not clearly indicate that. But in Matthew's version there is no
doubt that the disciples are concerned not merely with the date
of the destruction of the temple but with Jesus' glorious return
and the end of the age. Possibly, in the life-situation of Jesus,
they see the events superimposed, for Jews considered the
temple to be one of the foundations of the world, and the end
of the one would be the end of the other. Jesus refuses to answer "when." Moreover, although he does not expressly separate the temple destruction from the final end, he no longer
pays attention to the former and focuses his attention on the
latter. This suits Matthew's purpose well, for by his day the
destruction of the temple was a matter of historical record,
fulfilling the prediction of Jesus. But the second coming and its
delay was a burning issue, and the disciples' question here could
have been spoken easily by any member of Matthew's community.

The Greek word behind "your coming" is *parousia*, used by Paul and other NT writers to describe Jesus' glorious return. In the Greek-speaking empire, it was used for the visitation of the emperor or king to one of the provinces or cities, an event accompanied with great pomp and circumstance, sometimes with acclamations hailing the monarch as a god. It is an important word for Matthew, for he alone among all the evangelists uses it, four times in this eschatological discourse (here and 24:27, 37, 39). His picture of the end-time is dominated by the figure of the glorious, returning Son of Man.

Instead of answering with a date or signs, Jesus answers with events that will *not* be signs and with warnings instead about the interim. Beware of those who pretend to be the Messiah, whether this be a different Messiah than Jesus, or one who claims to be Jesus himself returned, or someone sent by him ("in my name"). In first-century Palestine several messianic pretenders appeared. Capturing the momentary enthusiasm of zealous Jews, they led many to destruction. By Matthew's time, the Zealots had led the whole nation to disaster.

Nor should wars, famines, or earthquakes be read as signs of the imminent end. They are rather only the beginning of "the birthpangs." This OT expression refers to sufferings endured by the people prior to their deliverance. Matthew's community had lived through the Jewish-Roman war that ended in the destruction of Jerusalem and the temple in 70 A.D. Not even that momentous event predicted by Jesus should be interpreted as a sign that Jesus was about to return.

## The Persecuted Church (24:9–14)

9 "Then they will deliver you up to tribulation, and put you to death; and you will be hated by all nations for my name's sake. ¹⁰And then many will fall away, and betray one another, and hate one another. ¹¹And many false prophets will arise and lead many astray. ¹²And because wickedness is multiplied, most men's love will grow cold. ¹³But he who endures to the end will be saved. ¹⁴And this gospel of the

kingdom will be preached throughout the whole world, as a testimony to all nations; and then the end will come.

When Jesus was asked by his disciples in Acts 1:6 about the time of the coming of the kingdom, he responded that it was not for them to know, but that they would be his witnesses in Jerusalem, throughout Judea, in Samaria and even to the ends of the earth (Acts 1:8). Witnessing there implies preaching but also a willingness to suffer for the faith. Here those elements are reversed, the prediction of suffering coming first. The anonymous "they" refers to any persecutor, Jewish or gentile. They will deliver up Jesus' disciples just as their persecutors "delivered up" John the Baptist (4:12) and Jesus (17:22). Some will be put to death.

At this point (the middle of v. 9) Matthew skips a long passage from Mark because he already used it in the missionary discourse in 10:17–22. In the second half of v. 9, Matthew resumes from Mark but adds the word *nations*, indicating that the persecution of the disciples will come not only from the Jews but from gentiles as well. And then, in v. 10–12, Matthew inserts a description of the turmoil to be expected within the Christian community itself. Many will "fall away," literally, be scandalized, that is, unable to endure the storms without and within, abandoning the faith and the Christian community as a result. It is not merely the weak who succumb to persecution but many of the strong as well. Earlier Jesus had said that persecution should be a source of rejoicing (5:10–12), but here the severity of the persecution brings about the break-up of fraternal relationships. I know of one convert who, when arrested and jailed for his conversion, denied that he was a Christian at all. He had been reported to the authorities by a fellow Christian who held a grudge against him! A literal fulfillment of Jesus' prediction that Christians would betray and hate one another.

False prophets, against whom Jesus had warned already in the Sermon on the Mount (7:15–20), will appear within the community, adding confusion to an already discouraged flock. They will teach falsehood and proclaim their own gospel, to which other Christians under the pressure of crisis will be exceptionally vulnerable. But the final scandal will be the explosion of moral anarchy even within the church. The word translated by the RSV "is multiplied" is the one used in the Greek OT to express the rampant spread of sins, crimes, prostitution, infidelities, especially the expansion of evil before the flood (Gen 6:5) and the destruction of Sodom and Gomorrah (Gen 18:20). When confronted by the wickedness of others on all sides, the Christian who had been taught to live by love, will be prone to join the crowd—or, if the wickedness was aimed at him personally, to requite in kind, to avenge himself. In either case, most Christians' love will grow cold. The churches addressed in the book of Revelation have already experienced a beginning of this cooling of love (Rev 2:4) as well as false prophecy and immorality (Rev 2:20–21). Not having an object here, "love" must be taken as defined by Jesus with its vertical direction to God, implying covenant fidelity, and its horizontal direction to neighbor, implying loyalty even under persecution. The perfection of this love would be to refuse to betray a brother or sister even to save oneself. But such love will grow cold. Does this mean Christians will become calculating and restrictive in their care for one another, doing only such acts of kindness as would be "safe"? Surely that, but since love has the characteristics of fire, for it to grow cold probably does not mean merely a weakening but rather an extinguishing. When a fire is cold, it is dead.

The call to the individual Christian surrounded by persecution, hatred, betrayal, rampant lawlessness, and lack of love, is to persevere despite all. It will be the ultimate test of covenant love. One may have to stand alone, or with the support of only a few. But that perseverance will mean salvation.

But there is also bright hope. The church, embattled though it may be, will continue to preach the gospel throughout the world. It will be a testimony (*martyrion*) to all nations, either in their favor or against them, depending on their response. Only when this missionary activity has been completed will the end come. This is Matthew's addition and clarification to the eschatological discourse as found in Mark and Luke. It

directs the attention of Christians to the mission of evangelization and away from a sterile attempt to calculate the time of
the Lord's return.

## Flight and Tribulation (24:15–22)

15 "So when you see the desolating sacrilege spoken of
by the prophet Daniel, standing in the holy place (let the
reader understand), ¹⁶then let those who are in Judea flee
to the mountains; ¹⁷let him who is on the housetop not go
down to take what is in his house; ¹⁸and let him who is in the
field not turn back to take his mantle. ¹⁹And alas for those
who are with child and for those who give suck in those
days! ²⁰Pray that your flight may not be in winter or on a
sabbath. ²¹For then there will be great tribulation, such as
has not been from the beginning of the world until now, no,
and never will be. ²²And if those days had not been shortened, no human being would be saved; but for the sake of
the elect those days will be shortened.

From the cosmic scene the view now shifts to concrete
historical signs that commend flight from Jerusalem. In the
book of Daniel (9:27; 11:31; 12:11), the "desolating sacrilege"
(sometimes translated, "the abomination of desolation" or "desolating abomination"—NABR) referred to the altar of Zeus
which the Greek King Antiochus IV set up over the altar of
holocausts in the Jerusalem temple (see 1 Macc 1:54) as part
of his program of harassment of the Jews. He offered swine's
flesh on the altar and put to death anyone found observing the
Jewish religion. In Matthew the image is a veiled reference to
something within the contemporary experience of the Christian
community, as the parenthetical "let the reader understand"
demonstrates.

To what contemporary event does it refer? It could hardly
be the erection of the Roman standards in the temple area
when the temple was burned, for then it would be too late to
flee. Nor could it be the statue to himself as Zeus which the
Roman emperor Caligula ordered to be erected in the temple,
for that would be too early. Caligula ruled from 37 to 41 A.D.

The best suggestion is that it refers to the desecration performed by the Zealots, whose politics overcame their piety when in 67–68 A.D. they went through the farce of installing a clown by the name of Phanni as high priest. About this time too, the Zealots began to hinder those who sought to leave the city. Whatever the origin of the saying and the reference, the early church historian Eusebius relates that the Christians in Judea, warned by prophecy, fled to Pella across the Jordan.

Haste will be important, as the three images urge. Pregnant and nursing mothers will suffer most. Winter in Judea is not only cold; it is the rainy season, and swollen wadis would make swift travel difficult and dangerous. The disciples should also pray they not have to escape on the sabbath. This phrase has been taken by some scholars as an indication that Matthew's community still observed the Jewish sabbath restrictions on travel or at least that somehow a saying from an early Jewish stage of the community managed to survive Matthew's pen. However, Matthew's retaining the word for that reason hardly squares with the freedom from Sabbath restrictions we find earlier in the gospel, and especially would it seem a useless remark in view of the fact that some rabbis taught that sabbath travel to save life would be permitted. The most logical meaning, then, is that, should the Christians have suddenly to travel on the sabbath, they would be conspicuous to their fellow Jews and the Zealots.

Verses 21 and 22 tag onto the command to flee, and therefore apply to the horrors of the siege and destruction of Jerusalem, gruesomely detailed by the contemporary Jewish historian Josephus (*The Jewish Wars*). But they are also projected to the future of the church, the final tribulation, which will be extremely severe but nevertheless reduced by the mercy of God for the sake of the elect, those who have remained faithful through it all.

## False Christs and False Prophets (24:23–28)

[23]Then if any one says to you, 'Lo, here is the Christ!' or 'There he is!' do not believe it. [24]For false Christs and false prophets will arise and show great signs and wonders, so as

to lead astray, if possible, even the elect. ²⁵Lo, I have told
you beforehand. ²⁶So, if they say to you, 'Lo, he is in the
wilderness,' do not go out; if they say, 'Lo, he is in the inner
rooms,' do not believe it. ²⁷For as the lightning comes from
the east and shines as far as the west, so will be the coming
of the Son of man. ²⁸Wherever the body is, there the eagles
will be gathered together.

We have met the warnings against false Messiahs (24:5)
and false prophets (7:15–20; 24:11) before. Here, though, what
marks them as signs of the final times is their ability to seduce
by false signs and wonders even, if possible, the elect. Some
of those who appear to be the holiest and therefore the safest
will fall for their seduction. It will be some safeguard to remember that Jesus has warned about them beforehand.

The peculiar Matthean v. 26 about the desert or the inner
rooms is interesting. The NT itself refers to three different
leaders of revolts in the first century, Theudas (Acts 5:36), Judas the Galilean (Acts 5:37), and "the Egyptian, who led four
thousand assassins into the desert" (Acts 21:38). The desert
was the cradle of Israel, and the prophets had foretold that
renewal and restoration would start in the desert (Hos 2:16–
17). It would be the most logical place for a Messianic pre-
tender to organize a resistance movement. (The freedom
fighters of Israel's 1947 war of liberation organized themselves
there.) Seeing that Jerusalem was doomed, one thousand Zealots withdrew to the mountain fortress of Masada in the desert
where they held out against the Romans for three years, finally
committing mass suicide to avoid the disgrace of surrender.
Matthew's community had lived through that tragic page of
Israel's history immediately after the fall of the temple.

On the other hand, there were the mystery religions scattered throughout the empire in the first century. Many of them
had rites of initiation which would invite the initiate to the
"inner room" of revelation, and some of them syncretized with
Jewish beliefs. Some Jews also believed in a "hidden Messiah"
to be revealed at the moment of God's pleasure (see John 7:27).
The coming of the Son of Man will be different. Unlike his first
coming as an infant who had to be searched out by the Magi,

the second coming will be public and not localized. It will be a brilliant, even cosmic type of event.

The reference to eagles gathering where the body is has often been taken by commentators to refer to the symbols of the Roman army that conquered Jerusalem. This is possible, but it does not fit well the context here, which has to do not with Jerusalem but with false messiahs and the coming of the Son of Man. Since "body" means "carcass," "eagles" should really be translated "vultures." The saying was originally probably a proverb meaning, "Where one thing is found, there is always another." Some scholars hold that the image is another affirmation of the public character of the Son of Man's parousia—as obvious as vultures circling in the sky. Others, finding this too strained, have proposed it as a sign of God's ineluctable judgment on sin. A simpler explanation is that those who rush to false messiahs are like vultures attracted to carrion.

## The Glorious Coming of the Son of Man (24:29–31)

29 "Immediately after the tribulation of those days the sun will be darkened, and the moon will not give its light, and the stars will fall from heaven, and the powers of the heavens will be shaken; ³⁰then will appear the sign of the Son of man in heaven, and then all the tribes of the earth will mourn, and they will see the Son of man coming on the clouds of heaven with power and great glory; ³¹and he will send out his angels with a loud trumpet call, and they will gather his elect from the four winds, from one end of heaven to the other.

The long awaited climax now arrives. The great tribulation over, cosmic signs will follow. Jesus is speaking prophetic language used in the OT to dramatize the cosmic significance of historical events—the fall of Babylon (Is 13:10) or of Edom (Is 34:4), a plague of locusts (Jl 2:10), or the death of Pharaoh (Ez 32:7). Here, however, it is no longer the fall of Jerusalem that is being dramatized but the "close of the age" (24:3; 28:20). It was popular belief in Jesus' day that the sun, moon and stars were ruled by heavenly beings which influenced people's lives.

In apocalyptic language, the darkening of the sun and moon
and the falling of stars means the release of these powers on
earth (Rev 6:12–13; 8:10–12; 9:1; 12:4). Exactly what historical
form these events will take is not specified, because in apocalyptic language every significant struggle on earth is merely
the earthly counterpart of a battle in the heavens, and it is not
easy to distinguish what elements belong to the heavenly and
which to the earthly scene. The point is that the last act of
history is the revelation both of the evil powers that have been
at work all along and the Son of Man whose coming will banish
them completely (2 Thes 2:3–12). The reader will be given a
foretaste of this cosmic victory in the signs that accompany the
death and resurrection of Jesus (27:51–54; 28:2).

Here, that central and all-determining moment of history
is evoked by the Matthean phrase, "all the tribes of the earth
will mourn." On hearing that phrase, any Jew who knew the
Scriptures would think of Zech 12:10–12: "When they look upon
him whom they have pierced, they shall mourn for him, as one
mourns for an only child . . . On that day . . . the earth shall
mourn, each tribe by itself . . ." (See also Rev 1:7; John 19:37).
The Son of Man who comes on the clouds of heaven to claim
his cosmic victory is the same one who was pierced upon the
cross. Those who have rejected him will mourn, not for him
but for themselves. Those who have accepted him and lived by
his message will rejoice, for when he comes in great power and
majesty, they will be gathered from the farthest corners of the
earth into his kingdom.

## The Time of the Coming (24:32–36)

32 "From the fig tree learn its lesson: as soon as its
branch becomes tender and puts forth its leaves, you know
that summer is near. 33So also, when you see all these
things, you know that he is near, at the very gates. 34Truly,
I say to you, this generation will not pass away till all these
things take place. 35Heaven and earth will pass away, but
my words will not pass away.

36 "But of that day and hour no one knows, not even the angels of heaven, nor the Son, but the Father only.

This is a notoriously difficult passage to interpret. It brilliantly illustrates the problems with which scholars wrestle: What was the original meaning of Jesus? Were these sayings originally grouped together, or have they been assembled by Mark or someone before him? How does Mark understand these sayings? How does Matthew, who follows Mark here, understand them in the light of his overall theology? And finally, what do they say to us today?

It will be helpful to note that the sayings of v. 32–35 are tied together by "catchword composition." This is a technique frequently used in oral tradition to tie sayings together by a word or phrase common to both, even when the sayings otherwise have nothing in common. To use a humorous example, if the pastor in his announcements from the pulpit would be using this technique, he might say, "Today is the feast of St. Joseph. St. Joseph was a carpenter. Carpenters make confessionals. And confessions will be heard tonight at 6 o'clock." I remember listening to the sermon of an Archbishop who was a master of catchword composition. His sermon was as encyclopedic as it was long, but anyone who expected logical connections between his sayings was at a total loss to find them. Now in the period of oral transmission of the sayings of Jesus, this was a serious method of cataloguing the sayings of Jesus, and the method can be illustrated here:

| | | |
|---|---|---|
| v. 32: Fig tree | > | near |
| v. 33: near | > | all these things |
| v. 34: all these things | > | pass away |
| v. 35: pass away | > | heaven and earth/my words |

Now Matthew, like Mark before him, was a preserver and transmitter of tradition, and at times the concern to preserve the tradition was greater than a concern for clarity. Thus our modern passion for logic and contextual clarity in these sayings, which may well have been uttered by Jesus in several different contexts, then were gathered by an oral transmitter by the technique of catchword composition, may be greater than that of the evangelists who preserved them. The early transmitters of the tradition seem to have had a faith in the power of individual sayings of Jesus which could then be contextualized according to each new situation of the audience.

Even so, let us do the best to discover what Matthew understood the meaning to be when he incorporated this block of catchword sayings.

The parable of the fig tree is fairly clear. The appearance of buds on the fig tree in spring heralds summer (Greek: *theros*) and the harvest (Greek: *therismos*). So "all these things" (that is, all the preliminary events Jesus has foretold in the preceding sections: destruction of the temple, appearance of false Messiahs and false prophets, wars, famines, earthquakes, the spread of wickedness, the freezing of love, the great tribulation) are signs that "he" or "it" (the Greek may be translated either way) is near. "It" could be the final judgment; "he" could be the Son of Man.

If "all these things" in v. 34 means the same as in v. 33, then "this generation" will witness all of the above. But who belongs to "this generation"? Some scholars take the meaning qualitatively as the "evil and adulterous generation" Jesus describes in 12:39 and 16:4 and note that if Jesus elsewhere understands this generation as collectively including all those who shed innocent blood from Abel to Zechariah the prophet (23:35–36), it could conceivably also include all the wicked till the end of time. But this is forced, for the good people will presumably also witness "all these things."

There is a better way to understand in what sense Jesus' generation will witness all those events that will herald and even perhaps usher in the coming of the Son of Man. It lies in the distinction between *chronological* time and *proleptic* (or "rehearsal") time. Both kinds of time are measured in relation to something else to give us perspective. Chronological time, or calendar time, measures events by relating them to the movements of the sun, the moon, seasons, and clocks. The only perspective chronological time gives us is a flat past, present, and future. It makes no judgment about the relative importance of the events. Blowing my nose is of no less importance than the eruption of Vesuvius. Proleptic time gives events perspective by relating them to coming events of climactic importance, such as the end of the world, the final judgment, the consummation of the kingdom. In proleptic time, one event is an anticipation or a rehearsal for the other. The earlier event somehow contains or makes imminent the later one. A close call with death may be more significant for a person's life than the moment of real, physical death, if, as often happens, it radically changes his way of living thereafter.

We may now understand in what sense "all these things" contain the end. In Jesus' understanding, crises of the type he has enumerated, are rehearsals for the end. For a person of faith, the end happens whenever an event confronts him with the ultimate meaning of life and the world. That is why "this present generation" experiences "all these things." Clinging to the words of Jesus, which transcend everything that is perishable, the Christian knows the ultimate meaning of whatever segment of historical events confronts him. Crises and especially persecutions make the coming of Jesus imminent, "at the gates." What is ultimately important is not what the future holds but who holds the future.

In v. 35, Jesus returns to chronological time, saying that the mystery of the final moment is hidden in the Father. It has not even been given to the Son as revealer to know it. And with this statement, the ground is cut from under every attempt to predict the time of the Second Coming in chronological terms—a directive which some Christian sects have known more in the breach than in the practice.

## THE PRESENT: WATCH! (24:37–25:30)

From this point onward, Matthew leaves Mark, picks up his Q source, and adds some material of his own. The theme of the future recedes to the background, giving way to the critical importance of the present as a time of readiness for the coming of the Lord.

## Introduction: The Peril of Unreadiness (24:37–44)

37 As were the days of Noah, so will be the coming of
the Son of man. 38For as in those days before the flood they
were eating and drinking, marrying and giving in marriage,
until the day when Noah entered the ark, 39and they did not
know until the flood came and swept them all away, so will
be the coming of the Son of man. 40Then two men will be in
the field; one is taken and one is left. 41Two women will be
grinding at the mill; one is taken and one is left. 42Watch
therefore, for you do not know on what day your Lord is
coming. 43But know this, that if the householder had known
in what part of the night the thief was coming, he would
have watched and would not have let his house be broken
into. 44Therefore you also must be ready; for the Son of man
is coming at an hour you do not expect."

Here Jesus relates three parables or examples of people
who were not ready when something dreadful happened. Matthew introduces the noun *coming (parousia)* twice here, showing again how important he considers this event. In the time
of Noah, people were going about their daily business (Jesus
does not say they were sinning) when they were swept away
by the flood. The implied lesson is that the disciples, like Noah,
should live in this world always ready for the next and not so
engrossed in the cares of the world and the pursuit of riches
that they are deaf to the word of God (13:22). The coming of
the Son of Man, at a moment least expected, should find them
ready.

The second example concerns two men and two women at
work. "One will be taken, one left" means that one, who is
prepared by doing the good works of the Christian life, will be
taken into the kingdom. The other will be left outside. Though
we should not draw any percentage conclusion from this, the
real possibility of the damnation of some is a stark warning.
The word "watch" means to stay awake, as watchmen would at
night. "Vigilance" means perseverance in faith and good works.

The final example is that of the person whose house is
broken into because he was not awake and watching. The Son

of Man will come at an unexpected hour. Obviously the point of the parable is the unexpected hour of Jesus' coming, not that Jesus is a thief—though for the unprepared it may well seem a violent intrusion.

## The Good and the Wicked Servant (24:45–51)

45 "Who then is the faithful and wise servant, whom his master has set over his household, to give them their food at the proper time? [46]Blessed is that servant whom his master when he comes will find so doing. [47]Truly, I say to you, he will set him over all his possessions. [48]But if that wicked servant says to himself, 'My master is delayed,' [49]and begins to beat his fellow servants, and eats and drinks with the drunken, [50]the master of that servant will come on a day when he does not expect him and at an hour he does not know, [51]and will punish him, and put him with the hypocrites; there men will weep and gnash their teeth.

Matthew had a pastoral problem which was not so acute at the time of Mark: the delay of the Lord's second coming. In this parable and the two following Matthew deals with the contrasting responses of disciples to the delay—on the one hand, fidelity, good works and industrious use of gifts; on the other, self-indulgence, laziness and pusillanimity. This first parable is addressed, amazingly, to church leaders who should be setting the example of the proper attitude in their care of the Lord's household. They are to feed the other disciples, not at their own convenience, but whenever the disciples need it. The servant who is found fulfilling this office will be blessed with charge of *all* the possessions of his Lord. But the one who tyrannizes the other disciples or wastes his time in self-indulgence will be startled at the Lord's coming and will be as severely punished as the hypocrites, Matthew's tag for the Jewish leaders who have rejected the gospel. The place of "weeping and gnashing of teeth" is the place of damnation.

## The Ten Girls and the Wedding Feast (25:1–13)

**25**"THEN THE kingdom of heaven shall be compared to ten maidens who took their lamps and went to meet the bridegroom. ²Five of them were foolish, and five were wise. ³For when the foolish took their lamps, they took no oil with them; ⁴but the wise took flasks of oil with their lamps. ⁵As the bridegroom was delayed, they all slumbered and slept. ⁶But at midnight there was a cry, 'Behold, the bridegroom! Come out to meet him.' ⁷Then all those maidens rose and trimmed their lamps. ⁸And the foolish said to the wise, 'Give us some of your oil, for our lamps are going out.' ⁹But the wise replied, 'Perhaps there will not be enough for us and for you; go rather to the dealers and buy for yourselves.' ¹⁰And while they went to buy, the bridegroom came, and those who were ready went in with him to the marriage feast; and the door was shut. ¹¹Afterward the other maidens came also, saying, 'Lord, lord, open to us.' ¹²But he replied, 'Truly, I say to you, I do not know you.' ¹³Watch therefore, for you know neither the day nor the hour.

At the time of the parousia and judgment (such is the meaning of the introductory "then"), the situation of those awaiting the kingdom will be like this story. I attended a tribal wedding in India quite similar to this story. At a given signal in the early afternoon, the bride and her party left her family's house to meet the groom and his party and escort them to the bride's house. The groom's arrival was a parousia of sorts, as the bride's party went to welcome him.. Thus began festivities that would last through the entire night and on through the week. In this gospel story, of course, the details are symbolic. In the NT the kingdom is a wedding feast (22:1-14; Rev 19:9), Jesus is the bridegroom (9:15) the church is the bride (Rev 21:2, 9, 17; Eph 5:25-26). All the girl-attendants are expecting the groom, but not all are prepared for his *delay*. The five "foolish" ones are different from the cruel and self-indulgent servant in the preceding story. There, observing the delay, the servant acts dishonorably. The foolish girls, on the contrary, do not take the possibility of a delay seriously. The "wise" girls do, and as a result take extra oil with them.

As the hour grows late and the bridegroom does not arrive, all the girls fall asleep. This is not a mere whimsical detail. The verbs for "slept" and "rose" were commonplace in the NT for death and resurrection. When Matthew uses the second of these independently of his sources, he means a real rising from physical death (9:25; 10:8; 16:21; 17:9). It is likely, then, that he too means "slept" to signify death. This, of course, was the real situation for Matthew's community as it had been for the Thessalonians—some members had died before the Lord's return (1 Thes 4:13–18). At the parousia, some Christians will be dead, some alive, but *all* must meet him.

When the foolish, realizing they have no oil, ask the wise for some, the wise in their continued wisdom point to the obvious fact that sharing at this point would risk extinguishing all lamps and ruining the feast. While the foolish leave to get oil, the wise go out and processionally escort the groom into the feast. The door is shut and locked, symbol of the final judgment. Entrance through the door is no longer merely difficult (7:13–14); it is impossible. The returning girls' cry, "Lord, Lord," is also the cry of those disciples in 7:21–22 hoping to gain entry because of their prophecies and miracles. To them, as to the foolish maidens, the Lord says, "I never knew you." There, the false disciples were condemned for not bearing fruit (7:15–20), that is, for not doing the will of the Father, which means performing the works of mercy (25:31–46). Like the scribes and the Pharisees who preach but do not practice (23:3) and the foolish man who, hearing the word of Jesus, did not act on it (7:26–27), the foolish girls have not *done* the agenda Jesus prescribed for his disciples. In 5:14–16 the lamp held high was an image for the good works to be done by the disciples in the sight of the world. The oil here, then, used for lamps, is surely good works. Jesus' final command to *watch* does not here mean "stay awake" (all the girls slept) but rather, "Be prepared by good works for the coming whose time you do not know."

## The Parable of the Talents (25:14-30)

14 "For it will be as when a man going on a journey called his servants and entrusted to them his property; ¹⁵to one he gave five talents, to another two, to another one, to each according to his ability. Then he went away. ¹⁶He who had received the five talents went at once and traded with them; and he made five talents more. ¹⁷So also, he who had the two talents made two talents more. ¹⁸But he who had received the one talent went and dug in the ground and hid his master's money. ¹⁹Now after a long time the master of those servants came and settled accounts with them. ²⁰And he who had received the five talents came forward, bringing five talents more, saying, 'Master, you delivered to me five talents; here I have made five talents more.' ²¹His master said to him, 'Well done, good and faithful servant; you have been faithful over a little, I will set you over much; enter into the joy of your master.' ²²And he also who had the two talents came forward, saying, 'Master, you delivered to me two talents; here I have made two talents more.' ²³His master said to him, 'Well done, good and faithful servant; you have been faithful over a little, I will set you over much; enter into the joy of your master.' ²⁴He also who had received the one talent came forward, saying, 'Master, I knew you to be a hard man, reaping where you did not sow, and gathering where you did not winnow; ²⁵so I was afraid, and I went and hid your talent in the ground. Here you have what is yours.' ²⁶But his master answered him, 'You wicked and slothful servant! You knew that I reap where I have not sowed, and gather where I have not winnowed? ²⁷Then you ought to have invested my money with the bankers, and at my coming I should have received what was my own with interest. ²⁸So take the talent from him, and give it to him who has the ten talents. ²⁹For to every one who has will more be given, and he will have abundance; but from him who has not, even what he has will be taken away. ³⁰And cast the worthless servant into the outer darkness; there men will weep and gnash their teeth.'

The abbreviated beginning of this parable means, "The kingdom of heaven is like . . ." or, better, "The coming of the Son of Man will be like . . ." Since in the Hellenistic world the talent was the largest known unit of money, the master is, by modern standards, a millionaire. Going on a journey, he entrusts his entire property at home to three servants, "each according to his ability." This diversity makes one think of the charismatic grace which the risen Christ has distributed in a measured way to each member of the community for its upbuilding (Eph 4:7), a grace of ministry for which each will have to answer (1 Cor 3:12–15). If so, this parable, like that of the two servants above (24:45–51), concerns not the interior grace that saves but grace given to the one for the many. It would apply particularly to the leaders in the community (they have received more), but the principle of making the divine gifts fruitful applies to everyone.

Those who receive the five and the two talents work industriously to make them fruitful, doubling in fact the original investment. Their example makes all the more pathetic the third servant who buries his master's money (see commentary above on 13:44). The master is gone *a long time*. In the light of Matthew's dealing with the delay of the parousia, we could understand "longer than expected." But return he does. In their reporting all three address the master as believing Christians address Jesus, "Lord" (*kyrie*, which the RSV and the NABR translate "Master"). The two who worked industriously are not only rewarded in a material way but (and this detail is proper to Matthew, not found in the Lukan parallel, Lk 19:11–27) they are welcomed "into the joy of your Lord." Matthew here touches a vein of the tradition also found in Jesus' discourse at the last supper in John 16:22, that for the faithful disciple the return of Jesus will mean fellowship in his joy. This spiritual union with Jesus is greater than any material reward.

The tragic flaw in the third servant is a paralyzing *fear*. He knows that the master expects returns, but this knowledge does not fire him to industrious activity, as it did the other servants; it freeze him into immobility. The only activity of which he is capable is digging a hole to bury the talent. His end is the most tragic in the gospel: worthless, he is cast into the outer darkness with the damned. The proverbial observation that "the rich get richer and the poor get poorer" has its truth in the spiritual realm as well: used when they are given, the spiritual gifts grow and bear fruit; unused, they atrophy.

The reason for disuse in this case is fear. Christian spirituality has not given as much attention to fear as it has to other obstacles in the Christian journey. At a retreat I once asked the participants to call out fears which they found blocking them from growth and ministry. The names of fears came so fast I needed help to write them on the chalkboard, nearly a hundred of them. Risk is a law of life; to avoid risk can cheat the Christian not only out of fruitfulness but out of eternal life as well.

Lest the dour end of this parable erase all hope, it is worth remembering that fear too can be overcome by faith. Jesus is available in the midst of the storm, saying, "Why are you afraid, O you of little faith?" (8:26). The infidelity of the third servant in the last analysis was an unwillingness to claim in faith the power of Jesus available to him.

## The Last Judgment (25:31–46)

31 "When the Son of man comes in his glory, and all the angels with him, then he will sit on his glorious throne. [32]Before him will be gathered all the nations, and he will separate them one from another as a shepherd separates the sheep from the goats, [33]and he will place the sheep at his right hand, but the goats at the left. [34]Then the King will say to those at his right hand, 'Come, O blessed of my Father, inherit the kingdom prepared for you from the foundation of the world; [35]for I was hungry and you gave me food, I was thirsty and you gave me drink, I was a stranger and you welcomed me, [36]I was naked and you clothed me, I was sick and you visited me, I was in prison and you came to me.' [37]Then the righteous will answer him, 'Lord, when did we see thee hungry and feed thee, or thirsty and give thee drink? [38]And when did we see thee a stranger and welcome thee, or naked and clothe thee? [39]And when did we see thee

sick or in prison and visit thee?' ⁴⁰And the King will answer them, 'Truly, I say to you, as you did it to one of the least of these my brethren, you did it to me.' ⁴¹Then he will say to those at his left hand, 'Depart from me, you cursed, into the eternal fire prepared for the devil and his angels; ⁴²for I was hungry and you gave me no food, I was thirsty and you gave me no drink, ⁴³I was a stranger and you did not welcome me, naked and you did not clothe me, sick and in prison and you did not visit me.' ⁴⁴Then they also will answer, 'Lord, when did we see thee hungry or thirsty or a stranger or naked or sick or in prison, and did not minister to thee?' ⁴⁵Then he will answer them, 'Truly, I say to you, as you did it not to one of the least of these, you did it not to me.' ⁴⁶And they will go away into eternal punishment, but the righteous into eternal life."

This scene stands at the climactic summit of Jesus' entire public ministry. It is awesome, universal, final. The Son of Man, who has dominated the sayings of Jesus on the final times, comes in *his* glory. It is the glory of the Father, to be sure (16:27), but, like the divine power (28:18), it has been wholly given to the Son, who is enthroned as King no longer of Israel merely (Ps 2:6) but of the entire universe, receiving all the nations as his heritage (Ps 2:8). The ingathering that heretofore has been a symbol of the judgment (13:39, 48–50) now is the "round-up" of all the nations, gentiles and Jews. The master who has allowed good and bad to mingle in this world, even in the church (13:38–39, 47–50), now is the shepherd who separates the good from the wicked, a task elsewhere delegated to the angels (13:41, 49).

At this point there is no distinction between those in the church and those outside it. Judgment will not be based on titles or even on the cry, "Lord, Lord," but upon deeds. The image of sheep, which was used earlier for members of the church (7:15; 18:12–13), now applies to the righteous of any nation. The King (the first time Jesus has used this title of himself) proclaims to them, "Come." It is not the first time Jesus has said "Come." He had done so in the call of his disciples (4:19), and he had flung the call to all who were heavily burdened (11:28). But this is the final call, the "come" which makes the called the elect. They are "blessed." The beatitude echoes the opening lines of the Sermon on the Mount, those proclaimed blessed and promised the kingdom for their hunger for God and their deeds of mercy, justice and peace. As Israel of old was promised to inherit the holy land, these "inherit" the kingdom as the real children of the Father who has prepared it for them from the beginning of the world.

The reason for their blessed inheritance is their *deeds*. In this climactic passage, the Matthean Jesus hammers home a theme that runs through this gospel from the Sermon on the Mount onwards: holiness is not words, holiness is not geographical or genetic closeness to Jesus, holiness is not titles, holiness is not external show of piety. Holiness is *doing* the will of the merciful Father, which is love in action. The lyrical detailing of these deeds is climactic but not surprising, given the stress throughout the gospel on love and mercy. The real surprise is that the King says these deeds were done to *him*. The Lord has so identified himself with the hungry, the homeless, the naked, the sick and the imprisoned, that they are not only his brothers. They are the Lord himself in disguise, a disguise that now becomes a theophany.

"Brother" and "least one" were terms earlier used in the gospel for a member of the Christian community (5:22–24, 47; 7:3–5; 18:15–21). For this reason, some scholars have proposed that Jesus is proclaiming blessed those who offer hospitality to Christian missionaries, those already blessed by Jesus in 10:42 for giving even so much as a cup of cold water to those who come in his name. Surely there were Jews and gentiles who, though not becoming Christians, did such deeds of loving-kindness to the early Christian missionaries. But to highlight only those who have been kind to Christian missionaries would be rather anti-climactic in this cosmic finale. The deeds rewarded here also go beyond mere hospitality. The conclusion is astounding: In the matter of love Jesus cannot be domesticated. He identifies himself with the poor and the suffering of the entire world. The compassion he showed to the outcasts of Israel he now receives from any citizen of earth in any act of merciful love.

The sentence upon the reprobate could hardly be more severe: they are damned, they go to the eternal fire, they will join the devil and his angels and all because they would not show compassion on earth. They too are surprised that in the hungry and thirsty, the homeless, the naked, the sick and the imprisoned it was the Lord himself they were rejecting. They address the king as "Lord," as indeed they must now at this final revelation. The title does not mean these people are Christians, though indeed some of them surely are, if we are to take the threats elsewhere in the gospel seriously. The title is used by those who claim they did not realize it was the Lord they were rejecting; but that is no acceptable excuse. Refusal to show compassion to one's fellow human being is enough to merit damnation. The revelation in Jesus' teaching *now* is, like Scrooge's vision of Marlowe, a call to awaken to the presence of God in the poorest of the poor.

Matthew beautifully avoids monotony in his last repetition of the "corporal works of mercy" by abbreviating the verbs and concluding, "and did not minister to thee?" The verb *minister*, also translated *serve*, evokes the ministry of Jesus as servant and the call to his disciples to be servants as well (20:25–28). Also, by reversing the good and the bad in the final line, Jesus concludes the whole scene on the positive note of the entry of the righteous into eternal life. Once more we see what Jesus means by that righteousness which must exceed that of the scribes and the Pharisees if his disciples are to enter the kingdom of heaven (5:20). It is love in action.

A theological question of great import arises from this text. If at the final judgment all people are judged on their acts of charity, if Christians who have done so find themselves brothers with non-Christians who have been saved by doing the same acts of love, and, conversely, if Christians as well as non-Christians can be lost on the common lack of deeds of love, then why the gospel, why baptism, why the church? It is a question which many ask themselves today, and this text is often cited in support of the question.

Every text of scripture must be interpreted in context, and first of all in the context of its author. This is the same Matthean Jesus who at the end of the gospel commissions his disciples to go to all the nations, to make disciples of them, baptize them and teach them to live the entire gospel. The question is: what advantage does the Christian have over the one who has not heard the gospel? First of all, the challenge of the gospel, including this text, is enormous, beyond normal human capacity to live. We saw this already in the Sermon on the Mount. Yet Jesus says it must be lived in its entirety ("Teach them to observe *all* I have commanded you" 28:19). What makes the impossible dream possible? It is the presence of Jesus promised to his church (28:20). Not only therefore is the Christian constantly confronted by this passage on the final judgment, he has the power of Jesus available to enable him to live up to Jesus' high expectations. If others manage to do it outside the church, it can hardly be without God's saving grace working in them, a grace Christians know to bear the name Jesus. By the same token, however, Christians will be judged all the more exactingly because of the superabundance of gifts that has been given them—*they* have received the ten talents! Theirs is the responsibility of the superabundantly gifted. ■

# The Climax:

## Jesus' Passion and Resurrection (26:1–28:20)

The alternation of story and discourse, which has been the structure of the gospel up to this point, has not been a static one. A plot has been developing in the material which now reaches its climax. The passion-death-resurrection of Jesus is the central event of the entire gospel, that which gives all the rest, both teaching and narrative, its final meaning.

### Jesus Introduces his Passion (26:1–5)

**26** WHEN JESUS had finished all these sayings, he said to his disciples, ²"You know that after two days the passover is coming, and the Son of man will be delivered up to be crucified."

3 Then the chief priests and the elders of the people gathered in the palace of the high priest, who was called Caiaphas, ⁴and took counsel together in order to arrest Jesus by stealth and kill him. ⁵But they said, "Not during the feast, lest there be a tumult among the people."

Matthew has furnished us with such a wealth of Jesus' sayings throughout his gospel, that we might be tempted to think of his work as primarily a collection of Jesus' teaching. Not so. Although the opening line, "When Jesus had finished. . . ," is Matthew's usual transition from discourse to narrative, the addition of "all" to "these sayings" alerts us to a key theological point. *All* refers not merely to the last discourse but to all the teaching of Jesus throughout the gospel. Hence, the teachings of Jesus are not merely those of a wise religious man, even a divine man. Illustrating by his own example that the teacher must *do* and not merely teach (5:19; 23:3), Jesus will now give himself in the supreme act of love, and the Father's response in raising him from the dead will seal with divine authority all that Jesus has taught. And this is what makes the teachings of Jesus different from those of any man who has ever lived. Matthew understands this well, but he is still so enamored of Jesus the speaker that, unlike Mark, he uses Jesus' own words to open the curtain on the passion story. Jesus announces and introduces his disciples to the passion (v. 2). It is almost as if he gives his permission for the first act to begin. In this original fourth passion prediction Jesus himself ties his passion to the Passover celebration and, by implication, his sacrifice to that of the paschal lamb. Matthew is also more historically precise than Mark when he says that the chief priests and *elders* (the components of the Sanhedrin) gathered with *Caiphas*, the high priest (also named by the Jewish historian Josephus, *Ant.* 18,2,2). The expression "took counsel together" echoes the messianic Psalm 2:2: "The rulers take counsel together, against the Lord and against his messiah." The expression "during the feast" can have two meanings, the chronological one, which is the most obvious (not during the festival time), the other topographical (not in the midst of the festival crowds). If the first, their plan does not succeed, or at least it will be changed in mid-course, for Jesus dies, as he prophesies, on the festival. If the second, then their plot does succeed as far as the arrest is concerned, but that apparent success only fulfills the word of Jesus and the plan of God.

## The Anointing in Bethany (26:6–13)

6 Now when Jesus was at Bethany in the house of Simon the leper, [7]a woman came up to him with an alabaster flask of very expensive ointment, and she poured it on his head, as he sat at table. [8]But when the disciples saw it, they were indignant, saying, "Why this waste? [9]For this ointment might have been sold for a large sum, and given to the poor." [10]But Jesus, aware of this, said to them, "Why do you trouble the woman? For she has done a beautiful thing to me. [11]For you always have the poor with you, but you will not always have me. [12]In pouring this ointment on my body

she has done it to prepare me for burial. [13]Truly, I say to you, wherever this gospel is preached in the whole world, what she has done will be told in memory of her."

This first event of passion week was a precious memory in the early church because it contrasted so poignantly with the hatred of Jesus' enemies which precedes and the betrayal by Judas which follows. All we know about Simon the Leper is his name. Perhaps he had been healed by Jesus, for if he is present, he could hardly be hosting a banquet if he were still afflicted with the quarantining disease. Bethany was less than an hour's walk east of Jerusalem. Matthew drops Mark's detail that the ointment is "pure nard," made from a root native to India, and simply says it was "very expensive." Pouring oil on the head of a guest was, like washing his feet, a gesture of hospitality (Ps 23:5), both very welcome in the hot and dry climate of Judea. Ointment would be kept in an earthenware jar with a long neck which, when broken, would facilitate pouring. While Mark says that "some" of those present react to the "waste" of the precious ointment, Matthew specifies that it is the disciples who say so. They have perhaps been too well-trained by Jesus, over-zealous young disciples unable to appreciate the deeper meaning of what is happening before their eyes. In any case, Jesus, aware of what his disciples are saying, defends the woman's action as a "beautiful deed." The reason he gives, that "the poor you have always with you but you do not always have me," addressed to the disciples, may be important to Matthew as a justification for expending for worship moneys that could be given to the poor. On the other hand, adding immediately that the woman was anointing Jesus' body for burial, something that would be done only *after* death, may indicate that Jesus is poorer than the poorest, for death is upon him. Taken with the following story of Judas' betrayal, there may be an echo here of Psalm 41, where the poor just man cries out, "Blessed is he who considers the poor! The Lord delivers him in the day of trouble; . . . thou dost not give him up to the will of his enemies . . . even my bosom friend in whom I trusted, who ate of my bread, has lifted his heel against me. But thou, O Lord, be gracious to me, and raise me up!"

Matthew does not record either Nicodemus' anointing of Jesus (Jn 19:39–40) nor the women going to the tomb on Sunday morning to do so (Mk 16:1). All the more then, does the Bethany anointing in Matthew gain a sacramental meaning. Like the institution of the Eucharist at the last supper, this gesture also done at a meal anticipates and prophesies the death of Jesus. It also heralds the proclamation of the gospel throughout the world. Luke says that the Eucharist is to be repeated in *memory* of Jesus (Lk 22:19). Here, the gospel (all that Matthew has given to us) will be proclaimed and in it, this story will be related in memory of *her*.

## Judas Plots Betrayal (26:14–16)

14 Then one of the twelve, who was called Judas Iscariot, went to the chief priests ¹⁵and said, "What will you give me if I deliver him to you?" And they paid him thirty pieces of silver. ¹⁶And from that moment he sought an opportunity to betray him.

Matthew's slight editing of Mark here puts the phrase "one of the twelve" like a headline at the very beginning, as if to record the shock that Jesus would die not merely through the machinations of the authorities but by the collusion of one of his intimate company. Further, in Matthew, Judas asks "How much money will you give me?" underlining the venal nature of his plot, and the priests' answer, "thirty pieces of silver," echoes Zech 11:12, where after Zechariah makes a dire prophecy, the sheep-merchants count out his wages, thirty pieces of silver. The Lord then directs Zechariah to throw the thirty pieces into the temple treasury, as Judas will do in 27:9–10. Receiving the money, Judas now looks for his chance to betray his Lord.

## The Passover: Jesus Foretells Judas' Betrayal (26:17–25)

17 Now on the first day of Unleavened Bread the disciples came to Jesus, saying, "Where will you have us prepare

for you to eat the passover?" ¹⁸He said, "Go into the city to a certain one, and say to him, 'The Teacher says, My time is at hand; I will keep the passover at your house with my disciples.'" ¹⁹And the disciples did as Jesus had directed them, and they prepared the passover.

20 When it was evening, he sat at table with the twelve disciples; ²¹and as they were eating, he said, "Truly, I say to you, one of you will betray me." ²²And they were very sorrowful, and began to say to him one after another, "Is it I, Lord?" ²³He answered, "He who has dipped his hand in the dish with me, will betray me. ²⁴The Son of man goes as it is written of him, but woe to that man by whom the Son of man is betrayed! It would have been better for that man if he had not been born." ²⁵Judas, who betrayed him, said, "Is it I, Master?" He said to him, "You have said so."

Originally Passover and the feast of the Unleavened Bread were separate festivals, the latter beginning immediately after the former and lasting for a week. In practice, however, the feasts merged into a week-long feast called Passover. Here "the first day of Unleavened Bread" means the day on which the Passover lambs were sacrificed in the temple in preparation for the meal that evening, with which the feast officially began. Thus Matthew, like Mark and Luke, situates Jesus' death on the day of Passover itself, unlike John who places it on the eve of Passover, at the very hour the paschal lambs are being slaughtered in the temple. The difference is a very involved question which the scholars continue to dispute. The common point of all the gospels is that Jesus' death is tied to the Jewish feast of Passover, which gives it a rich theological meaning. Matthew underscores this connection in v. 18, by the words, "My time is at hand. I will keep Passover at your house . . ." "My time" is not the time of the meal but the time of Jesus' suffering and death, clearly linked with the Jewish festival. "My time" in Matthew is very close to "my hour" in John's gospel.

Only the twelve join Jesus for this intimate meal. Again Jesus announces what is going to happen. To the prophecy of betrayal each disciple answers with the Christian address,

"Lord," with the exception of Judas who uses the Jewish address, *rabbi*, the same title he gives Jesus when giving him the
identifying kiss in the garden. Dipping the hand in the dish
simply means reaching into the one common plate to take a
morsel of food. The one who will betray Jesus belongs to the
intimate circle of disciples and is sharing the very table with
Jesus. If we recall how table-fellowship was in some way the
"sacrament" of Jesus' preaching—that is, Jesus' visible sign
that the Father makes all welcome at the table of the kingdom,
an innovation which the Pharisees could not tolerate ("Why
does your teacher eat with tax collectors and sinners?" 9:11),
the betrayal by Judas is all the more poignant, for it is the
price Jesus will pay for embracing and trusting all in his company. Jesus knows his disciples too well, however, for the betrayal to come as a surprise. Deep sadness and disappointment,
yes, but not surprise.

The "woe" which Jesus pronounces underlines the two levels at which the mystery of the passion is at work. On the one
level, there is the darkness and violence of men who plot and
scheme and look for a time. On the other, there is Jesus who
already stands somehow in the divine council of the Father's
will, as indicated in the scriptures. Thus there is the awesome
mystery of human freedom and the powers of darkness, and
yet at the same time the divine plan working through human
weakness and even the worst of human malice to achieve its
designs.

## The Last Supper (26:26–29)

26 Now as they were eating, Jesus took bread, and
blessed, and broke it, and gave it to the disciples and said,
"Take, eat; this is my body." [27]And he took a cup, and when
he had given thanks he gave it to them, saying, "Drink of
it, all of you; [28]for this is my blood of the covenant, which
is poured out for many for the forgiveness of sins. [29]I tell you
I shall not drink again of this fruit of the vine until that day
when I drink it new with you in my Father's kingdom."

We are not told of the departure of Judas into the night (John 13:30), but we may assume that he leaves to pursue his plan while Jesus celebrates the Eucharist with his disciples. Since, according to the synoptics, this is a passover meal, Jesus seemingly inserts his institution of the Eucharist at suitable points already provided by the Jewish ritual—the sharing of unleavened bread at the beginning, and the third ceremonial cup toward the end of the meal. The latter, called the cup of blessing (see 1 Cor 10:16), was accompanied by the prayer, "Blessed art thou, Lord, our God, King of the universe, who dost create the fruit of the vine." It is clear, then that when Matthew says, before the bread and the cup, that Jesus "blessed," he does not mean he invoked some special power upon the elements; rather Jesus says a prayer of praise and thanksgiving to the Father.

Matthew stresses the commands, "eat" and "drink." It must have come as a shock to the Jewish disciples to hear that they should eat the body of the Lord and drink his blood (a shock echoed in John 6:52, 60), for the only parallel in Jewish liturgy was the communion sacrifice, in which "those who eat the victims enter into communion with the altar" (1 Cor 10:18). It must have been especially shocking to be told to drink the blood, for this was forbidden in Jewish sacrifices, and in this case it is human blood that will be drunk. It is obvious we are in the midst of sacrificial-meal terminology, where the body and blood, however real, are symbolized by the bread and wine, consumed in a way that is not cannibalistic but appropriate for a banquet.

But the Eucharist is more than a communion sacrifice. It is a covenant meal, as is clear from v. 28, "the blood of the covenant." Jeremiah's prophecy of a *new* covenant (Jer 31:31) forms the background of the eucharistic formulas we find in Luke 22:20 and 1 Cor 11:25, where the word *new* is used. But Matthew harks back to the Exodus covenant of blood by which the people liberated from Egypt became the Lord's (Ex 24:6–8). That covenant-blood-sacrifice, like all of the old law, was prophetic (11:13), and Jesus is now fulfilling the reality of which that was the sign. Though the forgiveness of sins is not mentioned in the Hebrew text of Ex 24:8, the Aramaic Targum translates, "Moses took the blood and sprinkled it upon the altar *to make atonement* for the people." Thus it is likely that the understanding of Jesus' sacrifice as atonement was already prepared by this and other OT texts. Paul will speak of the shedding of Jesus' blood as the expiation for all sin (Rom 3:25). The note of forgiveness of sins is already contained in Mark's "for many," but Matthew makes it specific by adding "for the forgiveness of sins." Matthew, as we noted in 3:1–6, avoids saying that the baptism by John was for the forgiveness of sins (Mk 1:4), since he wants to make clear that all forgiveness comes through Jesus, and specifically through the shedding of his blood.

But the Eucharist is, in its turn, prophetic, for it is an anticipation, in sign and symbol, of the banquet of the kingdom. It is the "bread of tomorrow" enjoyed today (see above on 6:11), of which Paul speaks thus: "As often as you eat this bread and drink this cup, you proclaim the Lord's death until he comes" (1 Cor 11:26). This orientation to the future as well as to the past and present has been captured in the Catholic liturgy's acclamation immediately after the consecration prayer of the Mass. J. Jeremias in *The Eucharistic Words of Jesus*, points out that Jewish Christians, living in the tradition that the Messiah would come at Passover, would pray and read scripture until three o'clock in the morning, and if Jesus had not returned by that time they would celebrate Eucharist—the best thing the church can do "until he comes."

Finally, Matthew's version of Jesus' words has, typically, "*my Father's* kingdom," just as Jesus will address God in the garden as "My Father" (26:39, 42). In Matthew there are more than twenty occurrences of *Father* for God, over against two in Mark and some ten in Luke. Only John outdoes Matthew in this matter, though in John the Father is almost uniquely the father of Jesus rather than "your Father." It is significant for Matthew that the Eucharist points not only to Jesus' coming sacrifice but to its fruition ultimately in union with the Father.

## Peter's Denial Predicted (26:30–35)

30 And when they had sung a hymn, they went out to the Mount of Olives. ³¹Then Jesus said to them, "You will

all fall away because of me this night; for it is written, 'I will strike the shepherd, and the sheep of the flock will be scattered.' ³²But after I am raised up, I will go before you to Galilee." ³³Peter declared to him, "Though they all fall away because of you, I will never fall away." ³⁴Jesus said to him, "Truly, I say to you, this very night, before the cock crows, you will deny me three times." ³⁵Peter said to him, "Even if I must die with you, I will not deny you." And so said all the disciples.

At the end of the Passover meal, after the sharing of the fourth cup of wine, it was customary to sing the second part of the Hallel, Psalms 116–118. Anyone who has not read these psalms in the context of this moment in Jesus' life should do so, for they are rich in allusions to suffering, death and victory which Jesus must have surely understood as fulfilled in him: "The snares of death encompassed me . . . I suffered distress and anguish . . . 'O Lord, save my life . . .' I shall walk before the Lord in the lands of the living. . . . I kept my faith, even when I said, 'I am greatly afflicted'; I said in my alarm, 'No man is dependable.'. . . Precious in the sight of the Lord is the death of his faithful ones . . . I shall not die but live, and recount the deeds of the Lord. . . . The stone which the builders rejected has become the cornerstone . . ."

This is surely not the first time in his life that Jesus sang, but it is the only recorded instance in the gospels that he did. It contrasts sharply with the somber prediction which Jesus now makes. *All* the disciples will stumble in their faith tonight, and Matthew makes it clear in a way that Mark does not that it is *because of me.* The phrase will be echoed by Peter's "because of you" in v. 33. By the time of Matthew's gospel it is quite clearly the person of Jesus that is the source of persecution (see also 5:11).

What Matthew does with the text of Zech 13:7 is interesting. The Hebrew text reads: "Strike (singular) the shepherd and the flock will be scattered." The Greek OT translated: "Strike (plural) the shepherds and seize the sheep." Matthew's use of the first person singular, "I will strike" intends to show that it is God who will strike Jesus, and the disciples are the flock that will be dispersed—all his intimate friends! They will not be able to believe that God would allow this to happen to their cherished Messiah and their own messianic hopes. That is Jesus' prediction—though he adds a clear prophecy of the resurrection, that he will go before his sheep into Galilee, where he will proclaim the new age of the church. The disciples for the moment cannot believe they could possibly fall away, Peter as usual taking the lead and saying "Never!"

Mark has the cock crowing twice, Luke and Matthew once. The difference is easily explained by the time of night. The Greeks and Romans called the watch between midnight and 3 a.m. "the cockcrow," since the first crow of the cock usually occurred during that time. Mark specifies both times, whereas Matthew and Luke consider the second crowing the only one worth noting. Jesus' repeated and more specific prediction wrings from Peter the self-assured denial of denial even in the face of death, and it is echoed by all the disciples.

## Jesus' Prayer in Gethsemane (26:36–46)

36 Then Jesus went with them to a place called Gethsemane, and he said to his disciples, "Sit here, while I go yonder and pray." [37]And taking with him Peter and the two sons of Zebedee, he began to be sorrowful and troubled. [38]Then he said to them, "My soul is very sorrowful, even to death; remain here, and watch with me." [39]And going a little farther he fell on his face and prayed, "My Father, if it be possible, let this cup pass from me; nevertheless, not as I will, but as thou wilt." [40]And he came to the disciples and found them sleeping; and he said to Peter, "So, could you not watch with me one hour? [41]Watch and pray that you may not enter into temptation; the spirit indeed is willing, but the flesh is weak." [42]Again, for the second time, he went away and prayed, "My Father, if this cannot pass unless I drink it, thy will be done." [43]And again he came and found them sleeping, for their eyes were heavy. [44]So, leaving them again, he went away and prayed for the third time, saying the same words. [45]Then he came to the disciples and said to them, "Are you still sleeping and taking your rest? Behold, the hour is at hand, and the Son of man is betrayed into the

hands of sinners. ⁴⁶Rise, let us be going; see, my betrayer is at hand."

"Gethsemane" means "oil press," a piece of equipment understandably found in an olive orchard. Confronted by the horror ahead of him, Jesus turns to prayer, personal and alone. As he had done previously, he separates Peter, James and John and has them go with him some distance, as he did on the mount of the transfiguration (17:1). Why those three? Peter is Jesus' close associate, whose denial of Jesus and later repentance will be all the more poignant. James and John had said they could drink the Lord's cup (20:22), and it is about that cup that Jesus will now pray.

Jesus begins to be sorrowful and troubled. His verb for "be sorrowful" is milder than Mark's "be greatly distressed," but it corresponds better to what Jesus says in the next verse, "My soul is very sorrowful, even to death," which is almost a direct quotation of Psalm 42:5. To Mark's "watch" Matthew adds "with me," perhaps an indication of Jesus' desire for support. More likely, though, it is an exhortation to the *disciples* to follow his example in turning to prayer in order to emerge victorious in the trial. Jesus falls prostrate and addresses God once again as "My Father." "Cup" stands for "lot," here the suffering which Jesus had already prophesied using that image (20:22). In the OT it often stood for the cup of suffering allowed or sent by God, a cup which could be taken away (Is 51:17–23), but one which sometimes had to be drained even by those who did not deserve it (Jer 49:12). Jesus prays as any human being would pray, for life as he humanly experiences life. Jesus knew what Roman crucifixion was, but in addition there was a spiritual suffering even greater: betrayal by a friend. The rest of his weak disciples will desert him, Peter will deny him, for many his death will be useless, and, a motive not often mentioned in books of piety, the sorrow for Jerusalem and its fate for not knowing this time of grace. It was a time of real wrestling with the Father, yet ending in final submission to his will.

The disciples' sleeping betrays their complete lack of awareness of the gravity of Jesus' situation—and theirs. For Matthew they symbolize those disciples who are not awake when their Master comes (24:42–44). Jesus addresses all the disciples ("Could you not watch" is plural in the Greek) in the person of Peter. In the final petition of the Lord's prayer he had taught them to pray to be spared in time of testing; the disciples do not pray, they do not even watch Jesus pray, and thus they will not be ready for the test. In the second round of prayer, Jesus does not petition any longer to be delivered from the cup; he surrenders to the Father's will in the explicit words of the prayer he had taught the disciples (6:10), and so also presumably in the third round. Although it is not clear whether Jesus bothers to wake his disciples when he comes to them the second time, they never heed his warning to stay awake and pray. The festive Passover meal, with its multiple cups of wine, has left them lethargic. Jesus rouses them for the last time and announces the next act of the passion. "Is betrayed" is better rendered by the NABR, "is handed over," the passive voice indicating that God, and not merely Judas, is handing him over.

It is significant that, unlike the baptism and the transfiguration, there is no heavenly voice of reassurance. The answer to Jesus' prayer is the appearance of the betrayer and the mob. This is not the kind of prayer experience we would expect in one whom we have come to know as the Son of God. The author of Hebrews contemplates this mystery: "In the days of his flesh, Jesus offered up prayers and supplications, with loud cries and tears, to him who was able to save him from death," and then he adds, paradoxically, "and *he was heard* because of his reverence" (Heb 5:7 RSV and NABR). How was Jesus heard? Not by removing the cup of the passion but, once he had gone through it, by raising Jesus from the dead. It is *through* death and not by escape from it that Jesus wins the victory.

There is a great lesson here for disciples of every age. Jesus taught that we should ask, seek, knock and believe with faith that we would receive. He healed people who came to him. And he gave the power to heal to his disciples, and the gift of healing to the church. Yet the agenda of God is often beyond what our limited vision can see. And even when prayer for a specific healing is answered, that is only part of God's agenda, which is ultimately resurrection and the restoration of all creation. Like Jesus' prayer, ours too will be answered with victory but not always in a way that will remove the impending cross.

## Jesus Is Arrested (26:47–56)

47 While he was still speaking, Judas came, one of the twelve, and with him a great crowd with swords and clubs, from the chief priests and the elders of the people. ⁴⁸Now the betrayer had given them a sign, saying, "The one I shall kiss is the man; seize him." ⁴⁹And he came up to Jesus at once and said, "Hail, Master!" And he kissed him. ⁵⁰Jesus said to him, "Friend, why are you here?" Then they came up and laid hands on Jesus and seized him. ⁵¹And behold, one of those who were with Jesus stretched out his hand and drew his sword, and struck the slave of the high priest, and cut off his ear. ⁵²Then Jesus said to him, "Put your sword back into its place; for all who take the sword will perish by the sword. ⁵³Do you think that I cannot appeal to my Father, and he will at once send me more than twelve legions of angels? ⁵⁴But how then should the scriptures be fulfilled, that it must be so?" ⁵⁵At that hour Jesus said to the crowds, "Have you come out as against a robber, with swords and clubs to capture me? Day after day I sat in the temple teaching, and you did not seize me. ⁵⁶But all this has taken place, that the scriptures of the prophets might be fulfilled." Then all the disciples forsook him and fled.

The betrayer announced by Jesus is now identified as Judas, again poignantly tagged as "one of the twelve." With him is a *great* crowd, armed because they are expecting trouble, if not from Jesus, then from his disciples. Returning to the title "betrayer," as if the name Judas was too painful to repeat, Matthew relays Mark's detail about identifying Jesus in the darkness by a kiss, a normal greeting a disciple would give his teacher. Judas again addresses Jesus as *Rabbi* (as in 26:25), as if all he had learned as a disciple about Jesus' true identity is now repressed, and with the Greek greeting *chaire*, meaning

"rejoice." Whether this is Matthew's way of Greeking the Aramaic greeting *shalom* ("peace") or is a historical remembrance
that Judas spoke Greek, there is a bitter irony in the greeting,
just as there is in the kiss (noted in Luke's, "Do you betray
the Son of Man with a kiss?" Lk 22:48). Jesus' response, after
the cool "Friend" (20:13; 22:12), may be translated, as the RSV
does, "Why are you here?" or, with the NABR, "Do what you
have come for." Given Jesus' foreknowledge, the latter translation seems preferable. It would be another instance of Jesus,
at a deeper level, permitting the plot to proceed.

As Jesus is seized, one of the disciples attacks the slave
of the high priest and cuts off his ear. John identifies the disciple as Peter and the slave as Malchus. If Matthew knows this
tradition he does not use it; his interest seems to be to give a
lesson to all disciples, especially those of his day, on the matter
of violence. Majestically, as if there were plenty of time, Jesus
tells the disciple to put his sword away. Then he gives a mem-
orable teaching in the form of a proverb. Violence provokes
violence; Jesus himself who preached non-violence (5:38–39)
now practices it. Matthew no doubt wants his persecuted community, tempted to avenge itself, to hear this prohibition from
the Lord.

A third explanation follows in the form of a rhetorical question. If Jesus requested it and the Father so willed, an army
of angels would come to his defense. In the last analysis, it is
not a surrender to the blind forces of fate but a surrender to
the Father's will, forecast in the Scriptures, that places Jesus
in the hands of his enemies. These words are addressed to the
disciples (and through them to Matthew's church).

Now Jesus turns to the crowds and asks them why they
had to capture him by stealth and arms, when he was available
daily in the temple. There he "sat" (Matthew's favorite word)
teaching. "Day by day" suggests the kind of longer teaching
ministry in Jerusalem which we find in John's gospel, suggesting that Matthew has abbreviated Jesus' temple ministry for
his editorial purposes.

Verse 56 is for Matthew a theological headline. Jesus had
already mentioned the fulfilling of the scriptures in v. 54. He
returns to it here again by specifying the scriptures *of the*

*prophets.* No specific prophecy is mentioned, though Jesus has spoken earlier of Zechariah's prophecy that the shepherd would be struck and the sheep scattered (26:31). And, as a matter of fact, as soon as Jesus says this, his disciples abandon him and flee. But Matthew, who loves to cite specific passages, here sees what has happened and all that is about to happen as a fulfillment of *all* prophecy. It is significant that with the exception of 27:9–10, Matthew does not in the passion account interrupt the flow of events to insert his scriptural tags. There will be strong scriptural allusions, but we will miss the typical Matthean, "This happened that there might be fulfilled what was spoken by the prophet . . ." The reason for this is that Matthew sees the passion, death and resurrection of Jesus as the fulfillment of all the OT scriptures, law as well as prophets, and not merely of individual passages. See 5:18 and our excursus on the fulfillment of the law, pp. 72–73.

## Jesus before the Sanhedrin (26:57–68)

57 Then those who had seized Jesus led him to Caiaphas the high priest, where the scribes and the elders had gathered. [58]But Peter followed him at a distance, as far as the courtyard of the high priest, and going inside he sat with the guards to see the end. [59]Now the chief priests and the whole council sought false testimony against Jesus that they might put him to death, [60]but they found none, though many false witnesses came forward. At last two came forward [61]and said, "This fellow said, 'I am able to destroy the temple of God, and to build it in three days.' " [62]And the high priest stood up and said, "Have you no answer to make? What is it that these men testify against you?" [63]But Jesus was silent. And the high priest said to him, "I adjure you by the living God, tell us if you are the Christ, the Son of God." [64]Jesus said to him, "You have said so. But I tell you, hereafter you will see the Son of man seated at the right hand of Power, and coming on the clouds of heaven." [65]Then the high priest tore his robes, and said, "He has uttered blasphemy. Why do we still need witnesses? You have now heard his blasphemy. [66]What is your judgment?" They answered, "He

deserves death." ⁶⁷Then they spat in his face, and struck him; and some slapped him, ⁶⁸saying, "Prophesy to us, you Christ! Who is it that struck you?"

Matthew again mentions Caiphas by name. Jesus is led to the high priest's quarters where the members of the Sanhedrin had already gathered. There is a technical problem here which we should first deal with. According to the judicial procedures detailed in the Jewish Mishnah, written about 200 A.D., there are apparently a number of irregularities in the trial of Jesus as given by Matthew and Mark: a night session of the court, a trial on a feast day, pronouncing a verdict at the same session at which testimony was taken. However, we do not know whether the stipulations of the Mishnah were in force at the time of Jesus. More importantly, it is quite possible that Mark and Matthew have for brevity combined a nighttime preliminary investigation (see Jn 18:13, 19–24) and a formal trial the next morning (see Lk 22:66–71).

Peter, who earlier fled, now manages to return, hopefully incognito, following Jesus at a distance until he enters the courtyard. Matthew does not mention the fire, only that Peter sits with the guards *to see the end.* "End" could mean the outcome of the trial, but to Peter, who now grasps the seriousness of the situation, and to the Christian reader it could mean the death of Jesus. The council's motives in Matthew appear even more murky as he records that they sought *false* testimony. Unable to find any false accusation, they finally find two witnesses (the minimum required by law) who apparently give correct testimony, that Jesus said, "I *am able* to destroy the temple of God and rebuild it in three days." They are presumably latching on to some claim of Jesus like that of 12:6, that he is greater than the temple, or that he has authority over the temple, as he has authority over the law, or that the temple would be destroyed—all of which are true. But Jesus does not answer their accusation, even when pressed by the high priest to testify for or against himself. He remains the silent Servant of Is 53:7, aware perhaps that whatever he would say would be misinterpreted and turned against him, and already resigned at a deeper level to the Father's will.

At length the high priest puts Jesus under oath. The meaning of "the Christ" is clear, the Jewish Messiah. But what is meant by "Son of God" here? Mark's version, giving the circumlocution, "Son of the Blessed One," is doubtless more original. Matthew gives its equivalent. On the lips of the high priest it may have been another way of describing the Messiah (although such a title was not a common one). For Matthew and his audience, however, the double title, Christ, the Son of God, has already been used by Peter and accepted by Jesus (16:15–17). The first part of Jesus' answer is elusive, perhaps because Jesus does not approve of oaths (5:33–37). "You have said so" may also be rendered, "The words are yours." It is a way of conditionally accepting the titles, but with the understanding that Jesus now wishes to give them by adding: *"But . . . you* (now plural) will see the Son of Man . . ." Just as Jesus corrected his disciples' false understanding of his mission by introducing the title *Son of Man,* so he does so now with the Sanhedrin. No need, however, to say that the Son of Man will suffer, for the sufferings have already begun, under the hands of the Sanhedrin itself. What needs to be affirmed is that the humble prisoner before them is indeed the one who will "sit at the right hand of the Power." This is, on the one hand, a reference to Psalm 110:1, where the words "Sit at my right hand" are said by the Lord to the Messiah. That Jesus should claim that would simply be to affirm that he is the Messiah. But by saying "the right hand of the *Power,*" parallel to "the clouds of heaven," he is claiming to be the heavenly Messiah, an equal participant in the divine glory. This is clearly a reference, in Matthew's mind, to Jesus' resurrection, which the early church understood to be his enthronement as Messiah (Acts 2:34–36). The Sanhedrin may not *see* him thus enthroned in the same way the disciples will see him, but they will see, beginning even now (*ap'arti*), the cosmic signs that testify to it (the darkness, earthquake, rending of the temple veil). The Son of Man will also come with the clouds of heaven in his glorious return, when every eye will *see* him, including those who have pierced him (Rev. 1:7).

This is the claim the high priest was looking for. Without waiting for the opinion of his councilors, he declares Jesus

guilty of blasphemy—*then* he asks their opinion. "He deserves
death" is the most they can answer, since by Roman law they
were forbidden to put anyone to death themselves. Matthew
changes the "some began to spit . . ." of Mark to "*they* began
to spit *in his face*," thus involving the Sanhedrin more directly
and contemptuously in the abuse, which may indeed have been
carried out by lackeys. The mocking invitation to the "Christ"
to prophesy was doubtless motivated by Jesus' claims before
the high priest. At this point it may be necessary to assume
Jesus was blindfolded (a Markan detail Matthew has omitted),
so that he would not be able to identify the ones who struck
him.

### Peter Denies Jesus, Then Weeps in Repentance (26:69–75)

69 Now Peter was sitting outside in the courtyard. And
a maid came up to him, and said, "You also were with Jesus
the Galilean." [70]But he denied it before them all, saying, "I
do not know what you mean." [71]And when he went out to
the porch, another maid saw him, and she said to the bystanders, "This man was with Jesus of Nazareth." [72]And
again he denied it with an oath, "I do not know the man."
[73]After a little while the bystanders came up and said to
Peter, "Certainly you are also one of them, for your accent
betrays you." [74]Then he began to invoke a curse on himself
and to swear, "I do not know the man." And immediately
the cock crowed. [75]And Peter remembered the saying of
Jesus, "Before the cock crows, you will deny me three
times." And he went out and wept bitterly.

Matthew's camera now swings outside to the courtyard
where Peter has been sitting with the guard. It is not the guard
but a young girl who accuses Peter of being *with* Jesus the
Galilean—*with* here being a mark of discipleship. Peter denies
it not merely before the girl but in front of them all, with an
apparent spontaneity and openness that makes us think he has
suddenly become a different person. Sensing the danger to his
person, he withdraws to the gateway, where he is accosted by

another girl, who addresses the bystanders with a similar accusation that Peter is one of Jesus' intimate disciples. This time Peter goes beyond his earlier guarded statement that he did not know *what the girl meant*. He takes an oath, expressly forbidden by Jesus (5:33–37) and says "I do not know the man," thus falling into that public denial of Jesus which means he will not be acknowledged before the Father in the final judgment (10:32–33). Finally the bystanders come up to Peter and bring against him his Galilean accent as proof "you are one of them." The gravity of this third denial is that Peter, in addition to swearing, invokes a curse, probably upon himself, repeating "I do not know the man." At once the crowing of the cock reminds Peter of Jesus' prophecy. He leaves the crowd, goes out and weeps bitterly.

Matthew holds up Peter to his community as a tragic example of the truth of Jesus' words. Unaware of his own weakness, boastful of his fidelity, uncommitted to prayer, Peter falls in a most serious way. But he is also an example of repentance, of the good news that the most serious of sins can be forgiven. If he contrasts with Jesus witnessing unto death before the Sanhedrin, he also contrasts with Judas, who does not know the restoring power of repentance.

### Jesus Handed Over to Pilate (27:1–2)

**27** WHEN MORNING came, all the chief priests and the elders of the people took counsel against Jesus to put him to death; ²and they bound him and led him away and delivered him to Pilate the governor.

It is not clear whether the Sanhedrin's trial went through the night or whether it was reconvened the next morning. At any rate the final sentence is not handed down till morning. Since under Roman rule the Sanhedrin had no power to execute any one, they *hand over* Jesus to Pilate, whom Matthew calls repeatedly the *governor*. Thus is fulfilled Jesus' prophecy in 20:18–19: "The Son of Man will be delivered (=handed over, betrayed) to the chief priests and scribes, and they will condemn him to death, and deliver him (=hand over) to the Gen-

tiles . . ." In an inscription discovered at Caesarea by the sea,
Pilate bears the title *Prefect*. He ruled from 26 to 36 A.D.

## Disposing of Blood Money (27:3–10)

3 When Judas, his betrayer, saw that he was condemned, he repented and brought back the thirty pieces of
silver to the chief priests and the elders, ⁴saying, "I have
sinned in betraying innocent blood." They said, "What is
that to us? See to it yourself." ⁵And throwing down the
pieces of silver in the temple, he departed; and he went and
hanged himself. ⁶But the chief priests, taking the pieces of
silver, said, "It is not lawful to put them into the treasury,
since they are blood money." ⁷So they took counsel, and
bought with them the potter's field, to bury strangers in.
⁸Therefore that field has been called the Field of Blood to
this day. ⁹Then was fulfilled what had been spoken by the
prophet Jeremiah, saying, "And they took the thirty pieces
of silver, the price of him on whom a price had been set by
some of the sons of Israel, ¹⁰and they gave them for the
potter's field, as the Lord directed me."

The flow of Jesus' trial is interrupted at this point to tell
of the fate of Judas. It is interesting to speculate what precisely
led Judas to realize his mistake. Was he at heart a zealot who
hoped Jesus would at the last moment exercise his divine power
and establish the kingdom, Judas thus hoping to force Jesus'
hand? And when he saw that Jesus really meant what he said
about the cross, realized that he himself had been the unwitting
instrument of his death? The only indication Matthew gives is
that the change in Judas occurred "when he saw that Jesus was
condemned." Though the RSV translates "repented," the verb
Matthew uses is not the usual *metanoien*, but *metamelesthai*,
which he used of the second son in 21:30 who "thought better"
of his earlier decision, and of the priests and elders who did
*not* "change their minds." Perhaps Matthew intends a nuance
here: Judas' repentance was not full repentance, which would
have thrown itself on the mercy of God. It was a deep human
regret, but filled with the kind of pride that would not permit

him to forgive himself in the process of accepting the forgiveness of the Lord. He would be his own judge and executioner. He nevertheless makes a human confession to those who hired him, that he has betrayed innocent blood. The priests would shrug off their responsibility: that's not our problem—it is yours. Pilate will use the same expression in v. 24 to say, "It's not my responsibility, it is yours." Judas throws down the money in the temple and leaves to hang himself, as Ahithophel did after the failure of his plot against King David (2 Sam 17:23).

At this point we must mention the variant tradition about the death of Judas found in Acts 1:18–20, where the land is purchased by Judas himself, and his death is attributed to a fall which caused his body to burst and his entrails to spill out. Acts agrees with Matthew that the field was called "field of blood," because it was associated with the violent death of Judas. It is likely we have a common tradition about Judas' violent death (a kind of poetic and biblical justice, Ex 21:14) and the "field of blood" in the valley of Hinnom, which was differently explained in popular tradition, one strain of which was known to Matthew and fitted better his "fulfillment" purposes, as the text from Zechariah (below) shows.

The priests, who have no scruple about getting rid of Jesus, suddenly have serious scruples about the money, which they admit is "blood money." Probably reasoning from Deut 23:18, which forbade bringing into the temple money gained through such sinful activity as prostitution, they decide to dispose of it to buy the potter's field.

The passive "thus was fulfilled" shields the Lord from any direct intervention in the tragedy, just as it did in the slaughter of the innocents in 2:17. The scripture text is actually not from Jeremiah but from Zechariah 11:13, with some differences. We will look at the text first, and then endeavor to discover why Matthew attributes it to Jeremiah. In the original Hebrew, we read, "And the Lord said to me, 'Cast it unto the potter (*hayyôser*),' the handsome price at which they valued me; and I took the thirty pieces of silver and cast them into the house of the Lord unto the potter (*hayyôser*)." Modern translations (e.g. the NAB) assume that the original reading was not potter but the near-sounding *ha'ôsar,* meaning "treasury." An early scribe, feeling it derogatory that the price rejected by the prophet should have landed in the temple treasury, substituted "potter" for "treasury." Matthew cleverly combines both textual traditions to connect the treasury, the potter's field and the field of blood in the local tradition.

Why should Matthew attribute the text to Jeremiah? The atmosphere of judgment and condemnation we find here is, of course, a common one in Jeremiah. The themes of the potter (Jer 18:2–6) and buying a field (Jer 32:1–44) also appear there. But the most relevant passage is Jer 19:1–11. There the Lord tells Jeremiah to buy a potter's earthen flask, to go with the elders and the priests to the Valley of Hinnom and there to proclaim judgment upon the people for having, among other things, shed innocent blood. The place thereafter will be called the Valley of Slaughter, and it will become a burial place. The similarities with the situation of Judas, and the broader theme of the judgment upon Jerusalem itself, are clear. Matthew, then, has simply run together two prophetic scenes: the one explicit from Zechariah, the other implicit from Jeremiah. He leaves to the reader to make the connection between the two—a task that would have been relatively easy for a Jewish audience. When the priests buy a field for strangers, they give gentiles a hold on the promised land; thus unwittingly they let Jesus' blood buy the right of the gentiles to inherit the promises made to Israel.

### Jesus Is Tried before Pilate (27:11–26)

11 Now Jesus stood before the governor; and the governor asked him, "Are you the King of the Jews?" Jesus said, "You have said so." [12]But when he was accused by the chief priests and elders, he made no answer. [13]Then Pilate said to him, "Do you not hear how many things they testify against you?" [14]But he gave him no answer, not even to a single charge; so that the governor wondered greatly.

15 Now at the feast the governor was accustomed to release for the crowd any one prisoner whom they wanted. [16]And they had then a notorious prisoner, called Barabbas. [17]So when they had gathered, Pilate said to them, "Whom

do you want me to release for you, Barabbas or Jesus who is called Christ?" [18]For he knew that it was out of envy that they had delivered him up. [19]Besides, while he was sitting on the judgment seat, his wife sent word to him, "Have nothing to do with that righteous man, for I have suffered much over him today in a dream." [20]Now the chief priests and the elders persuaded the people to ask for Barabbas and destroy Jesus. [21]The governor again said to them, "Which of the two do you want me to release for you?" And they said, "Barabbas." [22]Pilate said to them, "Then what shall I do with Jesus who is called Christ?" They all said, "Let him be crucified." [23]And he said, "Why, what evil has he done?" But they shouted all the more, "Let him be crucified."

24 So when Pilate saw that he was gaining nothing, but rather that a riot was beginning, he took water and washed his hands before the crowd, saying, "I am innocent of this man's blood; see to it yourselves." [25]And all the people answered, "His blood be on us and on our children!" [26]Then he released for them Barabbas, and having scourged Jesus, delivered him to be crucified.

Pilate questions Jesus: "Are you the king of the Jews?" To admit to this title on Pilate's terms would be equivalent to treason, for it would amount to challenging the emperor's authority. For the Christian reader of Matthew, however, the title is full of meaning. Used first by the gentile Magi who were well disposed towards Jesus (2:2), it is repeated here from the mouth of a gentile governor, who is, in Matthew's view, as well disposed towards Jesus as his weak character permits. Jesus answers in his enigmatic way: "You have said so" or "The words are yours," indicating that Jesus would define his identity, even as Messiah, in different terms. The chief priests and elders plunge in with their accusations, but Jesus, in fulfillment of the prophecy about the suffering Servant (Is 52:7), keeps silent, even after subsequent probing by Pilate. The governor's amazement at this echoes the amazement of the powerful at the suffering Servant (Is 52:14–15). The very silence of Jesus here, like his words elsewhere, occasions the next step in the passion drama, a change in tactics on Pilate's part.

Although we do not have any record of the practice outside
of the gospels, it was a common custom in the ancient world
to grant amnesty to certain prisoners as a special mark of a
festival. Even today, in Nepal, certain prisoners will be released on the king's or queen's birthday. The particular prisoner that occurs to Pilate is a man who, according to Mark,
had committed murder *in the insurrection*. Matthew assumes
his readers are aware of this well-known fact; he does not repeat it. He simply calls the man a "notorious" prisoner. If he
were part of a Zealot rebellion against Rome, releasing him to
the Jewish crowds on the festival would play into their nation-
alistic hopes. On the other hand, he was a public criminal, and
Pilate may have assumed, wrongly, that the people, knowing
Jesus' innocence and popularity, would ask for his release. Pilate has not calculated on the influence the priests have already
exerted upon the crowds who, though favorably impressed with
Jesus, now are confronted with a choice: to accept Jesus as
their spiritual Messiah, or to go with the Zealot surge of na-
tionalism, which doubtless would have been high at Passover.
Their attachment to Jesus, for all its enthusiasm, may well have
been so tainted (as had been that of the disciples) with nation-
alistic hopes that, when push came to shove, they would choose
a Zealot over a prophet who eschews a political kingdom.

There is irony even in the name of the prisoner. Barabbas
means "son of the father." It may even be that his first name
was Jesus, a common enough Jewish name being the same as
Joshua's, for in a few manuscripts "Jesus Barabbas" appears,
and it seems more likely that Christian piety would have removed the name than that it would have been inserted by a
later hand. Because of the uncertainty in the manuscripts, the
NABR encloses "Jesus" in brackets before "Barabbas." However that may be, Jesus of Nazareth is the real son of the
Father, Barabbas is his foil.

Pilate then tosses to the crowd the option of choosing between Barabbas or Jesus, who is called *Messiah*. The envy of
which both Mark and Matthew speak refers to the rise in power
and influence which the leaders have perceived in Jesus. Before
they have a chance to answer Pilate, Matthew provides an interlude with the message from Pilate's wife about a dream in

which she suffered much because of this "just man." In her mind, the word may mean merely innocent, but for the Jewish reader of Matthew, the word would invoke the many OT passages that spoke of the suffering of the just, and perhaps even the title used in the early church for Jesus as "the Just One" (Acts 3:14). Matthew, for whom dreams are a medium of revelation (1:20; 2:13, 19), understands this to be God's message to Pilate.

But Pilate cannot withstand the crowd, which has been whipped up by the priests to demand the release of Barabbas. Acceding to their wishes for the Zealot has not solved Pilate's problem. In what is hardly thinkable in a Roman official, Pilate asks the *crowd* what he should do. This may be simply the synoptics' way of dramatizing the situation; but we must remember that Jesus is not a Roman citizen and Pilate, who has engaged the crowds, now wants to deal ingratiatingly with them. In recording that *all* say of Jesus, "Let him be crucified," instead of Mark's "Crucify him," Matthew shifts the responsibility more clearly upon the crowd. Pilate's final effort to save Jesus on the basis of undisproved innocence fails, as the shouts of the crowd prelude a riot.

Pilate then washes his hands in front of the crowd, a Jewish custom derived ultimately from Deut 21:6–8. There the law prescribes that in the case of an unsolved murder, the elders of the city nearest the corpse are to wash their hands over an animal sacrificed in expiation and declare, "Our hands did not shed this blood, and our eyes did not see this deed," and thus be absolved from the guilt of bloodshed. The psalmist speaks of washing his hands among the innocent (Ps 26:6; 73:13). It seems implausible to many scholars that the gentile Pilate would have thought of performing such a Jewish ritual here. Was it suggested to him by an aide knowledgeable of Jewish customs? Or is this a literary dramatization by Matthew for his Jewish readers of the meaning of Pilate's subsequent declaration of disengagement? In any case, Pilate declares his innocence and lays the responsibility upon the crowd. Surely this does not absolve Pilate of guilt; but in the Matthean context it does sharpen the responsiblity of the crowd, who even exclaim, "His blood be upon us and upon our children."

The latter expression is a difficult one for moderns to feel comfortable with. We must remember, though, the actual historical situation in which Matthew was writing. Matthew has witnessed the destruction of Jerusalem in 70 A.D., and he sees it as the result of his people's rejection of Jesus, the prince of peace, in favor of the Zealot rebellion prefigured by the insurrectionist Barabbas. The self-imposed curse anticipates the tragic results of this choice. In the wake of the Jerusalem disaster, Matthew is also at grips with Pharisaic Judaism over the question of whether they or the church is now the true people of God. As in the epistle to the Romans, it is not a question of the responsibility of individual Jews but of the direction and role in salvation history of the collectivity. In that context we can understand the statement of Vatican Council II that guilt for Jesus' death is not attributable to all the Jews of his time nor to any Jews of later times. In a deeper theological sense, the sins of all the human race are responsible for the saving death of the Son of God.

Pilate then releases Barabbas and "hands over" Jesus to be crucified, allowing the executioners to carry out the will of the leaders applauded by the crowds. The scourging here is presented as a preliminary to crucifixion. John presents the scourging of Jesus before the public trial as an attempt by Pilate to placate the crowds and possibly to avoid crucifying Jesus (Jn 19:1). To the spiritual and emotional suffering Jesus has endured is now added the most excruciating physical torture.

## The Mocking of the King (27:27–31)

27 Then the soldiers of the governor took Jesus into the praetorium, and they gathered the whole battalion before him. ²⁸And they stripped him and put a scarlet robe upon him, ²⁹and plaiting a crown of thorns they put it on his head, and put a reed in his right hand. And kneeling before him they mocked him, saying, "Hail, King of the Jews!" ³⁰And they spat upon him, and took the reed and struck him on the head. ³¹And when they had mocked him, they stripped him of the robe, and put his own clothes on him, and led him away to crucify him.

Earlier, after the death decision by the Sanhedrin, Jesus was mocked as a prophet (26:67-68). Here he is mocked as king. The crowd of available soldiers goes through a mock investiture, crowning, homage and acclamation. Not having readily available the purple robe of royalty (Mark), the soldiers throw over Jesus' shoulders one of their own scarlet robes. Hailing him as king of the Jews, these gentiles unwittingly give Jesus a title Christians revere and forecast the day when other gentiles in great numbers will bend the knee adoringly before him. After the royal ritual, the soldiers resort to reviling him, using the reed that had been his scepter, to strike him on his thorn-crowned head. Then they dress him again in his own clothes, in preparation for the dividing of his garments beneath the cross, and lead Jesus to be crucified.

## Jesus Is Crucified (27:32-38)

32 As they went out, they came upon a man of Cyrene, Simon by name; this man they compelled to carry his cross. ³³And when they came to a place called Golgotha (which means the place of a skull), ³⁴they offered him wine to drink, mingled with gall; but when he tasted it, he would not drink it. ³⁵And when they had crucified him, they divided his garments among them by casting lots; ³⁶then they sat down and kept watch over him there. ³⁷And over his head they put the charge against him, which read, "This is Jesus the King of the Jews." ³⁸Then two robbers were crucified with him, one on the right and one on the left.

All three synoptics agree that soon after the procession to Calvary begins, a man named Simon of Cyrene, well known to Mark who mentions his two sons, was compelled to carry the cross after Jesus. A historical remembrance, no doubt, but also symbolic of discipleship grounded in the word of Jesus about carrying the cross after him (16:24). What Jesus carried, and what Simon assumed, was the *patibulum* or cross beam, which would later be affixed to the upright beam awaiting them at the crucifixion site. Golgotha, skull-place, may have received its name from the shape of the rocky mound today found in-

corporated into the Church of the Holy Sepulchre in Jerusalem.
It was outside the city gates, a detail which confirms the prophecy of Jesus (21:39) and is richly exploited in Heb 13:11–14 for
its OT symbolism and its inspirational value for discipleship.
The wine offered to Jesus is mixed with gall, recalling the
Greek text of Psalm 69:21: "They gave me gall (Heb. *poison*)
for food, and for my thirst they gave me vinegar to drink," the
latter detail being fulfilled later on. Jesus refuses, less because
he wills to endure maximum pain than because he wishes to
retain full consciousness for this supreme act of his life.

It is incredible that Matthew should describe the crucifixion of Jesus in a passing participial phrase! There was no need
to rehearse for his audience the gory details of the gruesome
rite they all knew well. It was first introduced by the Persians
as a refinement of the Assyrian practice of impalement, then
popularized by the Romans to stigmatize the crimes of non-
Roman slaves, bandits and traitors. Recently the first archaeological evidence of the practice was unearthed in a limestone
ossuary in Jerusalem. The skeleton of a young man in his twen-
ties, a contemporary of Jesus, revealed that both heel bones
had been pierced by a single nail, and each forearm by a nail.
The body seems to have been awkwardly twisted as it hung on
the cross. The specific practices probably varied. Ordinarily a
stob was provided to support the buttocks and thus prolong
the agony. Death would come through loss of blood and finally
through asphyxiation, the contraction of the chest muscles finally choking the victim. That is why the breaking of the victim's legs, by which the body received some support, would
hasten death.

The clothes of the victim were booty for the executioners.
Matthew focuses on this detail, quoting almost word for word,
without his formal citation, Ps 22:18: "They divide my garments
among them, and for my raiment they cast lots." Matthew adds
to Mark: "then they sat down and kept watch over him there."
The theme of watching in expectancy recurs frequently in Matthew. The disciples in the garden *fail* to watch, but Peter in
the courtyard sits and watches to see the outcome (26:38, 40,
58). The women sit watching the tomb (27:61). The guards
watch the tomb (27:66). Here, the soldiers' watching on Calvary

is important, because these Romans are the very men who, after the apocalyptic signs at the death of Jesus, will make the first gentile Christian confession that Jesus is the Son of God (27:54). Matthew even hints at this ultimate outcome by saying that *they* put over Jesus' head the charge, "*This is Jesus the King of the Jews*," ironically hailing Jesus as King, just as they will confess him as Son of God.

All four gospels relate the crucifixion of two others beside Jesus. The word *lestai* can mean robbers (RSV) or revolutionaries (NABR). In either case they fulfill in another way the suffering Servant prophecy, that the just one is reckoned among the wicked (53:9). Once again, Jesus lets go of all appearances of righteousness. He even endures a death which brought a curse by OT standards (Deut 21:22-23). As in his baptism he chose to enter the ranks of sinners, as during his ministry he made community with tax collectors, sinners and outcasts, so now at the very end, "he who knew no sin was made sin for us, that in him we might become the righteousness of God" (2 Cor 5:21).

## The Mocking of the Crucified (27:39-44)

³⁹And those who passed by derided him, wagging their heads ⁴⁰and saying, "You who would destroy the temple and build it in three days, save yourself! If you are the Son of God, come down from the cross." ⁴¹So also the chief priests, with the scribes and elders, mocked him, saying, ⁴²"He saved others; he cannot save himself. He is the King of Israel; let him come down now from the cross, and we will believe in him. ⁴³He trusts in God; let God deliver him now, if he desires him; for he said, 'I am the Son of God.'" ⁴⁴And the robbers who were crucified with him also reviled him in the same way.

One might expect that once his enemies had him nailed to the cross they would at least have enough human compassion to keep silence. But instead they choose to revel in the fact that the one whose religious power and influence they feared is now powerless before them. They "wag their heads" in typical biblical mockery, recall the words of the witnesses in 26:61, and invite Jesus to turn his supposed power to his own benefit. The last temptation of Jesus is a replay of the first, an invitation to use his power to serve his own interests. The mockers use the very words of the desert tempter, "If you are the Son of God . . ." (4:1–4). These words, which appear only in Matthew, give us a key to understanding the whole scene. The one mocked, scourged and crucified is indeed the Son of God, but not on the terms dictated by human script-writers, who are simply tools of Jesus' arch-enemy, Satan, as Peter had been in trying to divert Jesus from the cross (16:23).

The Jewish leaders gloat as well over Jesus' being powerless, unable to save even himself. They even say (in Matthew's version), "He *is* the King of Israel," a mocking but nevertheless ironic confession of his messiahship. Equally ironic is their promise to believe if he would come down from the cross, for if they had resisted the signs of mercy Jesus had given during his ministry, they would certainly not be converted by a sign of self-interested power. They echo Psalm 22:9, "He relied on the Lord; let him deliver him, let him rescue him, if he loves him" (NAB), and Wis 2:12–20:

> "Let us lie in wait for the righteous man, because he is inconvenient to us and opposes our actions; he reproaches us for sins against the law, and accuses us of sins against our training. He professes to have knowledge of God, and calls himself a child of the Lord. He became to us a reproof of our thoughts; the very sight of him is a burden to us, because his manner of life is unlike that of others, and his ways are strange . . . He boasts that *God is his father*. Let us see if his ways are true, and let us test what will happen at *the end of his life;* for if the righteous man is *God's son,* he will deliver him from the hand of his adversaries. Let us test him with *insult and torture,* that we may find out how gentle he is, and make trial of his forbearance. *Let us condemn him to a shameful death, for according to what he says, he will be protected.*"

The priests, scribes and elders conclude their mockery by repeating the title *Son of God*. The robbers or revolutionaries do the same, but for a different reason. Unlike the religious authorities who have the human power, they, like Jesus, have none. Like many prisoners and condemned criminals, they do not know how to release their hostility except by casting it at one they consider another criminal. Thus at the very end of his life Jesus, "God with us," shares human misery in yet another way, by receiving the abuse of fellow "criminals."

## The Death of the Son of God (27:45–54)

45 Now from the sixth hour there was darkness over all the land until the ninth hour. ⁴⁶And about the ninth hour Jesus cried with a loud voice, "Eli, Eli, lama sabach-thani?" that is, "My God, my God, why hast thou forsaken me?" ⁴⁷And some of the bystanders hearing it said, "This man is calling Elijah." ⁴⁸And one of them at once ran and took a sponge, filled it with vinegar, and put it on a reed, and gave it to him to drink. ⁴⁹But the others said, "Wait, let us see whether Elijah will come to save him." ⁵⁰And Jesus cried again with a loud voice and yielded up his spirit.

51 And behold, the curtain of the temple was torn in two, from top to bottom; and the earth shook, and the rocks were split; ⁵²the tombs also were opened, and many bodies of the saints who had fallen asleep were raised, ⁵³and coming out of the tombs after his resurrection they went into the holy city and appeared to many. ⁵⁴When the centurion and those who were with him, keeping watch over Jesus, saw the earthquake and what took place, they were filled with awe, and said, "Truly this was the Son of God!"

Matthew is now about to narrate the climactic moment of Jesus' life: the moment when he "yields up his spirit" freely into the hands of the Father. How proclaim the cosmic meaning of this event for Israel, the church and the world? Expanding on Mark, Matthew notes a number of apocalyptic events the Bible considers signs of the Day of the Lord or the end-time: (1) *Darkness at noon,* a phenomenon prophesied by Amos for the "day of the Lord": " 'And on that day,' says the Lord God, 'I will make the sun go down at noon, and darken the earth in broad daylight' " (Am 8:9). (2) *The coming of Elijah.* Although Matthew has made it clear that Elijah has already come in the person of John the Baptist, the Jews nevertheless still believed that Elijah would come before the day of the Lord (Mal 4:5). Their misinterpretation of Jesus' words (which Matthew has changed slightly from Mark's Aramaic *Eloi* to evoke the prophet more clearly, *Eli, Eli* . . .) brings this end-time figure into the scene. (3) *The tearing of the temple veil.* There were two veils in the temple, the outer one covering the entrance to the Holy Place, the inner one covering the Holy of Holies. According to Jewish tradition, the temple was one of the "foundations of the world." The rending of the temple veil declared the old economy of Israel at an end, opening access to God to all. It may also have signified the end of the temple itself, forecasting its later destruction. In any case, this was also an end-time symbol, the "changing of the ages." (4) *The earthquake* (proper to Matthew). In the OT, earthquakes were frequently associated with divine manifestations (Num 16:31; Ex 19:18; Jgs 5:4; Pss 18:8; 68:9; Joel 4:16) especially of the last days (Is 24:18–19). They are a frequent apocalyptic sign in the book of Revelation (Rev 6:12; 8:5; 11:13; 16:18). The earthquake will recur at the rising of Jesus (28:2). (5) *The raising of the saints* (proper to Matthew). Rabbinic tradition, which distinguished between "the present age" and "the age to come," considered the general resurrection of the just to be one of the threshold events marking the end of the present age and the beginning of "the age to come." Matthew's placing of a proleptic resurrection here reveals his desire to show that the death of Jesus is the end of the present age and the beginning of the age to come. Yet he is also aware that the raising of the saints is an effect not only of the death of Jesus but also of his own resurrection, which in the narrative has not happened yet. That is why Matthew somewhat awkwardly says they were raised on Good Friday but did not appear in the city until Easter Sunday, "after his resurrection." Whatever the historical kernel of this tradition, the verse is a christological statement about the meaning of time and human destiny in the light of the death and resurrection of the Son of God.

The fourth and fifth sign, proper to Matthew, tie the death and resurrection of Jesus intimately together. We are on the way to the fourth evangelist's equation of the "lifting up" of the Son of Man, his glorification, with the hour of the cross and the resurrection as one event.

While in Mark, the centurion alone comes to faith when he sees the heroic manner in which Jesus died, Matthew mentions not only the centurion but also *those who were with him,* thus anticipating the conversion of the multitudes of gentiles. And it is not the death of Jesus but the cosmic signs accompanying it which lead them to faith. True, by editing Mark's "he breathed his last" to read "he yielded up his spirit," Matthew makes the theological statement that Jesus died by a free surrender to the Father's will. But at this point Matthew has a more cosmic interest in the meaning of Jesus' death. The signs which forecast the end of Israel's hegemony as God's people also forecast the creation of the new people of faith. The surprise in the climactic Christian confession, "Truly this was the Son of God," is that it is made by gentiles. Previously the title was used only by the demons (4:3–6), and the confession made by the disciples (14:33) and Peter (16:16). If the church will be built *on* Peter for making this confession, it will be built *of* peoples of all nations who confess the crucified and risen one to be the Son of God.

## The Women Witnesses (27:55–56)

55 There were also many women there, looking on from afar, who had followed Jesus from Galilee, ministering to him; 56among whom were Mary Magdalene, and Mary the mother of James and Joseph, and the mother of the sons of Zebedee.

The first sign within the Christian community that a new age has begun is that women become witnesses, a thing which Josephus tells us was not allowed in Jewish law. Deserted by his disciples, Jesus is faithfully followed, if at a distance, by women who had ministered to him in Galilee and from there

followed him to Jerusalem. Some of these women not only witness his death but they will also witness his burial (27:61), the
tomb on Easter morning (28:1) and the first resurrection appearance of Jesus (28:9–10). Thus the mystery of the death and
resurrection of Jesus is carried in the eyes and the hearts of
women, who are the only disciples who give visual continuity
to the events.

## Jesus Is Buried (27:57–61)

57 When it was evening, there came a rich man from
Arimathea, named Joseph, who also was a disciple of Jesus.
⁵⁸He went to Pilate and asked for the body of Jesus. Then
Pilate ordered it to be given to him. ⁵⁹And Joseph took the
body, and wrapped it in a clean linen shroud, ⁶⁰and laid it in
his own new tomb, which he had hewn in the rock; and he
rolled a great stone to the door of the tomb, and departed.
⁶¹Mary Magdalene and the other Mary were there, sitting
opposite the sepulchre.

Mark explains why it was important to get the body of
Jesus down from the cross: it was preparation day for the sabbath, and unfitting that the burial be carried out on the sabbath
day. More importantly, however, Deut 21:22–23 reads: "If a
man has committed a crime punishable by death and he is put
to death, and you hang him on a tree, his body shall not remain
all night upon the tree, but you shall bury him the same
day . . ." Matthew notes two details about Joseph of Arimathea. He is a rich man. This may be an echo of the Greek
version of Is 53:9: "I will deliver up the wicked for his burial
and the rich for his death," but it is more likely that Matthew
records this detail for another, simpler reason. The poor and
criminals were often buried in the ground or in a common tomb
(2 Kgs 23:6; Jer 26:23). But the tomb of a rich man would be
easily identifiable, so there could be no mistake on Easter
morning exactly where Jesus was buried.

The second detail is that Joseph is clearly a *disciple of
Jesus*. Matthew eliminates the qualifications given by the other
evangelists, that he was a member of the Sanhedrin (Mark),

that he had not consented to their purpose and deed (Luke), that he was a secret disciple for fear of the Jews (John). For Matthew Joseph is simply a devoted disciple who wishes to perform this last loving deed for his master. The "great stone" was a circular one set in a groove that rolled downward on closing and would therefore be difficult to roll open. The two Marys begin the mourning by sitting facing the tomb; they will leave to observe the sabbath, then return on Sunday morning.

## The Guard at the Tomb (27:62–66)

62 Next day, that is, after the day of Preparation, the chief priests and the Pharisees gathered before Pilate ⁶³and said, "Sir, we remember how that impostor said, while he was still alive, 'After three days I will rise again.' ⁶⁴Therefore order the sepulchre to be made secure until the third day, lest his disciples go and steal him away, and tell the people, 'He has risen from the dead,' and the last fraud will be worse than the first." ⁶⁵Pilate said to them, "You have a guard of soldiers; go, make it as secure as you can." ⁶⁶So they went and made the sepulchre secure by sealing the stone and setting a guard.

This story is proper to Matthew. It is historical in the sense that it reflects the disputes between the Christians and the Jews about the truth of Jesus' resurrection, which grew increasingly bitter and were no doubt a major issue in Matthew's day. The Jews accused the disciples of fraud by stealing the body of Jesus, and this story is the Christians' answer to that accusation. Highly significant is that both parties assume an empty tomb.

"After the day of Preparation" means the sabbath, an unusual time for the priests and Pharisees to gather before Pilate, but there is obvious urgency in their mission. The appearance of the Pharisees here after a long absence reflects the struggle in Matthew's day between their leadership and the leadership of the Christian community over this issue, among others. The "last fraud" is the claim of the disciples that Jesus has risen from the dead. The "first" refers either to Jesus' prediction of

his resurrection recorded in v. 63, or in a more general sense
to his claim that the kingdom of God had come in him (12:28).
Pilate's response, "You have a guard" means either that he is
now giving them a guard of Roman soldiers or that they already have a Jewish guard and should use it. Pilate's ready
acquiescence reflects not only his willingness to keep peace
with the Jewish authorities but also the fact that at the time
of Jesus tomb violation was a notorious problem. A marble slab
from Nazareth dating probably from the first century tells of
the Roman emperor's insistence with the provincial governor
that he deal more effectively with tomb violation, even by in-
flicting the death penalty.

## *Fear Not—He has been Raised (28:1–8)*

28 NOW AFTER the sabbath, toward the dawn of the
first day of the week, Mary Magdalene and the other
Mary went to see the sepulchre. ²And behold, there was a
great earthquake; for an angel of the Lord descended from
heaven and came and rolled back the stone, and sat upon it.
³His appearance was like lightning, and his raiment white
as snow. ⁴And for fear of him the guards trembled and
became like dead men. ⁵But the angel said to the women,
"Do not be afraid; for I know that you seek Jesus who was
crucified. ⁶He is not here; for he has risen, as he said. Come,
see the place where he lay. ⁷Then go quickly and tell his
disciples that he has risen from the dead, and behold, he is
going before you to Galilee; there you will see him. Lo, I
have told you." ⁸So they departed quickly from the tomb
with fear and great joy, and ran to tell his disciples.

The fact of Jesus' resurrection formed the core of the early
preaching of the church (1 Cor 15:1–3; Acts 2:22–36, etc.); but
no one witnessed the actual moment itself, and the details of
what happened in the Christian community on Easter morning,
unlike the numerous details of the passion, apparently were of
no great interest to the earliest preachers. Like the infancy
narratives, the Gospel accounts of these events belong to a
later stratum of interest and composition and reflect the par-

ticular theological concerns of each evangelist. That is not to say they lack any historical basis. For one thing, it is extremely unlikely that anyone wishing to prove to a Jewish audience that Jesus had risen would have created women witnesses, whose testimony was unacceptable in Jewish practice. And, as we have already pointed out, the empty tomb was a fact that both believers and non-believers accepted.

That being said, let us pursue Matthew's interest in this account. The sabbath ended at sundown, at which time Mark apparently has the women go to the shops to buy spices with which they go early Sunday morning to *anoint* Jesus. Matthew skips this detail (Jesus was proleptically anointed at Bethany, 26:6–13), and reports that the women go to *see* the tomb, apparently to continue their mourning but also, unknown to them, to continue their role as witnesses. There is no hint that they expect a resurrection; only the priests and Pharisees have a concern to prevent a fraudulent one. Whether the women witness the earthquake or whether it happens before their arrival is not relevant. It is a repetition of the apocalyptic sign already given at the death of Jesus, the unmistakable mark of a theophany like that of Mount Sinai (cf. above on 27:51), a sign of the end of the present age and the beginning of the "age to come." Also belonging to the apocalyptic signs is the "angel of the Lord" who descends from the highest heaven. In the OT the angel of the Lord is often a substitute image for God himself; here the expression recalls the "angel of the Lord" who appears four times in the infancy narratives as a guide and interpreter of the events. He is described in language taken from Daniel for the appearance of God himself (clothing white as snow, Dan 7:9) or the angel Gabriel (face like lightning, Dan 10:6). He rolls back the stone, not to let Jesus out but to show that he is not there, and subsequently to let the women in. Then he sits on the stone triumphantly—God in Jesus has conquered death itself.

The effect on the guards is like that of the men with Daniel who tremble (Dan 10:7) or the apocalyptist who falls on the ground as if dead (Rev 1:17). Unlike the guards at the crucifixion, who were led to faith by the earthquake, these guards are stunned into unconsciousness, thus allowing the dialog of faith to unfold between the angel and the women.

The emphatic "Don't *you* fear" contrasts with the fear of the disbelieving guards. The women will receive the correct, consoling interpretation of the event. Though the RSV translates, "He has risen," the more exact translation of the passive form of the verb should be, "He has been raised," emphasizing the role of the Father. "As he said" repeats Matthew's theme that Jesus knew ahead of time the ultimate result of his death, and prophesied it (16:21; 17:23; 20:19). The angel invites them to "Come" and inspect the place where the body of Jesus had lain, then he tells them to go with haste to tell the disciples the Easter message: "He has been raised from the dead." The women will be witnesses to the other disciples; to use un-Matthaean terms, they are apostles to the apostles. Jesus is going ahead of the disciples, as he had foretold, into Galilee (26:32), scene of Jesus' major public ministry and launching pad for the universal mission. Instead of repeating "as he told you," the angel says, "Lo, I have told you." In Mark's account, the women are so frightened they say nothing to anybody, but in Matthew they depart fearful but also filled with *great joy*, an echo of the great joy experienced by the Magi on rediscovering the star (2:10). And they go as excited and obedient messengers.

### Jesus Appears to the Women (28:9–10)

> [9]And behold, Jesus met them and said, "Hail!" And they came up and took hold of his feet and worshiped him. [10]Then Jesus said to them, "Do not be afraid; go and tell my brethren to go to Galilee, and there they will see me."

The overjoyed women rushing to tell the good news to the disciples meet another surprise: Jesus himself. He greets them with the Greek word *chairete*, which the RSV translates, "Hail" but literally means "Rejoice!" Jesus confirms and enhances the great joy the women have already experienced from the angel's announcement at the sepulchre. They come forward and, in typical oriental style, grasp Jesus' feet. This custom is still widespread in the middle-east and South Asia. I recall seeing a wife welcome her husband in this way, and even on occasion I received such a homage myself (however uncomfortable I felt!). In the case of Jesus, the gesture is one of divine adoration. This element is theologically important for Matthew, for it shows that the women identify the risen one as the same Jesus they had known in his earthly life, and they can physically touch him. Jesus is not a ghost; his body, however spiritualized, is still a body.

As is typical in theophanies, Jesus' first words are "Fear not!" He confirms the mission given by the angels. They are not to tarry in this Taboric experience but must become missionaries to the disciples, whom he calls his *brothers*. The only other time Jesus called his disciples his brothers was in 12:49–50, where they are held up as the ones who do the Father's will. In abandoning Jesus to the passion, they proved unworthy of the title, but now the very victory of Jesus in the resurrection is the great act of reconciliation restoring them to this intimate relationship both with Jesus and with the Father. The great moment of reunion will take place where discipleship started, in Galilee of the gentiles.

There are several interesting parallels between this encounter and that of Jesus with Mary Magdalene in John 20:14–18: Mary Magdalene herself, a surprise meeting with the risen Lord, grasping Jesus' feet, the command, explicit or implicit, to release Jesus and go with the Easter message to the disciples, called brothers of Jesus. This, and the tradition common to all the gospels that the tomb was empty and that women were the first witnesses, shows that despite divergence of details in the accounts, there is a common core on which the gospels agree.

## The Counter-Resurrection Fraud (28:11–15)

11 While they were going, behold, some of the guard went into the city and told the chief priests all that had taken place. [12]And when they had assembled with the elders and taken counsel, they gave a sum of money to the soldiers [13]and said, "Tell people, 'His disciples came by night and stole him away while we were asleep.' [14]And if this comes

to the governor's ears, we will satisfy him and keep you out of trouble.". <sup>15</sup>So they took the money and did as they were directed; and this story has been spread among the Jews to this day.

The guards posted to watch the tomb were left unconscious; now they rouse themselves only to discover the tomb open and empty. The Jewish leaders, to whom they bring their report, bribe them to tell an excuse, reassuring them that they need fear nothing from Pilate. As with Judas, money achieves their purpose. And thus, Matthew concludes, the story that the disciples stole the body of Jesus is current among the Jews even when the gospel is published some 60 years later.

This story, sequel to 27:62–66, reflects the polemics between the Christian and Jewish communities in the latter part of the first century. It is, as Matthew himself testifies, the Christian answer to the Jewish accusation that the disciples stole the body from the tomb. It may be difficult to believe that Roman soldiers would confess to such a gross neglect of duty, or that they could testify to something that happened while they were asleep. This absurdity surely could not have escaped Matthew, but perhaps that is precisely the irony he intended. The Jewish leaders' "cover-up" is full of contradictions. It is, in Matthew's view, a lie, a counter-gospel with which the Christian missionaries have to contend in their evangelization of the *Jews*. Up to this point Matthew has used the word "Jews" only on the lips of gentiles; "Israel" is the term used by the Jews themselves and even by Jesus during his public ministry. Now, however, Matthew speaks as would a gentile, indicating that "Israel" is now just another nation ("the Jews") to be evangelized by the new Israel, the church. Another sign of the end of the old world and the beginning of the new!

## *Finale: The Great Commission (28:16–20)*

16 Now the eleven disciples went to Galilee, to the mountain to which Jesus had directed them. <sup>17</sup>And when they saw him they worshiped him; but some doubted. <sup>18</sup>And

Jesus came and said to them, "All authority in heaven and on earth has been given to me. ¹⁹Go therefore and make disciples of all nations, baptizing them in the name of the Father and of the Son and of the Holy Spirit, ²⁰teaching them to observe all that I have commanded you; and lo, I am with you always, to the close of the age."

This passage is of capital importance for understanding the message of Matthew. It is not only the conclusion of the gospel, nor is it only the drawing together of all its major themes. It proclaims a qualitative difference both for Jesus and the church in the age opened by the resurrection event. Every word is laden with meaning.

The disciples are "the eleven," a reminder of the absence of Judas, the tragic figure whose betrayal of Jesus paradoxically triggered the entire passion narrative. Unlike John, Matthew does not mention the still visible wounds of Jesus, but the resurrection glory nevertheless carries the wound of betrayal, both for Jesus and the church, a wound now transformed by the Father into surpassing victory. The disciples go to Galilee "of the gentiles" (4:15), bringing the conclusion of the gospel back to its birthplace, which will now serve as the launching pad for the mission to all the nations. In the command Jesus had given through the women (28:10), there was no mention of the mountain. Perhaps Matthew is here referring to another resurrection appearance or message, or perhaps he had simply left this detail out of the message given the women. In any case, the mountain is of great symbolic importance for Matthew. It was on the mountain that Jesus had been tempted by the devil to accept the offer of "all the kingdoms of the earth" (4:9); now his refusal of that temptation and his obedience to the Father's will has won for him all power in heaven and on earth. It was on the mountain that Jesus, the new Moses, had proclaimed the new law (5–7); here he will promulgate it. It was on the mountain of transfiguration that Jesus was revealed to the disciples as the Son of God, fulfillment of the law and the prophets (17:1–8), and then *came* to his disciples in a way that anticipated his coming to them here. Now the mountain becomes the place of victory, revelation, proclamation and commissioning, as Jesus *comes* in a proleptic parousia to his disciples.

They *see* the risen Lord, who bears the name Jesus rather than "Lord" (throughout the gospel) or "Son of Man" (the dominant title in chapters 24–26) or "Son of God" (the dominant title in chapter 27) because Matthew wishes to underscore the fact that the glorious figure before them is indeed the same Jesus they knew in the public ministry, not some other figure, however angelic or divine. When Jesus appeared to his disciples walking on the water, they worshipped him (14:33). And so they do here. Even so, "they doubted" (NABR). Some translations, like the RSV, give the equally possible translation, "Some doubted." Either way, this is a surprising statement by Matthew in this glorious, climactic scene. Is it possible that some or all of the eleven could doubt at a moment like this? Matthew's answer is *yes!* By doubt here he does not mean doctrinal doubt but that wavering between trust in Jesus' power and trembling at their own weakness so well dramatized by Peter's desire to walk on the water coupled with his "doubt" as he saw the wind and waves (14:31). Discipleship for Matthew is not a continuous Taboric rapture; it is a mixture of light and darkness, of power and weakness. The church, pruned by betrayal and apostasy, continues to be a mix of wheat and weeds, a net containing all kinds of fish, even while it enjoys the light of the risen one. And that mixture is found within the individual disciple as well. This is both warning and encouragement.

Jesus comes to them. From the rest of the scene we can understand this as an anticipated parousia, not indeed the final coming as judge of the world (cf. 25:31–46), but a coming that has elements of the final glory of the Son of Man. Clearly in the background of Jesus' self-description is Daniel's picture of the Son of Man, the Greek versions of which read: "*Authority* [power] has been given to him, and all the *nations* of the earth . . . shall serve him. His *authority* is an everlasting *authority* . . ." (Dan 7:14). Jesus had shown his authority during his ministry in teaching (7:28–29), in his forgiveness of sins (9:6) and in his miracles and exorcisms (12:24–28). Even so, he said that during his public ministry his authority was limited to the lost sheep of the house of Israel (10:6; 15:24). Now, however, in virtue of his resurrection, *all* authority is given him in heaven and on earth. In heaven: he is the final judge of all (25:31–46). On earth: this authority will be exercised through the church and through Peter (18:18; 16:19), as the sequence here confirms.

Unlike the first preparatory mission, however, where Matthew says Jesus *gave* his authority to his disciples (10:1), here Jesus tells them to go in the power of, or because of, his own universal authority. In a sense, the power isn't even delegated; it is simply Jesus exercising his universal power through the missionary church. The emphasis, however, does not fall on the command to "go," which is really in the participial form *going* in the Greek, but upon the words "make disciples." This is a particularly Matthean word, keyed to a concept Matthew has spent his whole gospel defining. To be a disciple is to follow Jesus, to share his life-style and his table, to listen to his word, accept it and live by it, to share his mission, to accompany him through the storm, to learn how to live in the community with other disciples, to forgive and be reconciled, to bear public witness to Jesus, and finally to make other disciples. This making of other disciples will be a process similar to the one by which Jesus made the first disciples. It will take time; it will take instruction and a period of formation. And inasmuch as even the first eleven disciples experienced their weakness after witnessing the resurrection, the work of becoming a disciple is never finished. Thus for Matthew the work of evangelization is more than "preaching the gospel to the whole of creation" (Mk 16:15) or preaching repentance and forgiveness of sins and witnessing (Lk 24:47-48). It is a lifetime of spiritual formation.

Those to be evangelized are "all the nations." This is a better translation than "all the gentiles," which would assume that the church of Matthew's day had given up on the mission to the Jews. The Jews are no longer "Israel," for they have rejected the good news offered in Jesus; they are now simply one of the nations of the earth, but they too are still to be offered the good news (see above on 28:15). Jesus, who during his public ministry limited himself and the initiatory mission of his disciples to the lost sheep of the house of Israel (10:6; 15:24), now repeals that limitation and sends his disciples to all the nations. It is, of course, the *people* of all the nations that are to be evangelized, as the Greek makes clear by using the masculine plural *autous* ("baptizing *them*") rather than the neuter *auta*, which would refer back to the nations as such. The initiation of all new disciples is to take place through baptism. We noted that in describing John's baptism Matthew avoided the term "for the forgiveness of sins" because that comes only with Jesus, through the shedding of his blood anticipated in the eucharistic cup (26:28). Likewise, we observed that in predicting the cup which James and John would drink with Jesus (i.e., his suffering, 20:22), Matthew omitted Mark's reference to this suffering being a "baptism," probably because the term has now become a technical one for the church's initiatory sacrament. Baptism thus replaces circumcision as the rite by which one enters the new people of God. Though the Jewish Christians seem to have continued the practice of circumcision along with baptism (see Acts 16:3), the determination not to impose this Jewish rite on the gentiles came only after a struggle in the early church (see Acts 15; Galatians).

The Trinitarian formula for baptism is surprisingly theological and concise for a first-century document. Though Acts speaks of converts being baptized in the name of Jesus (Acts 2:38; 10:48; 19:5), no precise formula is given in the New Testament other than this one. Though some scholars have claimed that Matthew's formula is a later intrusion of a liturgical text, the manuscript tradition is firm—that is, the text as it is appears in the oldest manuscripts we have. The first century Didache has it (7:1). In Jesus' own baptism, prototype of the Christian sacrament, the Father, Son and Spirit are already present. The high Christology of Matthew associates Father and Son in the greatest intimacy (11:27) and the term "holy spirit," already found repeatedly in the OT, occurs in John's promise that Jesus will baptize "with the holy Spirit" (3:11). Decades before Matthew wrote, Paul used a Trinitarian formula to conclude his correspondence to the Corinthians (2 Cor 13:13). Matthew is doubtless reporting a formula that was used in his community.

Parallel to baptizing, the disciples are commissioned to teach. Following as it does the steps of proclaiming and baptizing, the teaching here may refer to that given at length *after* the sacrament of initiation. In the early church there would have been *some* instruction prior to baptism, obviously, but it was mostly of a kerygmatic kind, that is, geared to bring the person to conversion and commitment of his life to Jesus the risen Lord. Fuller instruction was reserved for the time after baptism and it built on what the convert had already experienced in the sacrament.

When Jesus sent his disciples forth on the earlier mission, it was only to proclaim the kingdom, to cast out demons and to heal the sick (10:1, 7–8). Jesus himself had not completed his teaching. But now he has not only completed it; he has sealed it by the eschatological event of his death and resurrection, and the disciples, who have understood Jesus' words (13:51), are now to bring them to the entire world. They are not to water down his teaching: the disciples they form are to observe *all* the commands Jesus has given to the first disciples. When one considers the high ethical demands Jesus makes in the Sermon on the Mount, one wonders whether indeed it is humanly possible to do all that Jesus demands. Humanly possible, no. But Jesus does not expect his disciples to do it alone. Whence the next revelation, the promise.

In the OT, after commissioning the prophet or holding out to the people their call to fullfill his purposes, the Lord says: "Fear not, for I am with you" (Jer 1:8; Is 43:5). At the end of Matthew's gospel, as at the beginning, Jesus is Emmanuel, God with us (1:23), fulfilling the prophecy of Isaiah (7:14; 8:10). He has promised to be with his disciples whenever they gather in his name (18:20), a truth difficult to remember when tossed by storm (8:26) or wind and waves (14:31). Yet here the promise is not merely domestic or limited to support in trial and persecution. It is inseparably tied to the command to *go* and the command to *live* the word of Jesus.

That means two things: (1) The church will continue to experience the presence of Jesus to the extent that it is missionary. Jesus does not say, "Stay here and continue to enjoy my presence." He promises rather that as the disciples *go* he will be with them. The church that ceases to be missionary ceases to be the church of Jesus. Mission is a constitutive element of the church's very being. (2) The high demands of Jesus, the righteousness that must exceed that of the scribes and the Pharisees (5:20), is not "the impossible dream." Rereading the Sermon on the Mount and reflecting on one's personal weakness the disciple may well feel like Peter overwhelmed by the wind and the waves. But Jesus does not expect any of his disciples to walk his walk alone. It is the presence and the power of Jesus that makes the impossible dream possible. Paul speaks of grace or of the Spirit which makes possible living up to and beyond the demands of law and thus escaping its condemnation (Gal 5:16–26). For Matthew, the abiding spiritual presence of the person of Jesus *is* grace. In Luke's view of things, Jesus leaves his church through the ascension in order to send the Holy Spirit to empower the disciples to go forth and to live the new life. But in Matthew there is no ascension. Jesus does not leave the church. If by his resurrection he has entered the glory of the Father, he has also *entered the church* as a permanent spiritual presence.

To find Jesus in our daily life, therefore, we need only strive to live his word in the company of other disciples, and to carry that word to those who have not heard it. In the very process of doing so, we will discover Jesus, the crucified and risen Lord, glorious Son of God and coming Son of Man, as our Emmanuel, our companion God. ■